POISON IN THE IVY

THE AMERICAN CAMPUS

Harold S. Wechsler, Series Editor

The books in the American Campus series explore recent developments and public policy issues in higher education in the United States. Topics of interest include access to college and college affordability; college retention, tenure, and academic freedom; campus labor; the expansion and evolution of administrative posts and salaries; the crisis in the humanities and the arts; the corporate university and for-profit colleges; online education; controversy in sports programs; and gender, ethnic, racial, religious, and class dynamics and diversity. Books feature scholarship from a variety of disciplines in the humanities and social sciences.

POISON IN THE IVY

Race Relations and the Reproduction of Inequality on Elite College Campuses

W. CARSON BYRD

RUTGERS UNIVERSITY PRESS

New Brunswick, Camden, and Newark, New Jersey, and London

Library of Congress Cataloging-in-Publication Data

Names: Byrd, W. Carson, author.
Title: Poison in the ivy : race relations and the reproduction of inequality
    on elite college campuses / W. Carson Byrd.
Description: New Brunswick, New Jersey : Rutgers University Press, 2017. |
    Series: The American campus | Includes bibliographical references and
    index.
Identifiers: LCCN 2017008278 (print) | LCCN 2017033131 (ebook) | ISBN
    9780813589381 (epub) | ISBN 9780813589398 (Web PDF) | ISBN 9780813589374
    (hardback) | ISBN 9780813589367 (paperback)
Subjects: LCSH: Racism in higher education—United States. | College
    students—United States—Attitudes. | Universities and colleges—Social
    aspects—United States. | College integration—United States. | Elite
    (Social sciences)—United States. | United States—Race relations. |
    BISAC: EDUCATION / Higher. | SOCIAL SCIENCE / Discrimination & Race
    Relations. | EDUCATION / Inclusive Education. | EDUCATION / Multicultural
    Education. | SOCIAL SCIENCE / Ethnic Studies / General. | SOCIAL SCIENCE /
    Ethnic Studies / African American Studies. | SOCIAL SCIENCE / Sociology /
    General. | SOCIAL SCIENCE / Ethnic Studies / Asian American Studies.
Classification: LCC LC212.42 (ebook) | LCC LC212.42 .B97 2017 (print) | DDC
    378.1/982996073—dc23
LC record available at https://lccn.loc.gov/2017008278

A British Cataloging-in-Publication record for this book is available from the British
Library.

∞ The paper used in this publication meets the requirements of the American National
Standard for Information Sciences—Permanence of Paper for Printed Library
Materials, ANSI Z39.48–1992.

www.rutgersuniversitypress.org

Manufactured in the United States of America

For Kat, a soul molded by intelligence, strength, and grace

"One could not be a cool, calm, and detached scientist while Negroes were lynched, murdered and starved."

—W.E.B. Du Bois, *Dusk of Dawn*

CONTENTS

PREFACE

It may seem strange at first, but the current examination of how college students at many of the nation's highly selective colleges and universities interact and think about racial inequality began many miles away in the mountains of Virginia. The seed was planted in a region noted for its once-dominant furniture industry and the coal veins that lie below the mountains. In what was seen as a racially diverse community for the region, my hometown of nearly 7,000 provided a microcosm of how such diversity did not ensure interactions across racial and ethnic lines, nor did it mean inequalities were not prevalent in the community. A subversive norm of elitism intermingled with racial and class disparities, which somewhat solidified the norms of inequality and how people rationalized these differing positions and experiences in our community. From this mountainous hamlet, how colleges can shape whom people interact with, what they know about racial inequality in the world, and how they may contribute to the persistence of racial inequalities through identities, ideologies, and interactions slowly grew into what became this volume.

My hometown is the city center for two counties, literally split in half by the county line, and thus not actually existing in either. As soon as you leave the town limits, you hit farmland and mountains for miles. Stark socioeconomic differences exist in the community given global economic developments in the last three decades. Reflecting deindustrialization in the latter decades of the twentieth century and a precipitous drop in job opportunities during the recent recession, the median household income is less than $30,000, and nearly one-quarter of all residents live in poverty. Growing up, this community was one of the more racially and ethnically diverse areas of this segment of the Blue Ridge Mountains, with 15% of the community being nonwhite. Although the Latino population has grown in recent years, the town and surrounding counties have become even more predominantly white. As with many places throughout the South, the area's socioeconomic strains intertwine with a long history of racism. The evolving community dynamics around race and class were magnified in the small school district that serves this town, and it is there that I began to wonder how colleges shape people's views of racial inequality.

My little public school district included three schools. Two and a half, actually, as the middle school was connected to the high school. In all, less than 1,700 students were enrolled in the district when I attended school, and I graduated with less than 70 classmates. Typical high school class sizes shrunk as they moved from ninth to twelfth grade because families were forced to leave town as the factories closed down and classmates who were on work release soon dropped out to help support their families. Nearly two-thirds of all students received free or reduced-price lunches. During middle school, as in most middle schools across the country, cliques and groups formed, with many students using race and class to establish group boundaries that mimicked the broader community. These groups crystallized throughout high school and sometimes created racial and class strife in the hallways. Many of the issues around race baffled me as the same person who espoused hate for another based on the color of their skin would line up next to them on the line of scrimmage during a football game, happy to push their team to victory—only to ignore their teammates once they left the locker room because they believed them to be inferior.

The combined racial and class divides grew more evident as I moved through high school toward graduation. Several professional families, nearly all of whom were white, particularly those who doctors, had children around the same time I was born, providing a unique dynamic to our classrooms. When we entered high school and began picking activities, the race and class divides were evident in who played what sports and who joined what clubs. Those with means played golf and tennis and ran cross-country. Few nonwhite students were on these teams. The same could be found with the academic competition teams, yearbook, and other clubs. As academic tracking worked its supposed magic sorting students, those from higher income families were in the honors courses or attended governor's school to gain advanced mathematics and science preparation, and few nonwhite students were found in these classrooms. Most, teachers and community members included, thought this reality was simply natural, with the supposed "best and brightest" achieving the most, while those who did not care were relegated to their fate in lower tracks with fewer opportunities and lower expectations.

The importance of how college can shape a person's views of the world, not simply their knowledge, developed during this time as well. A few of my friends left school to attend a prestigious boarding school. When I would spend time with them during the summers, they talked of strange aspects of their education: prevalent college recruiters, test-prep courses, and private college guidance counselors, among other oddities given my educational experiences of the time. As many of my classmates were from wealthier, professional backgrounds, they began to talk about going to college as if it were simply the next step in life. Soon, college t-shirts and sweatshirts were adorned through the hallways for institutions I had barely recognized, even from my favorite time of year: the "March Madness" accompanying the NCAA basketball tournament. The world of college seemed light-years away from where I was living. Several institutions were within a few hours of my hometown, but even they seemed far out of reach to me, which made a place like Harvard or Stanford float through my mind as colleges attended only by people on television, since they were the only people I knew who walked on those campuses.

As former classmates would return home on break from college, something seemed different about them. Many who went on to college attended smaller liberal arts colleges and public universities around the state or across the border in North Carolina, while a select few matriculated to Charlottesville and attended the University of Virginia, or "T.J.'s University" as one of them often referred to it, bolstering its founder Thomas Jefferson. Many of these students spoke of groups, communities, and often their hometown differently than before. Although this is not wholly of concern since people further develop their views on various issues in general as they get older, it was how college seemed to influence these views that interested me. Admittedly, I carried with me an idyllic view of colleges and universities that held them up as the bearers of knowledge and social progress. College was, as the American education system as a whole is sometimes referred to, the "great equalizer" where people worked hard and achieved their dreams. Campuses were the land of infinite possibilities. At least, so I thought. My former classmates soon presented me with a different perspective on college life as the small echelon of our community who pursued higher education seemed to increasingly view the inequality around town as the result of individual efforts and the cultural attributes of people despite their personal experiences suggesting otherwise. Some of them would look down on former classmates for not attending college or perhaps starting a family rather than pursuing their interest in history or science. Increasingly, inequalities were framed as a "natural" reality, regardless of the efforts put forth by someone who "showed great promise" during high school. I was confused how people who were given many opportunities to learn about the world could begin narrowing their explanations about the inequalities and life experiences that surrounded them, even for their childhood friends. What was it about college that influenced these views?

This volume contains the study that is my contribution to not only the research literatures on racial inequality and higher education, but to our larger knowledge of how a society continuously diversifying as well as witnessing growing inequalities can be shaped by a small segment of the college-going population, given their disproportionate access to high-status educations and postgraduate opportunities in the labor market and politics. These campuses are sites of ongoing debate around issues of race and inequality while they also diversify themselves. As recent years have shown, elite college campuses can be sites of social change by supporting the demands of students of color to improve educational opportunities and student support services, and also working to remove racist images and namesakes that confront students as they pursue their educations. However, these institutions can also be sites of resistance and retrenched inequalities on campus, which can influence broader society. In this work, I show how the highly selective colleges and universities in the nation can buttress and reinforce narrow perspectives on racial inequality and stereotypical views of racial and ethnic minorities despite the increasing diversity that exists on these campuses, and the research and knowledge available to undercut such views. Further, I show how the patterns of interaction among elite college students take shape and can influence their views of groups and inequality in some ways, while not influencing their views at all in other ways. In the end, this is a story of how racial inequality is normalized through interactions among the "best and the brightest" students who can leave a lasting mark on society. It is a story of how the ivy-clad walls of idyllic college campuses can harbor a toxic social structure eroding the foundations of students' abilities to understand the racial inequality around them on campus and beyond those walls, which can reinforce and even increase racial inequalities in the future. It is a story of how racism and elitism can pervade society, from the quads of college campuses to my little mountain town in Virginia. Ultimately, the current volume grapples with how colleges, particularly those with the most resources and influence on the society we live in, can simultaneously be the "great equalizers" and also "engines of inequality."

This volume took a village of supporters to come to fruition over nearly ten years of conceptualization, analysis, writing, rewriting, editing, rewriting yet again, and a bit more editing for safe measure. A large debt of gratitude is owed to my editor, Kimberly Guinta, who looked at the original prospectus and chapter samples, and decided to give my project the chance to have life. An even larger debt is owed to my friend and colleague Matthew Hughey, whose willingness to sit down with me from time to time and discuss my project to improve its clarity of ideas and connections made this volume stronger, without question. Despite his overwhelming schedule, he always found ways to give me feedback and support.

Many thanks to my friends and colleagues who looked over different chapters, and provided instrumental feedback to strengthen the arguments and theoretical connections throughout the volume. I greatly appreciate the perspectives provided by Maggie Hagerman and J. T. Thomas, and the questions they raised to increase the depth of this book's discussions. Victor Ray supported this project since its infancy when we were graduate students and continued his support all the way through the end with feedback on chapters and words of encouragement. Thank you to Jahi Johnson and Thomas Ratliff for their support while I was working on parts of this project during graduate school when we were deeply immersed in our research worlds.

This project would not have been carried out without the vital support of Ellington Graves, who always challenges me to extend my analyses and theoretical connections, and would make time to sit down and talk through obstacles I was facing. I appreciate all of your friendship and advice over the years. Thank you to Jill Kiecolt and Mike Hughes for always challenging my analyses. Your critical perspectives and feedback over the years were essential to making this project as strong as it is now. Wornie Reed always asked me the straightforward questions of "What do the data say?" and "Why do these findings matter?" that assisted me with keeping the project in perspective and elaborating on a bigger picture about social inequality. Fabio Rojas, who developed into an important mentor after receiving an email about a blog post, added much to the theoretical connections in my young career, particularly with exploring sociological discussions of elitism, diversity, and higher education. Dave Brunsma, I greatly appreciate everything you have provided me as a mentor during and since my postdoctoral years. Thank you to the three mentors who opened my eyes to research and sociology in general: Laurie Pedersen, Tom Plaut, and Alan Bayer. Laurie and Tom pulled me out of the fog as I wandered around the quad of Mars Hill and helped me find my path. Alan, whom the world dearly misses, assisted me with developing my skills and tools to establish a solid sociological foundation for my career from our first meeting to our last. A special thanks to all of my colleagues from graduate school as we supported each other in pushing toward the finish line, and to the colleagues I have gained since that time such as Latrica Best, Rachelle Brunn-Bevel, Woody Doane, David Embrick, Melanie Gast, Kwame Harrison, Kasey Henricks, Ricky Jones, Shirletta Kinchen, Laura Moyer, Sarah Ovink, Anthony Peguero, Rashawn Ray, Louise Seamster, Jessica Welburn, and many others. All of our conversations over the years were and continue to be invaluable to me.

To my family, thank you for supporting my path through life even if you were not quite sure what I was doing in the past, currently, and most likely in the future. To my parents, there is nothing I could say to convey how much I have owed you over the years. From letting me channel my energies into little projects with Legos as a child, to (literally) running around over hill and dale throughout high school, college, and beyond through the development of my career, you have always provided support and a helping hand when times were tough. You have always supported me as I figured out life despite my imperfect record of decisions. To my not-so-little-any-more brother and sister, Spencer and Katelyn, I hope you find comfort in knowing that the world, as crazy as it may seem, holds great things ahead for you in the pages of books, experiences in life, and the dreams you hold for yourselves. This book was once a dream, so run toward your dreams and do not shirk at obstacles that life throws at you. Last, and certainly not least, thank you to Kat, whose love and support helped me revive not only a project, but a life I had once placed on a shelf to collect dust. I am always in awe of your brilliance, your passion for life, and importantly, your patience as I often struggle to maintain a balance between work and life. Here's to the pages we continue to write together in life after this book.

POISON IN THE IVY

1 · EASING INTO VIEWS OF RACE AND INEQUALITY IN EVERYDAY LIFE ON CAMPUS

One evening near the end of the fall semester 2009, three law students at Harvard University gathered for dinner in the dining hall of the Law School. Throughout the evening, the conversation ebbed and flowed among the friends on a range of topics, but an email sent by one of the law students to her friends following the dinner set the Internet on fire with fierce debate. In conjunction with a lively discussion of affirmative action (Lat 2010a), the third-year law student felt her position on race and intelligence needed clarification, and took the time to elaborate her thoughts in an email:

I just hate leaving things where I feel I misstated my position.

I absolutely do not rule out the possibility that African Americans are, on average, genetically predisposed to be less intelligent. I could also obviously be convinced that by controlling for the right variables, we would see that they are, in fact, as intelligent as white people under the same circumstances. The fact is, some things are genetic. African Americans tend to have darker skin. Irish people are more likely to have red hair. (Now on to the more controversial) Women tend to perform less well in math due at least in part to prenatal levels of testosterone, which also account for variations in mathematics performance within genders. [*sic*] This suggests to me that some part of intelligence is genetic, just like identical twins raised apart tend to have very similar IQs and just like I think my babies will be geniuses and beautiful individuals whether I raise them or give them to an orphanage in Nigeria. I don't think it is controversial of an opinion to say I think it is at least possible that African Americans are less intelligent on a genetic level, and I didn't mean to shy away from that opinion at dinner.

I also don't think that there are no cultural differences or that cultural differences are not likely the most important sources of disparate test scores (statistically, the measureable ones like income do account for some raw differ-ences). I would just like some scientific data to disprove the genetic position, and it is often hard given difficult to quantify cultural aspects. One example (courtesy of Randall Kennedy) is that some people, based on crime statistics, might think African Americans are genetically more likely to be violent, since income and other statistics cannot close the racial gap. In the slavery era, how-ever, the stereotype was of a docile, childlike, African American, and they were, in fact, responsible for very little violence (which was why the handful of rebel-lions seriously shook white people up). Obviously group wide rates of violence could not fluctuate so dramatically in ten generations if the cause was genetic, and so although there are no quantifiable data currently available to "explain" away the racial discrepancy in violent crimes, it must be some nongenetic cul-tural shift. Of course, there are pro-genetic counterarguments, but if we assume we can control for all variables in the given time periods, the form of the argu-ment is compelling.

In conclusion, I think it is bad science to disagree with a conclusion in your heart, and then try (unsuccessfully, so far at least) to find data that will confirm what you want to be true. Everyone wants someone to take 100 white infants and 100 African American ones and raise them in Disney utopia and prove once and for all that we are all equal on every dimension, or at least the really important ones like intelligence. I am merely not 100% convinced that this is the case.

Please don't pull a Larry Summers on me (Filipovic 2010).

Although these troubling comments from the law student regarding racial differ-ences in intelligence were condemned from those within and outside of the Law School (Lat 2010a, 2010b), consideration of the educational trajectory of this student points to how unsurprising her comments are among current students attending some of the most selective and influential colleges and universities in the United States. Arguably, these budding elites develop their patterns of inter-actions and racial ideology in a world framed by both more diversity and less mobility and equality. That is, elite college students' social worlds frame their interactions and views of race and inequality in disjointed ways. This framing of social interaction and race buoys their views of individuality and merit within and outside their social worlds. Students' racial ideology provides the rational-izations, justifications, and possible challenges to the reality of racial inequality around them (see Bonilla-Silva 2014, 1997). Ultimately, elite social worlds found on these highly selective college campuses downplay students' consideration of social structures perpetuating racial inequality in their social world as well as in broader society.

Prior to attending Harvard University's Law School, the student whose email is quoted above was an undergraduate student at Princeton. Her academics at

Princeton were buttressed by hands-on research within a department known for its commitment to studying inequalities in society. Majoring in sociology, she excelled in her academic pursuits and worked closely with a faculty member on their research examining race and inequality in higher education, specifically the influences of cross-race interactions on attitudes, behaviors, and perceptions among college students, which was incorporated into a larger volume examining elite higher education (North 2010).[1] Thus, this law student was actively involved in several ways with discussions of race and inequality in society during her undergraduate years. Yet her position stated in the above email to her friends is in stark contrast to the conclusions of the research she worked on with her faculty member. Her perception of race and inequality did not match the reality she was exposed to in her classes and research.

At the time of the email controversy, like many of her classmates at elite colleges and universities, the aforementioned student was set to work in an influential position in society, specifically under a judge on a United States Court of Appeals (Lat 2010a). The opportunity to work in such a position gives her the ability to help shape varying aspects of court decisions possibly influencing future policies. Thus, it is not hard to imagine a case about racial discrimination appearing on the docket for judgment, and this student's prejudicial position toward racial and ethnic minorities, particularly African Americans, could influence the materials she selects and the summaries she writes of research and legal outcomes to assist the judge with their rulings and positions. The opportunity to clerk for a high-ranking judge is a product of the privileged position of the student and her attendance at highly selective universities affording their students with such opportunities, which are not available to others (see Binder, Davis, and Bloom 2016; Rivera 2015). Importantly, this student and most who attend elite institutions of higher education are afforded the opportunity to develop their views of race and inequality in differing social worlds, whereby social interactions take on differing meanings and influence their racial ideology in varying ways that may seem counterintuitive at first, but fit a larger narrative of openness, individuality, and diversity framing social interactions and racial inequality today (Khan 2011, 194–199; see also Khan 2012, 361–377; Khan and Jerolmack 2013, 9–19). As these students move into lucrative positions in political and professional sectors of society at much higher rates than other groups in society (Domhoff 1978; Mills 1956; Zweigenhaft 1993; Zweignehaf and Domhoff 1991), these different experiences in the elite social world have important implications for society as a whole in relation to future progress toward racial equality.

The most selective and prestigious colleges in the United States are often emulated and mimicked in relation to their varying policies, programs, and general openness to diversity and inclusion (see DiMaggio and Powell 1983; Kraatz and Zajac 1996; Meyer and Rowan 2007). Such emulation and mimicry extends to efforts to produce and sustain racial diversity and inclusion among students, faculty, and staff on campus. However, the contemporary positions situating these institutions as ideal models are often ahistorical and miss the inequality and racism of past and contemporary eras on these campuses, which influence student experiences.[2] As this volume indicates, the most selective colleges and universities in the United States exhibit a structure and culture inhibiting current and future generations of students from learning about the reality of race and inequality afflicting society outside of their elite social world. This extends to their social interactions on campus across racial and ethnic lines as these students frame what they learn about people who are racially and ethnically different from themselves, befriend peers from different groups, and adjust their views of race and inequality, which will guide their thoughts, feelings, and actions throughout much of their lives. I argue that much of what guides current and future generations of alumni from elite colleges and universities is the "ease" with which students can rationalize race and inequality in their social world to mean meritocracy and individuality. These views are buoyed by their perspectives of themselves and their peers on campus. It is the context surrounding these students as "the best and brightest" which influences their view that most peers from different racial and ethnic groups on campus are "normal" given their high achievements in a variety of ways similar to what they, themselves, have experienced in their lives. Thus, racial inequality is rationalized as a result of people who grew up in previous unjust eras, were unlucky, or have different priorities in life leading them to not achieve as much as elite students.[3] For elite college students, the exceptions become the rules of racial inequality in a colorblind meritocracy in the decades following the civil rights movement. These views of themselves as the "best and brightest," which frame racial inequality using narrow and often highly individualistic perspectives, are perpetuated by the colleges and universities they attend, which are often emulated for their diversity efforts as central to Supreme Court cases around affirmative action and justification for such policies (Berrey 2015, 55–123).

An examination of elite colleges and universities in the United States expands upon Pierre Bourdieu's seminal work on elites and educational reproduction to identify how the social structures and "mental structures" or ideologies of elites and their institutions intertwine in everyday life.[4] As I discuss further below, it is important to keep in mind the prominent influence that racial ideologies and racism had on the creation and histories of elite colleges and universities (see Wilder 2013). Throughout history and into the contemporary era, these colleges have served as spaces to develop conceptions of "elite" identities and distinguish this segment of the population from broader society. Central to this volume is noting how the development of an elite identity is also interconnected with racial ideology, as these spaces were specifically created for and continue to be dominated by whites. The "consecrating" of elites by creating a clear separation from those not admitted to elite institutions reinforces their beliefs in uniqueness

(Bourdieu 1996, 102), which has important ramifications for understanding how they view race and inequality within their elite social worlds as well as outside in broader society.

This book examines college students in the United States' upper echelon of higher education to identify how elites develop inter- and intraracial networks and how these interactions influence their racial attitudes and beliefs. Furthermore, I examine how students' race-related social identities influence their interactions and racial attitudes during college as well. Central to the analyses of this volume are the following questions:

1. How often do elite college students interact across racial and ethnic lines in their everyday lives on campus?
2. Do patterns of interaction depend on the social situation (i.e., friendships, dating, roommates, student organization participation)?
3. What is the relationship between elite college students' inter- and intraracial interactions and their racial attitudes?
4. How do students' race-related social identities influence their social interactions and racial attitudes?
5. How does the conception and construction of "elite" intertwine with "whiteness" at elite colleges and universities to influence students' ideologies and social interactions?

These questions provide insight into how future generations of America's leaders and professionals interact across racial and ethnic lines, but also how they view race and inequality, and what should be done to pursue a course of equality. The "college years" are an important time of development for many people, not just the students who attend these highly selective institutions, and an examination of the colleges and universities that young elites frequently enroll in can shed light on how their social world shapes the larger one we all live in and experience, particularly in relation to race and inequality. Ultimately, at the heart of this book lies the question: What can the study of the social worlds on elite college campuses tell us about the prospects for racial equality in the United States? Moreover, as little is known about elites who are not the prototypical image of this group (i.e., white, male, and Protestant), meaning little is known about elites who are people of color, this volume also expands research on how elites influence one another, including newer members (see Khan 2012).

INEQUALITY IN BRICK AND IVY SOCIAL WORLDS
AFTER THE CIVIL RIGHTS MOVEMENT

Elites (i.e., the most socioeconomically privileged class) attend different colleges and universities from most in the United States (Bowen, Kurzweil, and

Tobin 2005; Espenshade and Radford 2009; Khan 2011; Massey et al. 2003; Zweigenhaft 1993). Colleges and universities considered "elite" are those with inordinate restrictions on who is accepted for enrollment, and they carry high levels of status, privilege, opportunity, and most importantly resources, which establishes this upper echelon of higher education as a highly sought-after commodity in society.[5] Furthermore, elite colleges and universities have relied, and continue to rely, on the admission of the most socioeconomically privileged students. These students are often legacy students, meaning their parents attended these institutions as well, averaging about one-third of the entering classes of Yale, for example, while receiving significant advantages in admissions overall at these institutions (Bowen, Kurzweil, and Tobin 2005; Karabel 2005; Massey and Mooney 2007; Soares 2007). Elite students are also increasingly from the wealthiest families, limiting the number of students from lower socioeconomic and racially diverse backgrounds who can gain admission to elite institutions (Bowen, Kurzweil, and Tobin 2005; Espenshade and Radford 2009; Karabel 2005; Soares 2007). These colleges are "often in the vanguard of innovative change in higher education" as well, which can influence many aspects of campus life (Espenshade and Radford 2009, 10). However, the value of attending an elite college is not limited to what is learned in the classroom or directly related to economic opportunity. The social world on these campuses is an extension of elites' larger experience within organizations and institutions oriented toward their lifestyles and views that have evolved since the civil rights era in the 1960s (see Khan 2012, 2015; Armstrong and Hamilton 2013). Students at these elite colleges further develop their views of race and inequality established during the influential years of socialization in childhood and early adolescence (see Hagerman 2014; Johnson 2015; Lewis 2003; Lewis-McCoy 2014; Pahlke, Bigler, and Suizzo 2012; Van Ausdale and Feagin 2001), framing their individual achievements with meritocracy and diversity in mind. Further, most affluent students grow up in households that hold conflicting views around meritocracy, wealth, and inequality such that they and their families are aware of their socioeconomic privilege and the inequality existing in society, but frame their lives outside of this larger, unequal social world and view their position as the product of their individual hard work and merit, not of their privilege (Hagerman 2014; Johnson 2015).

The study of elite colleges and the social worlds they contain takes on more importance when reflecting on the changes occurring since the 1960s regarding inequality, particularly in the US context. The examination of economic and racial inequality since the post–World War II era documents a boom in economic growth leading into the 1960s and 1970s, with reduced inequality, more social mobility for Americans on the whole, and more openness to racial diversity in the market (see Khan 2012; Zweigenhaft and Domhoff 1991). This decreasing inequality did not last, as changes in government and economic policies in the 1980s initiated a continuing increase of inequality and a decrease in social mobility prospects throughout the 1990s and into the twenty-first century. Elites during the last thirty years have experienced a solidification of their position at the top of the economic ladder, and are wealthier now than at any point since the early decades of the twentieth century.[6] Importantly, these changes followed the pinnacle of the civil rights movement as well as movements among women, immigrants, and gays and lesbians to secure a more stable foothold in society with more opportunity and less discrimination. As the rights movements pushed the nation toward more social equality, elites saw changes in their own groups as diversity increased in their ranks, particularly from the emerging global elite (see Bernstein and Swan 2007).

The shifts in who composes the elites influenced elite colleges and universities, and increasing racial and ethnic diversity is now found among students on these campuses. Specifically, following the rights movements of the 1960s and 1970s, elite higher education saw an increase in the racial and ethnic diversity on campus, although this increase rarely mirrored the larger national population (Bowen and Bok 1998; Bowen, Kurzweil, and Tobin 2005; Espenshade and Radford 2009; Massey et al. 2003). These changes in student body composition influenced numerous aspects of higher education in the United States, from the actual number of students of color enrolled to the support and academic programs offered on campus. Change did not occur smoothly, evenly, or with complete success, as colleges and universities often struggled, and in many ways continue to struggle, to create an inclusive and supportive environment for students (Bowen, Kurzweil, and Tobin 2005; Peterson et al. 1978).

Shamus Khan accentuates a consequential shift among elites, specifically among students, following the rights movements, which influenced their views of race, inequality, and themselves. Young elites emphasize highly individualized views of achievement and inequality in society, supporting the belief in a colorblind meritocratic system (Khan 2011, 2015; Khan and Jerolmack 2013). Khan found students espousing views following the overall shift in American society, particularly among whites, that emphasized individual and cultural explanations of racial inequality, while simultaneously downplaying structural explanations.[7] That is, young elites stressed a central tenet of Max Weber's Protestant ethic and the American Dream ideology by noting people must work hard to succeed in life because only the hardworking and most talented in society achieve high-status positions (Johnson 2015; see also Weber 1930). These beliefs work to justify and legitimate why elites are perceived as "elite," as only people who are the "best and brightest" are purportedly found at these prestigious institutions.[8] Importantly, Khan frames these views in line with the social world these young elites live in. Consistently throughout their young lives these students are told they are talented, intelligent, and special in a variety of ways, building off of one of the central themes of the twentieth-century rights movements to move away from essentialist and group-based views to perspectives emphasizing the individuality and diversity within groups.[9] This view frames inequality in society as natural through the identification of precocity or intellectual "gifts" and "talents" as well as the result of individual efforts (Bourdieu 1996, 20–21). Thus, racial inequality is not a matter of discrimination and systemic racism, but the result of the "cream rising to the top" as people who are seen as not working hard or not as talented as those in high-status positions justifiably occupy lower positions in the hierarchy.

The view of inequality among young elites emphasizes a colorblind perspective in a more racially diverse society. Through reliance on individualized and cultural views of inequality, young elites use the four frames of colorblind racial ideology to make sense of the results of both their social world and the larger social world of the nation. The research of Eduardo Bonilla-Silva indicates that a majority of whites, and a segment of racial and ethnic minorities, emphasize colorblind views of racial inequality by framing (1) society as one of "equal opportunity" and meritocracy (abstract liberalism frame), (2) patterns of social interaction such as residential segregation and low racial and ethnic minority enrollments in particular schools and colleges as "naturally occurring" (naturalization frame), (3) inequality as a result of inferior cultural aspects (i.e., deviant family structure, lack of effort, not valuing college education, etc.) among racial and ethnic minority groups (cultural racism frame), and (4) racism and discrimination as marks of past unjust eras of history, and not a relevant part of contemporary society that influences people's lives today (minimization frame) (Bonilla-Silva 2014, 73–100). These views are found not only in Khan's work among young elites, but also in the decreasing importance placed on racial discrimination as a factor contributing to inequality, and the increasing reliance on cultural and individualized views among elite college students in recent studies (Charles et al. 2009; Espenshade and Radford 2009; Massey et al. 2003; Sidanius et al. 2008).

Young elites enact privilege in their everyday lives by ignoring the importance of inequality's impact on accessing the social worlds they live in, regardless of a person's talents, intellect, or hard work (Khan 2011, 2015; Khan and Jerolmack 2013). Additionally, when explaining inequality in highly individualized and colorblind ways, young elites rationalize inequality, and specifically racial inequality, as a result of bad luck, differing life priorities, and living in an earlier unjust era that influenced a person's life trajectory.[10] Thus, these situations establish an "ultimate attribution error" overriding the logic used by young elites to explain inequality, particularly among whites. The use of the ultimate attribution error in combination with what Khan labels "availability bias" leads to greater understanding of how elites are disconnected from larger society, specifically in their understanding of inequality. Thomas Pettigrew describes the ultimate attribution error in conjunction with a person's racial prejudice, whereby the stereotyped views of racial and ethnic minorities guide people throughout their lives. When someone is faced with an experience or information countering their prejudiced views of a group, they rationalize the contradiction as the exception to their stereotypical beliefs: the person was "lucky" or had extremely high motivation, or the outcome was a result of special life advantages or manipulated situations (Pettigrew 1979). This rationalization buffers people's prejudicial views from change.

The reliance on individualized and colorblind views of inequality connects with the use of the ultimate attribution error on a regular basis to heighten the availability bias of young elites. That is, young elites are sheltered from larger realities in society, such as limited social mobility and resources, and increasing racial inequality (Khan 2011, 2015; Khan and Jerolmack 2013). These experiences are often structured around them before they are born, as affluent parents seek out particular neighborhoods and school districts using highly racialized and classed views of different schools and communities, which carry forward into college through parents assisting students financially and in other ways with pursuing particular activities that also shape students' perspectives of inequalities (see Armstrong and Hamilton 2013; Hagerman 2014; Hamilton 2016; Johnson 2015). The experience of young elites, specifically whites, with highly successful racial and ethnic minorities in their social world arguably establishes the "exception as the rule" for how they understand racial inequality in society. Therefore, the disproportionately low number of students of color in elite schools and colleges is not seen as evidence of racial discrimination and inequality in the larger society, which limits access to elite schools and colleges, but as the work of a fully functional meritocratic system. The students of color in these institutions are mostly seen as intelligent, hardworking, and talented individuals who succeed in a meritocracy, supporting young elites' general view of success and inequality.[11] Thus, these students' views buttress colorblindness and the minimization of racial discrimination. When young elites' social world intersects with the larger social world where a majority of people reside and racial inequality becomes more apparent, young elites rationalize inequality in colorblind ways with individualized and cultural explanations for why only some people make it to high-status positions or elite educational institutions. This is prominently found in Khan's interviews of elite boarding school students and their discussion of staff members of their school (Khan 2011, 52–64).

When we step back from this discussion of how young elites view racial inequality from a disconnected position, we see the larger importance of studying these students at elite colleges and universities for understanding what changes may lie ahead for efforts toward racial equality in society. Elite colleges and universities allow their students to further entrench their disconnected views of success and explanations for racial inequality, even with different diversity programs in place.[12] These institutions continuously emphasize how their students are the "best and brightest" of society. However, if these students who have so much to offer and are also offered so much by their advantaged positions do not receive or take advantage of educational opportunities inside and out of the classroom during their short time on campus to challenge such limited views of race and inequality in society, future policies will only serve to further exacerbate racial inequality as these students work in influential political and professional positions following graduation. Elite college students can learn in classroom settings about race and inequality, which can influence their views on such issues in society (see McClelland and Linnander 2006). However, a more influential aspect of the college-going experience can influence views of race and inequality more than actual coursework, that is, social interactions. This book examines how inter- and intraracial interactions among elite college students can influence their racial ideology, and vice versa. These experiences, while the main focus of this volume, do not discount the coursework students complete that can have an influence on their views of race and inequality. These courses are incorporated into the analyses in later chapters as part of students' race-related campus experiences outside of their social interactions. As noted more below, a wealth of research conducted since the beginning of the twentieth century points to the possible influence of social interactions on views of race and inequality. I argue, despite the consistent positive outcomes of interacting with different racial and ethnic groups found by these studies, that the "ease" with which young elites can interact across racial and ethnic lines at elite colleges actually perpetuates their disconnected views of race and inequality, and how they identify with regards to race, as their social world is continuously differentiated from broader society.

INTER- AND INTRARACIAL INTERACTIONS, PREJUDICE, AND SOCIAL IDENTITIES

The examination of students at elite colleges and universities, their interactions across racial and ethnic lines, and the ways in which these interactions influence their views of each other, call for a complex perspective to frame the analyses and findings. I use the in-depth work of intergroup relations research to examine these students and identify how their social interactions in college can set the stage for how they live their life with regards to race and inequality after graduation. In what follows, I provide a more detailed look at the intergroup contact theory utilized in this study. Additionally, I discuss the distinctions among forms of racial prejudice and why these distinctions are important to understand race and inequality in past, present, and future eras. Lastly, I describe the importance of considering students' social identity when examining their interactions and racial prejudice. As an integral theme of intergroup relations research, how students identify with racial and ethnic groups, positively or negatively alike, can influence whom they interact with during college and what they think about their peers.

During this important time, young elites, and college students in general, establish a self-fulfilling prophecy relating to their lack of cross-race interactions. This is evidenced in an annual study of thousands of entering college students across the nation, which found that students were less willing to interact across racial and ethnic lines in college compared to previous entering cohorts.[13] Research indicates college students fulfill this prophecy given their lack of cross-race interactions during the early years of college, which also mirrors similar trends in society as a whole (Charles et al. 2009; Espenshade and Radford 2009; Massey et al. 2003; Sidanius et al. 2008; McPherson, Smith-Lovin, and Cook 2001). Thus, college students ensure they do not readily cross racial and ethnic lines in social interactions, preferring to interact among peers of their own groups. As this book shows, the lack of cross-race interaction continues for students throughout the remainder of college, and in some cases this interaction decreases from already paltry levels. The limited amount of cross-race interaction among students hinders the knowledge of race and inequality, the reduction of prejudice, and the building of racial empathy, which are key effects of cross-race interactions.[14] Given the views among young elites of society as a colorblind meritocracy, social interactions may not fully connect everyday experiences with learning about racial and ethnic groups for the current generation of college students. In the end, studying "race relations" among students at elite colleges and universities is arguably a study in the unrelated as homogeneity, homophily, and racial hierarchy often overrun diversity and inclusion on campus; the spaces of interaction become structured to entrench negative and disconnected beliefs about race and inequality, while providing limited space for positive interactions and the changing of such views. In the end, the social structure reinforces the racial ideology of students, which influences their social actions and ultimately reinforces the social structure they are attempting to navigate. It is a fragile balance in a microcosm of society with important implications for the future.

Intergroup Contact Theory and "Easing" through Interactions

The current study examines the influence of social interactions among elite college students on their views of race and inequality. My approach, grounded in the commonly used intergroup contact theory (often referred to as the "contact hypothesis") and framed using the social structure and personality perspective, is not one of an experiment.[15] Rather, it is an investigation of how the theoretical and methodological approaches that are used to study such interactions and their effects can gloss over the important structural realities of how elite social worlds limit interactions across group lines from influencing views of race and inequality. Intergroup contact is face-to-face interaction between people of two clearly defined groups (Pettigrew and Tropp 2011). Gordon Allport (1954) noted that without any substantive interactions between group members with particular features contextualizing these situations, interactions would be "superficial." Thus, Allport established this perspective to understand what conditions create meaningful interaction between members of different groups to reduce prejudice. However, people often assume this perspective simply argues for putting a diverse group of people together in an effort to reduce racial prejudice, that contact in and of itself is sufficient for prejudice reduction, which misses the complexity of social interactions and the processes involved in prejudice reduction as outlined in the theory (Pettigrew 1998, 68). First, people involved in the interaction must have *equal status*.[16] Second, the people involved must have *common goals*. Third, the situation must exhibit *intergroup cooperation*, not conflict, to assist achieving goals among people of different groups (Sherif 1966). Fourth, *authoritative support* for intergroup contact must exist in society, because the support of authorities for intergroup contact influences the acceptability of such interactions. A fifth condition, *friendship potential*, was added by Thomas Pettigrew since these friendships allow for close and repeated interaction in many settings over time (Pettigrew 1998, 76).

Four interrelated processes within intergroup contact situations can increase the likelihood of reducing prejudicial attitudes among people. First, a person can learn about outgroup members (i.e., members of different racial and ethnic groups), countering stereotypical beliefs and producing positive results by changing attitudes toward a group. Second, interacting with an outgroup member can modify a person's expectations about how to behave in future interactions, and also influence their attitudes. Third, continuous cross-group interaction can lead to affective ties, influencing empathy toward other groups. Finally, a person can experience "deprovincialization," whereby they reconsider the distinctions they have made regarding who is considered an outgroup member, and possibly redefine group boundaries to include outgroup members (see Gaertner and Dovidio 2000; also Pettigrew 1998, 72–73).

An extensive meta-analysis by Thomas Pettigrew and Linda Tropp (2011) examined when and how intergroup contact can influence prejudice. Their research found that intergroup contact reduced many forms of prejudice (racial, ethnic, religious, etc.). Moreover, their analyses found intergroup contact could reduce prejudice when all of Allport's key conditions were not met, but that when each condition was met there were stronger prejudice-reducing effects in the studies. Pettigrew and Tropp's meta-analysis found affective prejudice measures were influenced more by intergroup contact situations than cognitive prejudice measures (discussed more below), and revealed that learning about an outgroup during an intergroup contact situation reduced people's prejudice levels, lowered anxiety for future cross-group interactions, and increased empathy levels with outgroup members. Thus, increasing knowledge of and emotional ties to outgroups has prejudice-reducing effects in many studies, highlighting the importance of affect in racial prejudice. Increasing positive emotions toward outgroup members can reduce negative and stereotypical views of that group (see Pettigrew 1997). Additionally, an "extended contact effect" and a "common fate effect" may influence students' views of racial and ethnic groups. In the first situation, having friends who are likely to have racially diverse friendships can indirectly influence the prejudice of a student (Wright et al. 1997; also Pettigrew 2009; Pettigrew and Tropp 2011). In the second situation, having a friendship with a member of another racial group may influence a person's view toward another racial group, as these two groups are thought to have similarities, and thus, to have a common societal fate (see Schuman et al. 1997; Tajfel 1982).

Unlike many studies of social interaction and prejudice reduction, this book engages with how multiple groups interact together on campus. An abundance of studies has examined whites' social interactions and racial ideology, but much less work has focused on minority group members' interactions and ideologies. People of color are more likely to have cross-group interactions given their small size and historical presence in organizations (e.g., selective colleges) (Blau and Schwartz 1984). Additionally, research has identified the contact-prejudice relationship to be weaker for racial and ethnic minority groups (Tropp and Pettigrew 2005). In line with this finding, other studies have found the interracial contact-closeness relationship for blacks to be weaker than for whites (see Ellison and Powers 1994; Tropp 2007). Although perceptions of discrimination mediated the interracial contact-closeness relationship for blacks, cross-race friendships led to increased interracial closeness, which may reduce the reliance on perceptions of discrimination to form intergroup attitudes (noted in Tropp 2007).

Different forms of interracial contact can reduce racial prejudice among college students: interracial friendships, interracial dating, participation in diverse student organizations, and living in diverse residential settings. These forms of interracial contact represent different levels of intimacy, trust, common interests, and the likelihood of sharing information about their racial or ethnic group with others. More intimate forms of contact such as interracial friendships can reduce racial prejudice more than other forms. Although previous research found these different forms of interracial contact influenced students' racial prejudice, their relative influence has not been investigated fully (see Sidanius et al. 2008). The current study examines the influence of each form of inter- and intraracial contact on college students' racial prejudice, and the interactions among the different forms of inter- and intraracial contact, using data collected from nearly four thousand students at 28 of the most selective colleges and universities in the United States. These interactions indicate how multiple forms of social interaction simultaneously influence students' later interactions and racial prejudice. Lastly, I examine the influence of taking courses in a variety of academic departments that expose students to different perspectives about race and inequality and influence their racial attitudes and beliefs throughout college. Although this is not traditionally considered a form of cross-group interaction, these courses do bring students of different racial and ethnic backgrounds together to specifically discuss race and inequality in varying ways.

This area of research tests the general hypothesis that increased interactions across racial and ethnic lines will decrease elite college students' racial prejudice toward different racial and ethnic groups. However, if young elites do attend colleges that perpetuate disconnected social worlds (as suggested above), then it is possible that interracial interactions may not influence their racial prejudice at all, or worse, may increase their prejudice toward different racial and ethnic groups. The social interactions of students at elite colleges are framed by their beliefs in meritocracy, diversity, and inequality, which limit their learning of and from different racial and ethnic groups, a major aspect of reducing racial prejudice. I argue it is the privilege afforded to young elites on such campuses, and the structure and culture of the campuses themselves, which allow them to "ease" through social interactions while maintaining their views of race and inequality. That is, the practice of privilege manifests itself among young elites in college through the ease of everyday life supported by their institutions (Armstrong and Hamilton 2013; Bourdieu 1996; Khan 2011).

Khan noted in his study of students at an elite boarding school in the Northeast that the embodiment of privilege is "ease," which is the ability to interact during numerous situations and regarding varying topics using an omnivorous knowledge of the world (i.e., a broad-reaching understanding of many aspects of culture, history, and life in general), particularly elite social worlds and their norms (Khan 2011, 15–16 and 77–113). Important for the current study is how the social interactions of students influence their "knowledge" of race and inequality, specifically how it adjusts their racial prejudice toward different groups. As I described earlier, inequality is framed in highly individualized ways that support the view of a colorblind meritocracy in understanding racial inequality. As Khan notes, "inequality is explained not by the practices of the elites but instead by the character of the disadvantaged. Their [disadvantaged people's] limited (exclusive) knowledge, tastes, and dispositions mean they have not seized upon the fruits of our newly open world" (Khan 2011, 16). This view of inequality is supported by the "exception as the rule" environment young elites develop in (described above), whereby students of color in elite schools and colleges are often seen as "normal," talented, and intelligent individuals who assist with showcasing an elite institution's diversity, not as those lucky enough to gain access to such institutions in a racialized society. When students encounter information or experience interactions not supporting their meritocratic views and understanding of racial inequality, they are able to ease through such interactions using the ultimate attribution error to rationalize that some people are not the "best and brightest" or have unfortunate situations not allowing them to take advantage of an equal opportunity society, which is why inequality exists. Also possible is another "exception to the rule" rationale used by whites in these social environments: racial and ethnic minority peers are not worthy of their places at these schools. This builds on the belief that affirmative action programs such as race-conscious admissions policies are "reverse discrimination," and in the current case, bring supposedly unqualified students of color to campus who were traditionally excluded from inclusion in these highly selective institutions (Bonilla-Silva 2014, 131–135). Both possibilities frame social interactions in such ways as to disassociate race and inequality from students' lives, allowing them to claim their individuality and merit in a growingly diverse social world. Thus, their supposed omnivorous knowledge of race and inequality is limited to their predominant experiences within the social worlds of elite schools and colleges, which are often marked by homophilous and segregated social networks reinforcing their views of race and inequality within the larger social world. Given that the dominant group of elite social worlds has been and continues to be whites (see Espenshade and Radford 2009; Karabel 2005; Massey et al. 2003; Soares 2007; Wilder 2013), I argue that this disconnected view of race and inequality is more crystallized among young white elites, and that even cross-race interactions rarely modify it during college. Additionally, the ease of privilege in elite social worlds is simultaneously the ability to navigate whiteness in spaces and organizations historically designed for white elites.[17] With this in mind, the often-used campus climate measures may actually reflect the boundary enforcement of whiteness in social worlds and indicate how successful young elites ease through these environments and are possibly sanctioned for not fitting the elite, white norm, which is found in other studies of young elites (see Khan 2011).

Racial Ideology as "Knowledge" of Race and Inequality

Studies of intergroup contact theory are most concerned with racial prejudice, a prominent component of racial ideology. Additionally, as racial ideology guides people throughout their lives, this ideology arguably forms the "knowledge" possibly modified through social interactions. Racial prejudice has two related components: an affective component and a cognitive component. The affective component of racial prejudice reflects negative emotions and feelings toward a group, while the cognitive component reflects a poorly founded or unfounded belief about a group, better known as a stereotype (Quillian 2006, 300; also Taylor and Pettigrew 2000). A debate about the necessity of both components to form prejudice exists, with some researchers noting that negative affect without a "faulty stereotype" may not necessarily constitute prejudice (Bobo 1988). Traditionally, social psychology focused on the cognitive component of prejudice, although the affective component adds a significant amount to researchers' understanding of prejudice (Pettigrew 1997). For example, researchers would ask about a person's support for particular racial stereotypes (e.g., lazy, unintelligent, violence-prone, etc.), whereas more recent research expands our understanding regarding intergroup contact effects on the feelings and emotions a person has that are related to other racial and ethnic groups. Moreover, recent studies of intergroup contact find cross-group interactions influence the affective component of prejudice more than the cognitive component (Tropp and Pettigrew 2011, 97–114).

Scholars argue traditional racial prejudice has evolved into a modern, more subtle form of racial prejudice following the civil rights movement (see Bobo et al. 1997; Bonilla-Silva 2014; Quillian 2006; Schuman et al. 1997). This subtlety in modern forms of racial prejudice typically is a result of defending traditional values (such as the belief in meritocracy and other values, which allow victim-blaming to occur in situations of failure by an outgroup), exaggerating cultural differences instead of claiming outright genetic inferiority or difference, and restricting positive emotions toward outgroups (Pettigrew and Meertens 1995). Allport's (1954) definition of prejudice was broadened by Pettigrew and Meertens, who note that prejudicial attitudes, which include racial stereotypes, allow for the justification of racial discrimination through the formation of "ideological clusters of beliefs" (Pettigrew and Meertens 1995, 58). An example of the use of racial attitudes to justify racial discrimination is found in the historical discussion of the rise of slavery in the United States.[18]

One conceptualization of modern racial prejudice is racial resentment, a stratification ideology using racial individualism by whites to explain racial inequality in society and their racial policy attitudes.[19] Racial individualism views a racial or ethnic group's position in society as a reflection of the group's effort and initiative. Racial individualism is a key component of racial resentment, which has slowly replaced the use of symbolic racism among scholars who view it as a more accurate understanding of modern racial prejudice (Hughes 1997; Kinder and Sanders 1996; Sears 1988; Tuch and Hughes 2011). The most recent perspective on this modern form of racial prejudice is a set of racial beliefs among whites developed through early socialization around race and racial issues, centering on the belief that blacks violate tenets of the Protestant ethic such as hard work and self-reliance (Sears 1988; Sears and Henry 2003; Tuch and Hughes 2011). This view of racial inequality by whites focuses on the individual and their group, while often dismissing structural explanations of inequality and increasing the level of disagreement with governmental efforts toward equal opportunity and racial equality such as affirmative action (Hughes 1997; Hughes and Tuch 2000; Kinder and Sanders 1996; Schuman et al. 1997; Tuch and Hughes 2011).

Racial resentment differs from other conceptions of modern prejudice such as subtle racial prejudice and laissez-faire racism (see Bobo, Kluegel, and Smith 1997; Pettigrew and Meertens 1995). Racial resentment more forcefully emphasizes the negative stereotypes and beliefs about blacks described above (Hughes 1997; Kinder and Sanders 1996). Subtle prejudice, however, does include negative black affect. Racial resentment also differs from laissez-faire racism, which emphasizes historical patterns of racial inequality in American society. Laissez-faire racism also uses Blumer's (1958) group position approach, which describes whites' subjective perception of blacks as a threat to their resources, status, and privileges.[20] Modern forms of racial prejudice have been noted to influence people of color in addition to whites (see Bonilla-Silva 2014, 199–224). This study examines how social interactions among elite college students intertwine with both their traditional, group-specific forms of traditional prejudice as well as the central component of modern racial prejudice, racial individualism.

RACE, SOCIAL IDENTITY, AND THE CONTINUUM BETWEEN BOUNDARIES

An important aspect of understanding young elites' social world in college and their views of race and inequality relates to how they identify themselves. More specifically, how elite college students connect with racial and ethnic groups, including their own, can influence their social interactions as well as their racial attitudes and beliefs. One particularly cogent framework for understanding how elite college students connect race and identity is through social identity theory. Social identity is a person's sense of belonging to a social category or group, and originates from a person's group membership.[21] Social identity theory developed out of the work of intergroup relations scholars, particularly Turner and colleagues (1987). This theory posits that people attempt to maintain a positive social identity, which derives from favorable comparisons of their ingroup with outgroups. Social identity theory builds off of self-categorization, whereby a person categorizes other people who are similar to them along some dimension (i.e., race, ethnicity, religion, gender, social class, etc.) as the "ingroup" (Stets and Burke 2000).

A person's social identity is activated in different contexts and situations, which include social interactions. People have multiple components of their identity, and these different components can override one another in different situations, meaning identity maintenance is a continuous process, and the salience of a person's identity may be activated in various ways based on the components of their identity and the situation at hand. Social categories precede individuals, and individuals are born into these structured group categories; however, social identity theory does not often consider the social structural characteristics influencing the activation of a group identity (Stets and Burke 2000). These categories are quite large, and have traditionally been constructed and reconstructed by one group of people (whites) to distinguish who is a member of their ingroup (see Bonilla-Silva 2014; Feagin 2010; Zuberi 2001). Scholars have identified several dimensions of group identification that point to the complexity of the identity maintenance process, such as closeness or attachment to a group (see Ashmore, Deaux, and McLaughlin-Volpe 2004). This study uses closeness to racial and ethnic groups as proxy measures of a student's social identity. The measures of closeness to specific racial and ethnic groups fit measures of attachment as well (also noted in Ashmore, Deaux, and McLaughlin-Volpe 2004).

Importantly, this approach to social identity does not limit analyses to whether or not a person identifies with a particular racial or ethnic group, but rather, to how connected or attached they are to each group. Thus, this research extends recent discussions by sociologist Matthew W. Hughey (2012) on racial identity as a continuum extending between boundaries of group memberships, and even within groups. People can modify their identity in different ways, and one identity maintenance strategy influencing a person's social identity is ingroup bias. Social identity theory hypothesizes that higher levels of identification with the ingroup by a person will lead to that person having more positive ingroup bias. Furthermore, a person's ingroup identification can influence their level of stereotyping and prejudice toward an outgroup (Stets and Burke 2000; Tajfel and Turner 1997). Thus, a person's social identity with one racial or ethnic group most likely leads to higher levels of prejudice toward other racial and ethnic groups.

As mentioned earlier, students are socialized and interact with each other during their childhoods leading up to their entrance into college, with race, racial prejudice, and racism in mind.[22] Through the social identity process and identifying with structured categories like race and ethnicity, people develop a working knowledge of the components of each category and the relationships between the categories, and they act according to this knowledge; thus, people "[act] in the context of, referring to, and reaffirming the social structure" (Stets and Burke 2000, 232; also Thoits and Virshup 1997). This knowledge can ultimately consist of prejudicial views of groups and how racial inequality exists in a world viewed as a meritocracy. Therefore, by the time students enter college, they have developed some degree of racial identity in regard to their closeness to and identification with a racial or ethnic group, which could directly influence their level of racial prejudice and the amount of social interaction they take part in during college.

During childhood and college, people refine their identification with racial and ethnic categories and the people they perceive to be members of such groupings, including when choosing friends (Doyle and Kao 2007; Harris and Sim 2002; Kao and Joyner 2004, 2007; Lee and Bean 2007). This occurs among elite college students as well. As noted in previous research, the socialization of people within elite institutions such as colleges and universities shapes the ideology of these individuals in particular ways, which are reinforced by their increasingly homophilous social networks and activities (Armstrong and Hamilton 2013; Bourdieu 1996; Domhoff 1978; Khan 2011). As elite college students progress through college, their views of race and inequality are directed toward certain perspectives benefiting elites' interests as a whole, and reinforce racial inequality given the history of what these interests typically hold for racial and ethnic minorities in society who are not among elites (Bartels 2008; Feagin 2010). Although Khan emphasizes the demographic changes of elites globally, he also notes elite institutions such as colleges and universities assist with supporting elites' overall advantaged position in society; their structure locks in the benefits of aligning oneself with elites and their associated positions and perspectives. This structure is entrenched to such a degree that "even as some new members join the elite, they do so within the context of the institutional arrangements that allowed for their ascent; thus, they often become committed to such arrangements" (Khan 2012, 366). The structure is framed by young elites as the product of a meritocratic and open system, which rationalizes inequality in individualized ways while simultaneously justifying their continued access to privileged positions and increasing their advantages through the credentialing of high-status degrees (Khan 2011; Khan and Jerolmack 2013). Elites actively work to define and isolate themselves using this framing and their experiences within elite social worlds such as the colleges and universities examined in this volume. Elite-created institutions such as colleges and universities, particularly those held in high esteem and considered the vanguard institutions to attend, are in line with Pierre Bourdieu's lifelong examination of social reproduction in society, which emphasizes the central influence that educational institutions have on the reproduction of inequality (see Bourdieu 1996; Bourdieu and Passeron 1990).

The highly individualized perspective of society and educational opportunity held by young elites can produce distinct patterns of identification with racial and ethnic groups. The reliance on such individualized perspectives of race and inequality suggests young elites are less likely to identify with racial and ethnic groups on the whole, conforming to colorblind views of society and the use of race today that are similar to the patterns found among the current generation of college-goers (better known as the "millennials") (see Apollon 2011; Bonilla-Silva 2014; Pew Research Center 2010, 2014). Natasha Warikoo (2016; Warikoo and Novais 2015) also finds elite college students, particularly whites, operate with views of racial identity that downplay structural aspects of racial inequality in favor of colorblindness. Students entering elite colleges and universities are more racially and ethnically diverse than they were in the past, and there has been a dramatic change in the number of women entering and graduating from such institutions. In addition, these students are wealthier than cohorts entering in the past (Bowen and Bok 1998; Bowen, Kurzweil, and Tobin 2005; Buchman, DiPrete, and McDaniel 2008; Espenshade and Radford 2009; Karabel 2005; Soares 2007). This increase in diversity is seen as evidence of the openness of society today compared with the past, allowing for an additional aspect to the ease of privileged social interactions in elite social worlds to influence young elites' views: the arguably increased presence of racial and ethnic minorities in their social world compared to childhood allows young elites, particularly whites, to dismiss or remain oblivious to discrimination and inequality within and beyond their elite social world. This could reinforce stereotypical views of racial and ethnic groups and how to address inequality. The current study extends research on reproduction among elites to examine how elite colleges and universities perpetuate racial inequality through social life on their campuses, and how interactions in elite social worlds can modify or reify their views of race and inequality in society as well as young elites' identification with these views and racial groups.

ELITE COLLEGES AND THEIR STUDENTS

In order to examine the patterns of social interactions and the racial attitudes and beliefs of elite college students, this study uses data from the National Longitudinal Survey of Freshmen (NLSF), a project designed by Douglas S. Massey and Camille Z. Charles and funded by the Mellon Foundation and the Atlantic Philanthropies. The NLSF has five waves of data following 3,924 freshmen from the fall of 1999 until their graduation from college in the spring of 2003, from 28 of the most selective colleges and universities in the United States (based on student SAT scores and class rank and the *U.S. News and World Report College Rankings*). Twelve of these institutions are located in the Northeast region of the country, eight in the Midwest, five in the South, and three in the West. Massey and colleagues, who collected the NLSF data, chose the sample of institutions to be comparable to Bowen and Bok's *College and Beyond Survey*, with the addition of the University of California at Berkeley as the main modification to the institutions included in the data collection.[23] The average percentage of Asian and Pacific Islander students enrolled at these institutions in 1998 was 13.1%, while 8.1% were black students, 5.0% were Latino students, and 69.2% were white students.[24]

The NLSF dataset contains a variety of items relating to racial prejudice, the campus racial climate, and intergroup relations. This dataset also contains extensive precollege information allowing for an examination of how young elites' social worlds prior to college influence their interactions with peers along with their views of race and inequality. The analyses in this volume are for students who finished college within six years of their first entrance at their original institution, meaning transfer students (even between institutions in the NLSF dataset) are not considered in this study. Each institution has its own racial climate, race-related history, and patterns of interactions, making a full investigation into young elites quite complicated when considering a student's experience in more than one college environment. With this in mind, the analyses of elite college students included 867 whites, 796 blacks, 835 Asians and Pacific Islanders, and 753 Hispanics and Latinos. Of these students, women were the majority within each racial and ethnic group, with the highest percentage among black students (68.1%), followed by Hispanics and Latinos (59.8%), Asians and Pacific Islanders (57.7%), and whites (52.2%).

Beginning with data from a few weeks prior to or within the first weeks of students' first semester in college, researchers collected a wealth of information relating to the family background, social interactions, academic experiences and outcomes, community and school resources and perceptions, racial attitudes, and social psychological outcomes of students. Then, in the spring of their first year and each of the three succeeding years, data were collected on the academic and social experiences of students on campus, their academic information including majors and grades, and their attitudes and views on various topics including race and inequality. The current study uses data across all five waves collected while students pursued their undergraduate degrees. A further discussion of these data and a list of measures utilized in this study are provided in the Appendix.

OVERVIEW OF THE BOOK

I provide a look at how the social characteristics and precollege experiences of the students who step onto campus at these highly selective colleges and universities influence their prejudice toward different racial and ethnic groups and views of inequality in Chapter Two. The nearly 18 years of socialization that students experience prior to college can provide fairly rigid frameworks for them to understand race and inequality. Through a series of analyses I show how various characteristics and experiences these students bring with them to college inform stereotypes of different racial and ethnic groups as well as how much students use individualistic explanations for why racial inequality exists in the world. This chapter concludes with a discussion of the influential factors shaping students' entering views of race and inequality, and explores why particular social characteristics of students such as gender, religiosity, and racialized social identities influence their views.

Chapter Three documents the patterns of social interactions among elite college students across their four years on campus. Elite college campuses are not thoroughly integrated, nor are they completely segregated. A complex racial hierarchy exists on campus for students to navigate with segregation, isolation, and some levels of integration found among student interactions. The characteristics and experiences of these students that influence whom they become friends with, date, and room with, and who is mostly likely to compose the student organizations they join during college, are explored through a series of analyses. Importantly, how students perceive and experience the campus racial climate is an integral factor in the relationships they form with their peers throughout their college years. This chapter lays the foundation for understanding how these campuses continue to support a circumscribed set of relations among student groups forming a racial hierarchy on elite college campuses around material opportunities and resources as well as perceived social desirability.

Chapter Four explores how the relationships formed on campus for elite college students across racial and ethnic lines can, and often cannot, influence their views of race and inequality when they leave college. Through a detailed series of analyses, I examine how influential life on campus is to the views of race and inequality among elite college students. Although not countering the long-standing literature of intergroup contact, these analyses indicate the importance of the larger campus racial climate surrounding students, which influences whom they interact with during college (as noted in Chapter Three), and also how influential these interactions can be on their views. Additionally, elite college students' racialized social identities are an important factor influencing their views on race and inequality in different ways depending on whom the students are considering in relation to their own group. This chapter provides a powerful discussion of what changes in views of race and inequality elite college students experience after their four years of college.

Chapter Five provides a thorough discussion of the findings from the analyses documented in the aforementioned chapters. I focus on the importance of how higher education institutions themselves can dictate the degree of interaction across racial and ethnic lines and solidify particular views of race and inequality. I explore how the framework of organizational racial habitus can assist us with understanding the elite social worlds of these students. This discussion brings together literature on how the culture and structure in these elite social worlds shape students' race-related experiences and correspondingly reproduce racial inequality in both student interactions and racial ideologies. Next, I discuss the importance of linking the racialized social identities of students to this organizational habitus of elite colleges and universities. How students identify with multiple groups and literally relate to one another through social interaction takes on new meaning and importance with this framing in mind. Finally, I examine what these findings and theoretical perspectives mean for understanding what is commonly referred to as "race relations" and their impact on students' racial ideologies.

I conclude in Chapter Six by providing a general narrative of the college-going experience of elite college students and how this experience shapes their views of race and inequality when they complete their degrees. Then, I discuss why further consideration of colleges' racial habitus sheds light on how these findings of students' interactions and views are somewhat unsurprising when we consider the mindset of young elites concerning diversity, individuality, and race on these campuses. With this in mind, I discuss the recent protests against racism and inequality on college campuses with a critical eye toward the rhetoric of the "educational benefits of diversity" framing many of these protests, which blinds people from understanding central issues at the heart of these protests. Finally, I consider the importance of pursuing organizational change within elite colleges and universities, and higher education as a whole, to create a more holistic education incorporating social interaction with their coursework to combat the reproduction of racial inequality.

2 · LIFE BEFORE COLLEGE

Factors Influencing Early Views of Race and Inequality

Which children grow up in poverty, which schools children attend, and what kinds of community resources and social networks are available to young people are factors strongly influenced by organizing aspects of race and racism. Educational institutions are not immune from complicity in organizing the life chances of a person based on the racialized social system that surrounds their walls and grounds. The influence of educational environments on a person's life begins early, as schools and colleges shape not only how people understand race, difference, and inequality but also how a person sees the world and how they navigate social interactions as they grow older.

The depth and breadth of how race and racism organizes our lives is found within educational institutions that shape the lives of children before they enter primary school and are designed to combat this aspect of our society. Researchers found that children attending preschools with a racially diverse population, a well-designed multicultural curriculum to build students' knowledge and acceptance of social differences among people, and teachers trained to combat stereotypical thinking, still exhibited racial stereotypes (see Van Ausdale and Feagin 2001). The teachers, despite their training, reinforced traditional notions of racial difference between students. These teachers also corrected students who described or understood themselves outside of traditional definitions of who is "white" and "black." For example, during an exercise where children were asked to create hands out of paper and color them to reflect themselves, a young black girl colored her cut-out hand pink. The teacher, somewhat befuddled, told the child she did not use the correct color, and the young girl pointed to the pink palm of her hand to justify why she colored her cut-out hand a similar color. In this brief example from Van Ausdale and Feagin's (2001) famous study, conceptions of racial identity and categorization were reinforced by traditional notions of race and difference among the teachers who were trained to counter such notions. These moments among preschool-aged children develop even as parents employ "colorblind" socialization approaches to race and racism (Pahlke, Bigler, and Suizzo 2012). Beyond the preschool years, however, socialization processes around race and inequality continue throughout primary and secondary education in the classrooms and on the playgrounds of both public and private schools in the United States, and have done so since the early years of the public school system (see Bettie 2003; Burkholder 2011; Khan 2011; Lewis 2003; Lewis-McCoy 2014; Perry 2002; Stoll 2013).

Further considering the example from the preschool classroom above indicates how what happens within educational institutions can reproduce aspects of racial socialization, which can also shape inequality in schools and beyond. This example illustrates how difficult it is to counteract a system of racism that consistently sends powerful racial messages to children, even when parents and educators attempt to raise and educate them to resist the racial status quo, which has traditionally been the focus of many parents of color (Hagerman 2014). Despite this early and sometimes inflexible socialization around race and inequality which children experience once they enter school, more information is needed on how the backgrounds of elite college students influence the development of their early views of race and inequality, and how their social backgrounds inform their social interactions when they enter college. As found in previous studies (Hagerman 2014; Johnson 2015; Khan 2011; Lewis-McCoy 2014), affluent students often discuss race and inequality from highly privileged positions, reinforcing traditional stereotypes of communities of color and highly individualistic explanations of inequality. As mentioned in the previous chapter, the availability bias existing for these students is structured around them throughout their precollege years as a majority of them come from affluent backgrounds and environments that can limit their understanding of race and inequality in the larger social world (Johnson 2015; Khan 2015). With this in mind, the factors influencing students prior to stepping onto a college campus are important to consider because these factors can shed light on what views about race and inequality students bring with them to college, and possibly why they hold such views.

LIFE BEFORE COLLEGE

Students at elite colleges often originate in privileged socioeconomic positions in society. However, the degrees of such positions are influenced by the traditional racial hierarchy in society, as seen below (Table 2.1). As this table illustrates, the mean for each student group is presented to identify what social backgrounds these students bring with them to campus. The differences between each student group are marked in the far right column. Several differences are worth mentioning.

TABLE 2.1   Social backgrounds of elite college students

Characteristic	Student Group				Means test
	White	Black	Latino	Asian & Pacific Islander	
Female	.52	.68	.60	.57	a,b,c,d,e
International student	.05	.08	.19	.30	a,b,c,d,e,f
Family socioeconomic status					
Mother's education	5.56	4.96	4.64	5.09	a,b,c,d,f
Father's education	5.96	5.06	4.98	5.79	a,b,c,e,f
Family income (in 2000 dollars)	112,773.62	74,364.39	82,145.33	101,672.49	a,b,c,d,e,f
Homeowner	.94	.73	.82	.88	a,b,c,d,e,f
Religious beliefs					
Protestant	.38	.70	.14	.27	a,b,c,d,e,f
Catholic	.29	.18	.69	.17	a,b,c,d,f
Other religious beliefs	.32	.12	.18	.56	a,b,c,d,e,f
Religiosity	5.14	6.47	5.34	5.45	a,c,d,e
Community segregation					
Predominantly white	.92	.41	.62	.88	a,b,c,d,e,f
Integrated	.07	.22	.16	.11	a,b,c,d,e,f
Predominantly minority	.01	.38	.22	.01	a,b,d,e,f
School segregation and type					
Predominantly white	.74	.44	.51	.70	a,b,c,d,e,f
Integrated	.24	.34	.29	.28	a,b,e
Predominantly minority	.02	.22	.19	.02	a,b,e,f
Private school	.29	.30	.34	.24	b,c,e,f
Region					
Northeast	.36	.32	.31	.32	b,c
Midwest	.25	.25	.19	.20	b,c,d,e
South	.20	.27	.22	.25	a,c,d
West	.19	.15	.27	.23	a,b,d,e

NOTE: Analyses conducted with nonimputed NLSF dataset.

[a] Significant difference ($p < .05$) between white and black students.

[b] Significant difference ($p < .05$) between white and Latino students.

[c] Significant difference ($p < .05$) between white and Asian and Pacific Islander students.

[d] Significant difference ($p < .05$) between black and Latino students.

[e] Significant difference ($p < .05$) between black and Asian and Pacific Islander students.

[f] Significant difference ($p < .05$) between Latino and Asian and Pacific Islander students.

There exists a prominent gender difference among elite college students: women were the slight majority among white and Asian and Pacific Islander students, while they were solidly the majority for black and Latino students who entered elite colleges. When we consider the status of students regarding their national origin, although over 90% of white and black students at elite colleges were from the United States, nearly 20% of Latino students and fully 30% of Asian and Pacific Islander students were from nations other than the United States. Turning to the households of these students, we find the parents of elite college students are well educated; most have at least a college degree (represented by a "5" in the coding of the data), with fathers having higher education levels than mothers. White students come from substantially more affluent households compared to the other student groups, who are fairly well off themselves, as evident in the average household incomes ($112,773) as well as the percentage of students who reported that their families owned their homes (94%). Although Asian and Pacific Islander students also come from fairly affluent, although significantly lower, socioeconomic positions in comparison to their white peers, Latino students are from families with less financial comfort than both groups, and black students are the least affluent of the four student groups. As we will see later in this chapter, these differences in households can influence students' views of race and inequality.

Religion can also shape how people view race and inequality in varying ways. Among elite college students, we find differences in religious beliefs as well as religiosity worth discussing further. Black students reported the highest following of Protestant denominations and Latinos the highest following of Catholicism, with Asians and Pacific Islanders reporting the largest following of other religions. With regards to religiosity (i.e., frequency of attending religious events and services), black students reported the highest levels, with the remaining three student groups reporting similar, lower levels of religiosity. Turning to the communities and the schools where young elites live and study prior to college, most whites live in almost exclusively white communities and attend schools with less than 30 percent students of color in their classes. Most Asian and Pacific Islander students also live in almost exclusively white communities and attend predominantly white schools. Latino students and black students are much more likely to live in communities and attend schools that are more racially integrated than their peers, while black students are also the most likely to come from segregated communities and schools where blacks and Latinos make up more than 70% of the population. Among all four student groups, one-quarter to one-third of students attended private schools prior to enrolling in college. Lastly, elite college students come from different regions around the nation, with the Northeast sending the most students on average across the four racial and ethnic student groups (see also Massey et al. 2003).

The social backgrounds of the students at elite colleges and universities illustrate the affluent socioeconomic positions these students have upon entering their first year of college. Financial difficulties are less likely to impede their academic and social progress in college, but such situations are more likely to occur for black and Latino students. Additionally, the predominantly white social worlds of elite colleges and universities correspond with the communities and schools that most white and Asian and Pacific Islander students have experience with prior to college. Thus, it is arguably easier for these two student groups to navigate the elite social worlds of these institutions and their patterns and norms of interactions, and to conform to the dominant views of race and inequality. On the other hand, black and Latino students are less familiar with such social worlds prior to college, which could influence whom they interact with, and how such interactions influence their views of race and inequality.

Overall, similar patterns of who attends elite colleges and universities match those of decades past despite the many societal changes following the rights movements in the twentieth century (Bowen and Bok 1998; Bowen, Kurzweil, and Tobin 2005; Buchman, DiPrete, and McDaniel 2008; Espenshade and Radford 2009; Karabel 2005; Soares 2007). In the succeeding sections, I examine what views of race and inequality students bring with them to elite colleges as well as their identification with different racial and ethnic groups. Then, a series of analyses identify what social characteristics and precollege experiences influence such early views of race and inequality among these students. These analyses point to a somewhat disturbing trend for intergroup relations scholars, as precollege friendships may not shape elite college students' views of race and inequality as much as previous studies suggest. Additionally, these analyses point to the importance of students' racialized social identities in shaping their early views of race and inequality, which are often left out of many examinations of such views.

RACE AND INEQUALITY VIEWS AT COLLEGE ENTRANCE AND THEIR CAUSES

A variety of social characteristics can influence the racial prejudices and views of inequality among elite college students before they arrive on campus. Prior to examining what factors influence these views of race and inequality, we need to explore the prejudice levels these students hold toward each racial or ethnic outgroup. That is, to understand the story of how college experiences may impact elite college students' views of race and inequality, we must first consider what views and experiences students bring with them to campus. Table 2.2 displays the average levels of traditional racial prejudice each student group held with regard to their three racial and ethnic outgroups in addition to their views on a related measure about the causes of racial inequality, whom they were friends with at college entrance, and a proxy measure for racialized social identity examining how close they felt their ideas and feelings were to those of four racial and

TABLE 2.2   Entering racial prejudice, racial individualism, cross-race friendships, and racialized social identity among elite college students

Variable	Student Group				
	Whites	Blacks	Latinos	Asian & Pacific Islanders	Means Tests
Traditional racial prejudice					
Anti-white	——	−.07	−.17	.68	d,e,f
Anti-black	.28	——	.12	1.06	b,c,f
Anti-Latino	.32	.10	——	1.12	a,c,e
Anti-Asian	−.57	−.86	−.86	——	a,b
Racial individualism toward					
Blacks	5.37	5.06	5.28	5.46	a,d,e
Latinos	5.10	4.84	5.35	5.28	a,b,d,e
Asian & Pacific Islanders	5.54	5.67	5.63	5.86	c,e,f
All three groups	5.33	5.20	5.42	5.53	c,d,e
Precollege friendships					
Whites	.79	.28	.54	.51	a,b,c,d,e
Blacks	.05	.56	.08	.06	a,b,d,e,f
Latinos	.04	.06	.26	.05	a,b,d,e,f
Asian & Pacific Islanders	.10	.07	.10	.36	a,c,d,e,f
Closeness to					
Whites	6.62	4.63	5.89	5.90	a,b,c,d,e
Blacks	5.42	6.69	5.22	5.04	a,b,c,d,e,f
Latinos	5.11	5.21	6.25	4.82	b,c,d,e,f
Asian & Pacific Islanders	5.45	4.26	5.00	6.34	a,b,c,d,e,f

NOTE: Means calculated using nonimputed NLSF data.
[a] Significant difference ($p < .05$) between white and black students.
[b] Significant difference ($p < .05$) between white and Latino students.
[c] Significant difference ($p < .05$) between white and Asian and Pacific Islander students.
[d] Significant difference ($p < .05$) between black and Latino students.
[e] Significant difference ($p < .05$) between black and Asian and Pacific Islander students.
[f] Significant difference ($p < .05$) between Latino and Asian and Pacific Islander students.

ethnic groups. Also included in the table is the proportion of friendships with each racial and ethnic group to provide a baseline for their precollege interracial interactions.

For the traditional racial prejudice rows, each value represents the average prejudice level among each student group using a difference score that compared how students rated racial and ethnic groups on four traits (intelligence, work ethic, self-support, and sticking to tasks) with their own group. Positive scores indicate more racial prejudice toward a group, while a negative score suggests students think more positively about a group compared to their own (i.e., positive racial bias).[1] The values in the racial individualism columns indicate how much each student group agreed on a scale combining two items discussing why blacks, Latinos, and Asians and Pacific Islanders may not achieve higher positions in society. Students reported their level of agreement on whether (1) a person of each group only has herself to blame for not doing better and they need to try harder to do better; and (2) a person of each group who is educated and does what is considered "proper" will get ahead in society. This scale ranged from strongly disagreeing with the statement (equaling 0) to strongly agreeing with the statement (equaling 10). This measure corresponds with a dominant perspective following the peak of the civil rights movement in the 1960s centering on individual efforts in an assumed equal opportunity society. This measure can also shed light on how elite college students understand the causes of racial inequality in connection with their beliefs in a meritocratic system solely rewarding hard work and achievement.

Figure 2.1 visually depicts students' entering levels of racial prejudice toward each group. Again, positive scores represent negative bias toward outgroups while negative scores represent positive racial bias toward an outgroup in comparison to a student's own group. From these analyses, we gather that each racial and ethnic student group held negative views toward each racial outgroup in relation to anti-black and anti-Latino prejudice. That is, each student group thought blacks and Latinos were less intelligent, hardworking, self-supporting, and able to stick to tasks compared to their own racial or ethnic group. Asian and Pacific Islander students held the highest levels of prejudice toward blacks, followed by white students and Latino students. A similar pattern existed for elite college students' prejudice toward Latinos, with Asian and Pacific Islander students having the highest levels of prejudice, followed by white students and black students. A mixture of views was held by students regarding whites. Black and Latino students held slight positive bias toward whites, meaning they viewed whites as slightly more hardworking, intelligent, self-supporting, and able to stick to tasks compared to their own groups. Asian and Pacific Islander students held negative views of whites, unlike other students of color. Not to be lost among these comparisons between student groups is the reality that these students hold differing views of racial and ethnic groups outside of their own, and unfortunately, these views are not of equals to themselves.

A different story exists when we examine the views of Asians and Pacific Islanders. White, black, and Latino students viewed Asians and Pacific Islanders positively compared to their own group at college entrance, with Latino students thinking the most positively of the three groups. Although one can only speculate at this point why students hold such positive views of Asians and Pacific Islanders, students' views may relate to the predominant myth of the "model minority" that surrounds these groups—that Asians and Pacific Islanders embody positive cultural traits leading to higher social mobility (see Chou

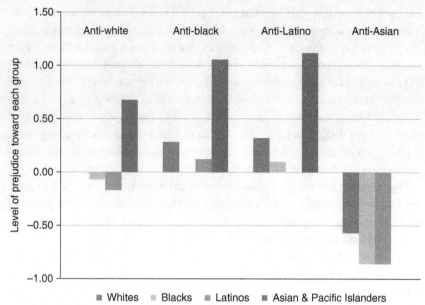

FIGURE 2.1. Entering racial prejudice among elite college students

and Feagin 2008; Lee and Zhou 2015). However, it is important to note that this myth is highly problematic, as it frames all Asian and Pacific Islander groups as successful in American society including in higher education, which simultaneously dismisses experiences of racism toward these groups and glosses over a contentious history of how Asians and Pacific Islanders were used as a "buffer group" between whites and blacks following the end of slavery (Chou and Feagin 2008; Kim 1999).

In relation to how students connect racial inequality and individual efforts, another story is found among these entering college students. As seen in both Table 2.2 and Figure 2.2, students across race and ethnicity slightly agreed that individual efforts were important factors for a person's social position for blacks, Latinos, and Asians and Pacific Islanders. At this point of their lives, students ever so slightly agreed that people have themselves to blame for not doing better in life and should work harder to achieve more, and students supported the belief that education and doing what is considered "proper" will lead to better life outcomes regardless of race. Variations exist in this general narrative across students of different races and ethnicities in relation to the specific group scales. The most notable is that black students slightly disagreed that individual efforts and doing what is "proper" as an educated Latino person will lead to better life outcomes. Taken together, general support among elite college students exists for the belief in meritocracy and the importance of individual efforts to improve social positions.

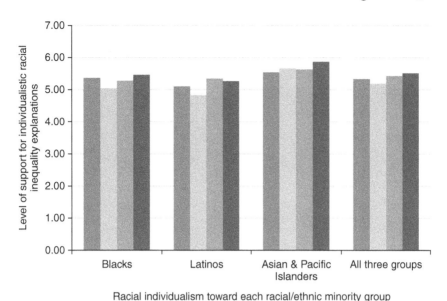

FIGURE 2.2. Racial individualism among elite college students at college entrance

The friendships of students throughout childhood can have a significant influence on their racial prejudice levels and views of inequality, as they can communicate important information and experiences among friends. Students of different races and ethnicities were connected to different groups of friends when they entered college, and these differences in their friendship networks were quite significant in the end. In the table, the proportions of their friendship networks are reported. These same proportions are displayed in Figure 2.3. For white students, almost eight out of ten of their friendships were with other whites (79%), while the second-highest amount of friends they had in their networks were among Asians and Pacific Islanders (10%). On average, white students had far fewer friends among blacks (5%) and Latinos (4%) at college entrance. Black students entered college with far fewer white friendships (28%), and many more friendships with other blacks (56%). Black students had few friendships among Latinos (6%) and Asians and Pacific Islanders (7%) when they came to college. For Latino students, slightly more than half of their friendships were with whites (54%) and about one-quarter of their friendships were with other Latinos (26%). Similarly, Asian and Pacific Islander students had slightly more than one-half of their friendships with whites (51%) and a little over one-third of their friendships with other Asians and Pacific Islanders (36%). Latino students were much less likely to have friendships with blacks (8%) and Asians and Pacific Islanders (10%) when they entered college. Among Asian and Pacific

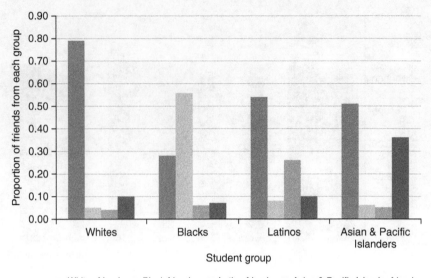

FIGURE 2.3. Average composition of elite college students' precollege friendships

Islander students, they also had low levels of friendships among blacks (6%) and Latinos (5%) when they entered college compared to their friendships among their own group and whites. Coupling these findings together, we identify a pattern of circumscribed interactions among elite college students along racial and ethnic lines that can hinder learning important information about group experiences and the histories of inequalities.

In general, students of each racial and ethnic group felt their ideas and feelings were closest to those of their own group instead of other groups. However, as also seen in Figure 2.4, none of the student groups indicated they were overwhelmingly close to members of their own group; they were moderately so. This suggests students' racialized social identity (i.e., their connection to a general group identity and perspective) was not wholly in line with that of their racial or ethnic group. Among white students, following their own group, they felt close to Asians and Pacific Islanders as well as blacks, and least close to Latinos. Black students felt closest to Latinos following their own group, then whites and Asians and Pacific Islanders. Latino students felt closest to whites following their own group, then blacks, and least close to Asians and Pacific Islanders. Among Asian and Pacific Islander students, following their own group, they felt closest to whites, then blacks, and least close to Latinos.

Overall, elite college students step onto campus with negative views toward racial and ethnic groups outside of their own with the important exception of how they view Asians and Pacific Islanders. If we return to the earlier notion posited at the outset of this volume that racial prejudice is often considered

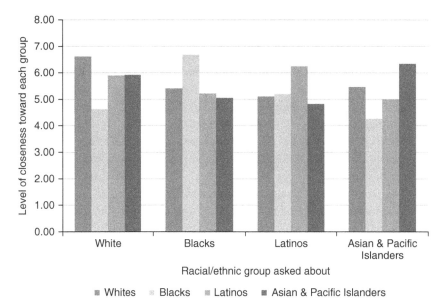

FIGURE 2.4. Closeness to each racial and ethnic group at college entrance among elite college students

"racial knowledge" by people given their reliance on racial stereotypes of different groups in comparison to their own group, elite college students view themselves and their racial or ethnic group as fairly superior to other groups at the beginning of college. Although black and Latino students were slightly more positively biased toward whites, Asian and Pacific Islander students held more negative views of whites. The obvious exception to this general trend is that white, black, and Latino students view Asians and Pacific Islanders as better than they view their own group. Again, this may result from the mythologized position of these ethnic groups as "model minorities" in society, which is highly problematic in its assumptions of group backgrounds, cultures, and experiences. These early perspectives also likely relate to the limited interaction elite college students have across racial and ethnic lines to break down these biased views of each other prior to college.

Important to note regarding prejudice levels is that elite college students do not view each other as equals when they enter college. Previous research notes a growing argument in popular discourse following the civil rights movement's peak in the 1960s around the idea that society is moving away from race and racial discrimination as important factors shaping the lives of Americans. Considering the views of elite college students, these findings alone counter the view that US society is postracial and postracism.[2] If this were so, then students would view each other as equals throughout their lives, but at this early point, they do not. Additionally, the less than complete agreement among students that individual efforts in a presumed meritocratic society are the major determinant of people's socioeconomic success provides further support for the idea that race has not "declined in significance," and students view factors external to the individual as continually influencing their life chances.[3] Students vary in the degree to which they hold racial and ethnic minorities individually accountable for their socioeconomic position, with only black students readily identifying factors outside an individual's control as more of an influence on their life chances.

However, simply because students entering elite colleges were not highly supportive of individualistic views of racial inequality, as found in previous studies of young elites, does not mean they acknowledged structural inequality (see Johnson 2015; Khan 2011; Khan and Jerolmack 2013). It is plausible that many elite college students step onto campus believing individual efforts are not as influential on social mobility because, as one affluent child replied in Johnson's study when asked how rich people become rich: "They were born with no money or they were born with lots of money and they got more" (Johnson 2015, 145). That is, students may believe more in a deterministic socioeconomic caste system whereby being affluent or being poor is more or less fixed in society, with little influence of individual efforts to overcome poverty and inequality. Such a perspective on inequality is informed by the highly affluent social environments elite college students originate from, increasing the availability bias of these students and limiting their understanding of racial inequality (Khan 2015). Further, despite the strong support of meritocracy and the impact of individual efforts found in the current and previous studies, the ease of privilege these students employ in their everyday lives and for understanding the larger social world as they grow older simultaneously allows them to navigate their elite social world while disconnecting their broad-reaching, omnivorous knowledge of society from understanding or even knowing the ground-level aspects of race and inequality (Johnson 2015; Khan 2011). This is evident in students' general support for racial stereotypes and individualistic views of inequality, which hinge on disadvantages of racial and ethnic minorities, shielding these budding elites from fully understanding the impact of intertwined white and socioeconomic privilege surrounding them every day on campus. More insidiously, these findings may relate to a certain degree of racial apathy among elite college students whereby they are indifferent to racial inequality as they do not relate to it, think it is "fixable," or possibly do not know much about racial inequality at all (see Forman 2004). With this in mind, I turn to exploring the social characteristics influencing elite college students' views of race and inequality.

Traditional Racial Prejudice

In order to identify how the social backgrounds of elite college students inform their prejudice toward racial and ethnic groups other than their own, several regression models were constructed to see how this precollege foundation sets the stage for how their views of race and inequality change during the impressionable years of college. Although previous research has considered how different social characteristics and experiences of students prior to entering college can influence their views of race and inequality, the current study expands these considerations to present a fuller picture of the early development of elite college students' racial ideology.[4] Below, three models for each student group were tested to identify what precollege characteristics influence students' views toward racial and ethnic outgroups and why racial and ethnic minority groups may not achieve more in life. For each form of traditional prejudice, the model contains the students' gender, skin color, whether they were an international student, their religious background, parental socioeconomic background, neighborhood and school segregation levels, whether they went to a private high school prior to college attendance, the region of the country they are from, the proportion of their friends who were either white, black, Asian or Pacific Islander, or Latino prior to college, and their entering racialized social identity measured by how close they felt toward their own group and each racial or ethnic outgroup.

Table 2.3 reports the social and precollege characteristics of white students and their influence on their prejudice levels at the beginning of college. The first column shows the impact of different characteristics on white students' anti-black prejudice. The second and third columns contain similar analyses for white students' anti-Latino and anti-Asian prejudice levels.

A somewhat concerning picture is present in the models for white students. Here, the models indicate that few precollege characteristics of white students significantly influenced their entering racial prejudice toward each racial and ethnic outgroup. Of those factors that did influence their views of different groups, they were inconsistent predictors spanning gender, skin complexion, and regional origin of white students, which indicates that the commonly used social characteristics of a person hold little explanatory power over what white students at elite colleges think of people of color when they first step foot onto campus. Additionally, the residential and school environments of these students had little influence on white students' prejudice toward people of color as well. Perhaps even more concerning is the lack of significance of any friendship measure, meaning that the precollege friendships of white students have no influence on their entering levels of racial prejudice, which counters much of the previous research on intergroup friendships and prejudice reduction (discussed further below).

Among white students, the most influential set of characteristics shaping their racial prejudice was their racialized social identity. In support of social identity theory, an ingroup-outgroup distinction was found for how closely white students saw their thoughts and ideas aligning toward two groups. White students who felt closer to other whites were more prejudiced toward blacks and Latinos at college entrance. The opposite was found for higher levels of closeness toward

TABLE 2.3   Factors influencing entering levels of prejudice among white students

Variable	Traditional racial prejudice		
	Anti-black	Anti-Latino	Anti-Asian
Social characteristics			
Female	−.090**	−.058	.040*
Darker skin color	.117***	.125***	−.055
International student	.021	−.023	−.049
Mother's education	.006	−.011	.030
Father's education	.005	.032	−.002
Family income	.044	.005	−.031
Parental homeownership	−.025	.018	.000
Catholic	−.009	−.007	−.022
Other religious beliefs	−.032	−.014	.025
Religiosity	.043	.057	−.017
Northeast region	−.073	.017	.071
Midwest region	−.057	.015	.137**
West region	−.042	.034	.055
Precollege environments			
Private high school	.036	.015	.025
School segregation level	.090**	.032	−.011
Neighborhood segregation level	.074*	.031	.036
Precollege friendships			
Whites	.042	.085	.140
Blacks	−.009	−.010	−.009
Latinos	−.048	.006	.061
Asians & Pacific Islanders	.004	.017	.067
Closeness to			
Whites	.385***	.303***	−.030
Blacks	−.367***	−.023	.044
Latinos	−.065	−.372***	.149*
Asians & Pacific Islanders	.035	.033	−.122*
Constant	−.348	−.442	−1.172*
Adjusted R²	.184***	.159***	.016*

NOTE: Standardized coefficients (β) reported in table. Models estimated with imputed NLSF data. Reference categories include: male, US citizen, Protestant, South resident, attended public high school.
*$p < .05$, **$p < .01$, ***$p < .001$.

these same groups, as feeling closer to blacks and Latinos lowered their prejudice toward both groups. Somewhat contrasting findings existed in the anti-Asian prejudice model. Higher levels of closeness toward whites were not significant in the anti-Asian prejudice model, but their closeness toward Latinos and Asians and Pacific Islanders was. White students who were closer to Latinos had higher levels of prejudice toward Asians and Pacific Islanders, while the opposite was found for those who felt closer to Asians and Pacific Islanders. Regardless of whom they were friends with, the friendships with other whites or with peers of different racial or ethnic groups did not influence their prejudice levels at college entrance.

The limited influence of students' precollege backgrounds and experiences continues when we examine the factors shaping black students' views of race in Table 2.4. Similar to white students, precollege friendships did not influence black students' prejudice toward other groups. Partial support for social identity theory exists among black students entering elite colleges, as those with higher levels of closeness toward whites and Latinos were less prejudiced toward those groups, while students who felt closer toward their own group were more prejudiced toward Latinos. However, the complexity of racialized social identity is seen across the anti-white and anti-Asian models for black students. It is not how close black students were to their own group that increased their prejudice toward whites at college entrance, but their closeness to Asians and Pacific Islanders. Interestingly, although higher ingroup closeness increased black students' prejudice toward Asians and Pacific Islanders, so did higher levels of closeness to Asians and Pacific Islanders, while higher levels of closeness toward whites reduced their prejudice toward this specific ethnic group.

Among Latino students in Table 2.5, their social characteristics and precollege experiences were slightly more influential on their levels of prejudice toward each racial outgroup. Similar to the findings for white and black students, few social characteristics and precollege environments or experiences influenced Latino students' racial prejudice toward other groups. However, friendships were found to influence Latino students in two models, as more friendships with blacks increased both students' prejudice toward whites and blacks. The influence of how Latino students identify with racial and ethnic groups is not only powerful toward this aspect of these students' lives, but so is the complexity of their relationships to their own and other groups. Partial support for social identity theory was found in the anti-black and anti-white models, as higher levels of closeness toward whites reduced Latino students' prejudice toward both whites and Asians and Pacific Islanders. Higher levels of closeness toward blacks increased Latino students' prejudice toward whites and Asians and Pacific Islanders, but reduced their prejudice toward blacks. More ingroup closeness increased prejudice toward blacks, but actually decreased prejudice toward Asians and Pacific Islanders for Latino students. Lastly, higher levels of closeness toward Asians and Pacific Islanders increased students' prejudice across all three models.

Turning to the influences on Asian and Pacific Islander students' prejudice at college entrance in Table 2.6, again, we find students' social characteristics and precollege experiences influenced their prejudice at low levels, far less than was

TABLE 2.4   Factors influencing entering levels of prejudice among black students

Variable	Traditional racial prejudice		
	Anti-white	Anti-Latino	Anti-Asian
Social characteristics			
Female	.033	−.025	−.002
Darker skin color	−.031	−.021	−.017
International student	−.034	.017	−.012
Mother's education	.010	.041	−.016
Father's education	−.035	−.054	−.002
Family income	.092	.003	.010
Parental homeownership	−.053	−.066	−.081*
Catholic	−.006	−.039	−.014
Other religious beliefs	.057	−.056	.048
Religiosity	−.023	.003	−.022
Northeast region	−.053	.046	−.089*
Midwest region	.010	.001	.062
West region	−.043	−.073	−.102*
Precollege environments			
Private high school	.064	.048	.057
School segregation level	.014	−.007	.055
Neighborhood segregation level	−.121**	−.097*	−.074
Precollege friendships			
Whites	−.048	−.012	−.075
Blacks	−.068	−.079	−.201
Latinos	.007	.014	−.027
Asians & Pacific Islanders	−.016	.011	−.039
Closeness to			
Whites	−.252***	−.088	−.102*
Blacks	.066	.123**	.142**
Latinos	.054	−.164**	−.043
Asians & Pacific Islanders	.173**	.091	.171**
Constant	.177	.376	−.690
Adjusted R^2	.156***	.018*	.033**

NOTE: Standardized coefficients (β) reported in table. Models estimated with imputed NLSF data. Reference categories include: male, US citizen, Protestant, South resident, attended public high school.
*$p < .05$, **$p < .01$, ***$p < .001$.

found even among their white peers. In line with their peers, precollege friendships did not influence Asian and Pacific Islander students' racial prejudice toward different groups. When considering students' racialized social identities, partial support existed for social identity theory in the anti-black and anti-Latino models, as more ingroup closeness increased prejudice and more outgroup

TABLE 2.5   Factors influencing entering levels of prejudice among Latino students

Variable	Traditional racial prejudice		
	Anti-white	Anti-black	Anti-Asian
Social characteristics			
Female	−.010	−.010	−.025
Darker skin color	−.044	−.011	.023
International student	.004	−.050	−.021
Mother's education	.053	−.043	.054
Father's education	−.023	−.098*	.026
Family income	−.031	−.051	.026
Parental homeownership	.018	.011	−.009
Catholic	−.017	.032	.028
Other religious beliefs	.004	−.005	.075
Religiosity	.004	.048	−.047
Northeast region	−.018	−.066	.055
Midwest region	.074	.080	.140**
West region	.100*	−.021	.111*
Precollege environments			
Private high school	−.040	−.063	−.021
School segregation level	.037	−.033	.004
Neighborhood segregation level	−.029	−.065	−.011
Precollege friendships			
Whites	.237	.087	.065
Blacks	.138*	.140*	.023
Latinos	.171	.100	.119
Asians & Pacific Islanders	.119	.095	−.065
Closeness to			
Whites	−.229***	−.009	−.164**
Blacks	.184**	−.250***	.275***
Latinos	−.067	.127*	−.187***
Asians & Pacific Islanders	.112*	.135**	.132*
Constant	−.642	.215	−1.392**
Adjusted R^2	.049***	.061***	.069***

NOTE: Standardized coefficients (β) reported in table. Models estimated with imputed NLSF data. Reference categories include: male, US citizen, Protestant, South resident, attended public high school.
*$p < .05$, **$p < .01$, ***$p < .001$.

closeness to each specific outgroup decreased prejudice. This indicates the need to consider other closeness measures as well. Higher levels of closeness toward whites increased Asian and Pacific Islander students' prejudice toward both blacks and Latinos. Higher levels of closeness toward Latinos decreased Asian and Pacific Islander students' prejudice toward blacks, while a corresponding

TABLE 2.6   Factors influencing entering levels of prejudice among Asian and Pacific Islander students

Variable	Traditional racial prejudice		
	Anti-white	Anti-black	Anti-Latino
Social characteristics			
Female	.052	−.017	−.005
Darker skin color	.036	.012	.042
International student	.010	.025	.003
Mother's education	.040	.034	.030
Father's education	.000	−.046	−.028
Family income	.021	.077	.079
Parental homeownership	.025	−.033	−.034
Catholic	−.047	−.019	−.044
Other religious beliefs	.020	.013	−.020
Religiosity	.097*	.104**	.081*
Northeast region	.027	−.105*	−.066
Midwest region	−.010	−.052	−.055
West region	−.039	−.073	−.058
Precollege environments			
Private high school	−.065	−.046	−.063
School segregation level	−.016	.035	.045
Neighborhood segregation level	.011	.029	.008
Precollege friendships			
Whites	−.075	−.063	−.163
Blacks	−.010	.047	.007
Latinos	.055	.011	−.013
Asians & Pacific Islanders	−.111	−.016	−.109
Closeness to			
Whites	.011	.217***	.175***
Blacks	.066	−.288***	−.122
Latinos	−.213**	−.131*	−.239***
Asians & Pacific Islanders	.084	.201***	.190***
Constant	.474	.501	.825
Adjusted R^2	.023*	.122***	.102***

NOTE: Standardized coefficients (β) reported in table. Models estimated with imputed NLSF data. Reference categories include: male, US citizen, Protestant, South resident, attended public high school. $*p < .05, **p < .01, ***p < .001$.

finding existed in the anti-Latino model, in which feeling closer toward blacks led to less prejudice toward Latinos. Only Asian and Pacific Islander students' level of closeness toward Latinos influenced their prejudice toward whites, as higher levels of closeness increased their prejudice.

These models indicate students entering elite colleges are influenced by various aspects of their social backgrounds in different ways that shape how they view people of different races and ethnicities, particularly their peers they meet on campus. This is important because these stereotypes can influence whom students interact with during college. However, many aspects of precollege life were not the overwhelming guides for elite college students' views of race. For example, men and women rarely differed in their views on race, with the only differences found being among white students. It is important to discern what characteristics generally influence elite college students' views of race, and as is seen below, how these students identify with different groups often dominates the construction of prejudicial views of race and ethnicity.

Phenotypic features of people such as skin color, hair, and facial features are often used as signals for group memberships and categorization. Previous research suggests that salient group categorization done by identifying individuals based on distinct physical features such as skin color can influence people's racial prejudice toward other racial and ethnic groups (Hewstone and Brown 1986; Pettigrew 1998). Students' skin color may serve as a salient group marker, particularly for blacks who have endured the "one drop rule" in American society (see Smedley and Smedley 2011). Additionally, differential treatment in relation to skin color significantly influences Latinos' and blacks' socioeconomic status and their life chances in the United States (Gomez 2000; Herring, Keith, and Horton 2004; Hughes and Hertel 1990). The current study explored how skin color may relate to views of racial and ethnic outgroups among elite college students. Interestingly, white students with darker skin complexions were more prejudiced toward blacks and Latinos. Although one can only speculate as to what these findings mean, there is the possibility that white students with darker skin complexions have experienced alienation or discrimination based on their darker skin complexion (and possibly other phenotypic characteristics) during childhood. These findings may likely result from white students with dark complexions being confused with or often compared to black and Latino peers, such as in some of the findings among multiracial adolescents, which increases their desire to differentiate themselves from both groups and takes the form of higher levels of prejudice toward them (see Harris and Sim 2002; Lee and Bean 2007). As mentioned earlier, this possibility is only speculative, but it could account for the significant findings in relation to white students' skin complexion.

The current study also explored how students' religion and religiosity may shape their views of race. Scholars have identified how Christianity and the Protestant ethic are associated with a view, particularly among whites, reflecting negative black affect (feelings and emotions) (Sears 1988; Sears and Henry 2003). Additionally, research indicates that following the Christian faith, particularly among evangelicals, can hinder whites' ability to "see" structural inequality facing people of color, and it significantly influences how they perceive different aspects of society relating to race.[5] In association with religion, students' level of religiosity (i.e., how important religion is in their life) can influence their views of race. A study at UCLA found religiosity to influence students' views of race, but did not fully incorporate religion and religiosity in analyses to examine the possible influences on students' views of race (Sidanius et al. 2008, 87–88). In the current study of elite college students, religion did not impact students' views of racial and ethnic groups, and religiosity was only slightly more influential for elite college students regarding their views of race, but only for Asian and Pacific Islander students. As we will see below, religion and religiosity contribute much more to our understanding of elite college students' views of racial inequality.

Beyond simply considering family income as a proxy measure for socioeconomic position, this study builds on previous research suggesting the importance of incorporating components of wealth such as homeownership and parental education, which could influence students' views.[6] The lack of research on students' personal and family characteristics, with the exception of truncated examinations of socioeconomic status, left the possibility of these characteristics influencing students' views on race and inequality unexamined. Despite these possibilities, this aspect of elite college students' social backgrounds rarely influenced their views of race. Related to the socioeconomic positions of students are their differing social environments such as neighborhoods and schools. Research is somewhat limited in this area, though previous studies point to the importance of neighborhoods and schools for influencing social interactions (see Fischer 2008; Locks et al. 2008; Saenz, Ngai, and Hurtado 2007). Khan's (2011; Khan and Jerolmack 2013) research on elite youth in boarding school also points to the possible importance of attending private schools prior to entering college. These students often exhibited strong support for individualistic views of racial inequality, and these highly exclusionary educational environments may also amplify the support of racial stereotypes and views of inequality (discussed further in the next section) among all students, regardless of race, compared to peers who did not attend such schools prior to college.

The level of neighborhood segregation had limited influences on students' views of race. White students from more segregated neighborhoods were less prejudiced toward blacks at college entrance, and black students from more segregated neighborhoods were less prejudiced toward whites and Latinos. School diversity was slightly more influential for these entering college students. White students who attended more segregated schools were also found to be more prejudiced toward blacks. When focusing specifically on private school attendance often experienced by young elites, attending a private school had limited influences on students' views of race, which suggests these schools provide their students with little education assisting with breaking down racial stereotypes in broader society. This, again, may indicate a possible state of racial apathy among students entering elite colleges, even those supposedly with more knowledge of the world and more access to information on societal issues such as those attending well-financed private schools (see Forman 2004).[7]

In relation to precollege social environments, the current study explored how the regional context of where students lived prior to college may influence their views of race. Although this possibility has been explored in previous research, this factor may distinctly affect students given the racial history across the country for communities of color beyond the commonly acknowledged history of racism toward blacks in the South. The precollege environments of students had a variety of influences on their views of race and inequality. The regional context of students shaped their prejudicial views toward racial and ethnic outgroups, and indicates the complexity of understanding how different racial and ethnic groups relate to one another. For example, a few of the analyses found students from the South were not the most prejudiced. White students from the Midwest had higher levels of prejudice toward Asians and Pacific Islanders, Latino students from the Midwest and West were more prejudiced toward Asians and Pacific Islanders, and those students from the West were also more prejudiced toward whites. These findings complicate the traditional North-South narrative of racial attitudes findings (see Bobo et al. 2012; Schuman et al. 1997), and of how people relate to one another as being dependent on their regional context around social interactions. Additionally, these findings point to the importance of understanding the history between different racial and ethnic groups that sheds light on why (1) the South, which is often demonized as the bearer of most prejudice and negative racial attitudes, is sometimes not the strongest supporter of racial stereotypes and individualistic views of inequality, and (2) racial prejudice and narrow views of inequality play out in varying ways throughout the United States overall and toward specific communities of color. Thus, the analyses above indicate that using the South as a means of comparison can gloss over the fact that, although one group of students may not be as prejudiced toward a racial or ethnic outgroup as their same-race peers from the South, they are still, in fact, prejudiced toward the same group and do not believe in their peers' equality to themselves.

Students generally build friendships from among their peers whom they meet in school and their neighborhoods. As noted previously, friendships can have prejudice-reducing effects (Pettigrew and Tropp 2011; Sidanius et al. 2008). However, the influence of childhood friendships on students entering elite colleges was quite limited in the analyses for traditional forms of prejudice. Only one set of friendships influenced students' prejudice toward a racial or ethnic outgroup. Latino students who had more childhood friendships with black peers were more prejudiced toward whites and blacks when they entered college. Despite the strong evidence that friendships can influence people's views of racial and ethnic groups, particularly those they do not identify with, this was a troubling early finding among elite college students given that these friendships had developed throughout most of their life at this point.

One last but highly important aspect of a student's background possibly influencing elite college students' views of race at college entrance is their racialized social identity. As noted in the previous chapter, a person's racialized social identity informs views of and connection to the racial ingroup as well as racial outgroups. These views can lead to varying degrees of ingroup and outgroup bias, which influence the support for racial and ethnic stereotypes as well as particular views of inequality such as highly individualistic views. However, previous studies of college students have not fully examined how students' racialized social identities inform their early views of race and inequality.[8] A complicated picture is found when we consider students' racialized social identity and their views of race. Although support for social identity theory (i.e., more ingroup closeness increasing prejudice and individualistic views, more outgroup closeness reducing prejudice and individualistic views) was found, partial and contrasting findings were present across all four student groups. These findings result from a more nuanced approach applied in the analyses considering multiple group connections simultaneously rather than relying on a narrow ingroup-outgroup ("us-them") approach. When we consider traditional racial prejudice forms, social identity theory was partially supported among elite college students, with the strongest support existing among white students. Generally speaking, these findings support the contention that more ingroup closeness increases prejudice while more outgroup closeness reduces prejudice toward racial and ethnic outgroups. However, for elite college students, particularly the students of color at the elite institutions, they rarely use the traditional ingroup-outgroup view of race. The current study indicates students, and arguably people in general, use a multigroup continuum positioning their racialized social identity in simultaneous relationship to each group. Thus, ingroup bias may not be the strongest influence on what groups a person identifies with, or it may not have any influence at all, as was found in several models. What is important is that students were actively relating to multiple groups, which is a result of a complex set of histories around race and ethnicity shaping students' considerations of how they relate to them.

The examination of how the social characteristics and precollege environments of elite college students impact their views of race provides a foundation for further analyses of how influential social interactions and other experiences in college are for these students. In general, little outside of students' racialized social identity influences their views of different racial and ethnic groups prior to entering college. However, a similar foundational picture is needed for how these precollege years shape elite college students' views of racial inequality. When we examine how these same social characteristics and precollege experiences influence students' view of racial inequality when they enter college, more information is garnered about how both early conceptions of identity and race-related experiences can influence students' views.

Racial Individualism

Although understanding the racial prejudice among elite college students when they enter college is important, it is also important to understand how they connect race and explanations of inequality. That is, it is critical to understand how strongly elite college students hold individualistic explanations for the unequal social positions of different racial and ethnic groups. Similar to the regression models for traditional racial prejudice among students, each model of racial individualism includes students' gender, skin color, whether they were an international student, religious background, parental socioeconomic background, neighborhood and school segregation levels, whether they went to a private high school prior to college attendance, region of the country they are from, the proportion of their friends who were either white, black, Asian or Pacific Islander, and Latino prior to college, and their entering racialized social identity measured by how close they felt toward each racial or ethnic group.

Table 2.7 displays the racial individualism models for white students and the factors that influence how these students view racial inequality as an individualistic phenomenon when they enter college. Unlike the results for the models of white students' entering levels of racial prejudice, far more social characteristics and pre-college experiences influenced their views of racial inequality. One notable characteristic that consistently influenced these views was gender: white women were less likely to support individualistic explanations for racial inequality compared to white men at college entrance. Religion and religiosity were important influences on white students' views of how individual efforts factored into racial inequality as well. White students who were Catholic, as compared to white Protestant students, were more supportive of individualistic explanations of racial inequality for Latinos at college entrance. White students who followed non-Christian religions were less supportive of such individualistic views of inequality when considering Asians and Pacific Islanders and overall. More religious white students were also more supportive of individualistic views of racial inequality across all four models. Unfortunately, none of the friendship measures significantly influenced white students' racial inequality views. The importance of racialized social identity was evident in these models, particularly the strength of ingroup bias. Higher levels of closeness toward other whites increased whites' support for individualistic explanations of inequality toward each specific group as well as overall.

In relation to black students' views of individual efforts as an important factor in racial inequality, Table 2.8 presents quite different results compared to those for their white peers. Fewer social characteristics and precollege experiences influenced black students' views of racial inequality, and those characteristics that did shape these views were inconsistent at best. However, the friendships

TABLE 2.7 Factors influencing individualistic views of racial inequality among white students at college entrance

| | Racial individualism toward | | | |
Variable	Black	Latino	Asian & Pacific Islander	Overall
Social characteristics				
Female	−.083*	−.116**	−.105**	−.108**
Darker skin color	.058	.040	.062	.057
International student	.066*	.083*	.120***	.095**
Mother's education	−.004	−.022	.013	−.005
Father's education	−.088*	−.085*	−.097*	−.095*
Family income	.048	.025	.025	.035
Parental homeownership	−.021	−.007	.005	−.008
Catholic	.064	.076*	.050	.068
Other religious beliefs	−.071	−.063	−.088*	−.078*
Religiosity	.102**	.128***	.084*	.111**
Northeast region	−.050	−.022	−.071	−.050
Midwest region	−.074	−.054	−.102*	−.081
West region	−.121**	−.088*	−.105*	−.111**
Precollege environments				
Private high school	−.141***	−.118**	−.087*	−.123***
School segregation level	.078*	.054	.087*	.077*
Neighborhood segregation level	.020	−.001	−.007	.005
Precollege friendships				
Whites	.127	.058	.054	.085
Blacks	.029	−.006	.017	.014
Latinos	.064	.051	.035	.054
Asians & Pacific Islanders	.135	.090	.101	.116
Closeness to				
Whites	.251***	.225***	.224***	.248***
Blacks	−.110	−.120	−.101	−.117
Latinos	−.002	.084	−.068	.006
Asians & Pacific Islanders	.013	−.029	.071	.018
Constant	2.742*	3.473**	3.983**	3.399**
Adjusted R²	.129***	.117***	.120***	.136***

NOTE: Standardized coefficients (β) reported in table. Models estimated with imputed NLSF data. Reference categories include: male, US citizen, Protestant, South resident, attended public high school.
*$p < .05$, **$p < .01$, ***$p < .001$.

among black students developed prior to college had an important impact among their precollege experiences. More friendships with whites, blacks, and Asians and Pacific Islanders reduced their support for individualistic explanations of racial inequality overall and additionally for Latinos and Asians and Pacific Islanders. Friendships with Latinos prior to college did not influence

TABLE 2.8   Factors influencing individualistic views of racial inequality among black students at college entrance

Variable	Racial individualism toward			
	Black	Latino	Asian & Pacific Islander	Overall
Social characteristics				
Female	−.037	−.068	−.074*	−.066
Darker skin color	.033	.014	.025	.027
International student	−.010	−.015	.014	−.004
Mother's education	−.035	−.052	−.048	−.050
Father's education	−.037	−.004	−.045	−.032
Family income	−.072	−.097*	−.012	−.068
Parental homeownership	.071	.108**	.100*	.103**
Catholic	.034	.053	.049	.050
Other religious beliefs	−.116**	−.071	−.094*	−.105**
Religiosity	.001	.034	.031	.024
Northeast region	.011	−.034	.000	−.008
Midwest region	−.011	−.068	−.044	−.045
West region	−.050	−.079	−.004	−.050
Precollege environments				
Private high school	−.019	.011	−.027	−.013
School segregation level	.071	.015	−.009	.030
Neighborhood segregation level	−.020	.001	.003	−.006
Precollege friendships				
Whites	−.198	−.288*	−.348**	−.307*
Blacks	−.186	−.292*	−.369*	−.312*
Latinos	−.016	−.058	−.105	−.065
Asians & Pacific Islanders	−.123	−.177**	−.197**	−.183**
Closeness to				
Whites	.220***	.209***	.089	.195***
Blacks	.007	−.027	.055	.013
Latinos	−.121*	−.086	−.011	−.083
Asians & Pacific Islanders	.058	.076	.013	.055
Constant	5.878***	6.463***	7.314***	6.453***
Adjusted R^2	.068***	.073***	.038***	.068***

NOTE: Standardized coefficients (β) reported in table. Models estimated with imputed NLSF data. Reference categories include: male, US citizen, Protestant, South resident, attended public high school.
*$p < .05$, **$p < .01$, ***$p < .001$.

black students' views of racial inequality. The power of black students' racialized social identity was evident in these models, particularly how they positioned themselves in relation to whites. Black students who felt closer toward whites were more supportive of individualistic explanations of racial inequality across all four models. Higher levels of closeness toward Latinos, on the other hand,

TABLE 2.9   Factors influencing individualistic views of racial inequality among Latino students at college entrance

| Variable | Racial individualism toward | | | |
	Black	Latino	Asian & Pacific Islander	Overall
Social characteristics				
Female	−.055	−.076*	−.045	−.063
Darker skin color	.018	.004	.029	.018
International student	.015	.027	.003	.016
Mother's education	−.002	−.021	−.029	−.018
Father's education	−.130**	−.139**	−.041	−.112*
Family income	.040	.060	.004	.038
Parental homeownership	.017	.004	−.015	.003
Catholic	.018	.044	−.006	.021
Other religious beliefs	−.028	.001	−.006	−.012
Religiosity	−.014	.004	.022	.004
Northeast region	.011	.003	.067	.028
Midwest region	.037	.010	.055	.036
West region	−.087	−.044	−.016	−.053
Precollege environments				
Private high school	−.041	−.074	−.052	−.060
School segregation level	.043	.068	.074	.066
Neighborhood segregation level	−.041	−.057	−.121*	−.077
Precollege friendships				
Whites	.059	.023	−.004	.028
Blacks	−.016	−.017	−.066	−.035
Latinos	.049	.038	.025	.040
Asians & Pacific Islanders	.004	−.012	.006	−.001
Closeness to				
Whites	.262***	.270***	.162**	.249***
Blacks	−.238***	−.260***	−.248***	−.266***
Latinos	−.026	.001	.093	.024
Asians & Pacific Islanders	.126*	.081	.088	.105*
Constant	4.791***	5.199***	5.362***	5.117***
Adjusted R^2	.073***	.070***	.035**	.064***

NOTE: Standardized coefficients (β) reported in table. Models estimated with imputed NLSF data. Reference categories include: male, US citizen, Protestant, South resident, attended public high school.
*$p < .05$, **$p < .01$, ***$p < .001$.

reduced black students' support for individualistic explanations of inequality for their own racial group.

Similar to black students, Latino students' views of racial inequality were influenced by few consistent social characteristics and precollege experiences, as seen in Table 2.9. Additionally, precollege friendships had no influence on students' support for individualistic explanations of racial inequality. Similar to the findings for Asian and Pacific Islander students noted below, how close these students were to whites and blacks was an important influence on their views of racial inequality. Across all four models, feeling closer toward whites increased Latino students' support for individualistic explanations of racial inequality, while feeling closer toward blacks decreased support for such explanations. Interestingly, higher levels of closeness toward Asians and Pacific Islanders increased Latino students' support for individualistic explanations for racial inequality overall and particularly toward blacks.

As seen in Table 2.10, although fewer social characteristics were consistent predictors of Asian and Pacific Islander students' views of racial inequality compared to those of their white peers, one exception was gender. Asian and Pacific Islander women were less supportive of individualistic explanations of racial inequality across all models compared to Asian and Pacific Islander men at college entrance. Also notable is the importance of regional differences among these students, as Asian and Pacific Islander students from outside the South were less supportive of such individualistic explanations for blacks, Latinos, and overall, while Asian and Pacific Islander students from the Northeast and Midwest held lower levels of individualistic explanation toward their own group. Only one friendship measure in one model influenced Asian and Pacific Islander students' views of racial inequality: more white friendships prior to college actually decreased Asian and Pacific Islander students' support for individualistic explanations of racial inequality for Latinos. Similar to the findings for other students, how close Asian and Pacific Islander students felt to whites at college entrance was an important factor in their support for individualistic explanations of racial inequality, but so was their closeness toward blacks. Across all four models, Asian and Pacific Islander students who felt closer toward whites were more supportive of individualistic explanations for racial inequality. However, higher levels of closeness toward blacks reduced their support for such explanations of racial inequality in each model except when specifically considering their own communities. These last findings, again, point to the important influence of students' racialized social identities on their views of racial inequality.

Similar to the models of elite college students' prejudice toward racial and ethnic groups when they entered college, the examination of racial individualism among these students points to a wide variety of characteristics and experiences these students have prior to stepping onto campus that can influence their views of racial inequality. Although these characteristics and experiences have more influence on elite college students' views of racial inequality compared to their racial prejudice, they still have much less of an impact on these views than one would expect. Perhaps what is most troubling is not that their school and neighborhood environments had little influence on their views of racial inequality when they entered college, but that their childhood friendships only influenced

TABLE 2.10 Factors influencing individualistic views of racial inequality among Asian and Pacific Islander students at college entrance

| | Racial individualism toward | | | |
Variable	Black	Latino	Asian & Pacific Islander	Overall
Social characteristics				
Female	−.080*	−.102**	−.078*	−.093**
Darker skin color	.007	−.005	.034	.013
International student	.058	.068*	.051	.063
Mother's education	−.076	−.108*	−.059	−.087
Father's education	−.111*	−.100*	−.088	−.107*
Family income	.074	.074	.114**	.094*
Parental homeownership	−.020	.013	−.018	−.009
Catholic	−.026	−.034	−.020	−.029
Other religious beliefs	−.032	−.015	.014	−.012
Religiosity	.046	.044	.093*	.065
Northeast region	−.126**	−.142**	−.105*	−.133**
Midwest region	−.112**	−.093*	−.087*	−.105**
West region	−.159***	−.147**	−.084	−.140**
Precollege environments				
Private high school	−.031	−.012	−.017	−.021
School segregation level	.057	.055	.077	.068
Neighborhood segregation level	−.012	−.027	−.027	−.023
Precollege friendships				
Whites	−.195	−.298*	−.128	−.222
Blacks	−.021	−.093	−.030	−.051
Latinos	−.060	−.085	−.037	−.065
Asians & Pacific Islanders	−.034	−.156	−.035	−.080
Closeness to				
Whites	.295***	.274***	.256***	.295***
Blacks	−.156*	−.173*	−.118	−.160*
Latinos	.073	.107	−.033	.053
Asians & Pacific Islanders	.035	.022	.069	.045
Constant	5.472***	6.299***	4.994***	5.588***
Adjusted R²	.114***	.106***	.085***	.115***

NOTE: Standardized coefficients (β) reported in table. Models estimated with imputed NLSF data. Reference categories include: male, US citizen, Protestant, South resident, attended public high school.
*$p < .05$, **$p < .01$, ***$p < .001$.

black students' view of the importance of individual efforts as a major influence on racial inequality in society, while also having a slight influence on Asian and Pacific Islander students' support for such explanations of racial inequality. Taken together, the views of race and inequality among elite college students when they enroll in college are shaped by several important precollege experiences and social characteristics, most importantly their racialized social identities. Below I summarize some of the main factors that consistently shape how students of different races and ethnicities view one another and understand the influence of individual efforts in racial inequality when they enter these colleges.

Similar to the examination of elite college students' views of race, the views of racial inequality among white men and women, but also Asian and Pacific Islander men and women, differed somewhat. Both white and Asian and Pacific Islander women were less supportive of individualistic views of racial inequality than white and Asian and Pacific Islander men at college entrance. It appears that masculinity shapes individualistic views of racial inequality, particularly for whites, as gender differences existed across both their views of race and inequality. Previous studies (Hughey 2011, 2012; also DiTomaso 2013) also noted how white masculinity influences views of racial inequality as well. This is arguably found in how white men view other racial and ethnic groups in relation to themselves to (re)produce and work toward an idealized white male self, discounting forms of femininity and other male selves. In this (re)production of the white male self, these young white men are distancing themselves from men of different races and ethnicities and women of all races and ethnicities to establish their identities as having "strong, autonomous, rational, neutral, objective, and meritocratic characteristics that commonly (yet never exclusively) characterize a dominant, idealized, or hegemonic form of masculinity and whiteness" (Hughey 2011, 134). However, these distinct gender differences among white students at college entrance are also part of a more complex and varied phenomenon whereby white men and women are not always found to differ in their views of race and inequality.[9] Gender differences also existed for black students, but on the whole, black and Latino students were much less split along gender lines in their views of racial and ethnic groups or their support for individualistic explanations of racial inequality.

As noted earlier, previous research indicates people following the Christian faith, particularly evangelicals, are often limited in their ability to understand the interconnections between race and structural inequality (see Emerson, Smith, and Sikkink 1999). Religiosity can shape views of racial inequality as well, which previous studies of college students also found (Sidanius et al. 2008, 87–88). Religion was more influential on elite college students' views of racial inequality than on their views of race. These findings were limited to white and black students. Although white Catholic students were more supportive of individualistic views of racial inequality for Latinos when compared to Protestants, white students following another religion, not Christianity, held less support for such views overall and when specifically considering Asians and Pacific Islanders. Similarly, black students who followed other religious beliefs were less supportive of individualistic views of racial inequality overall and regarding their own racial group and Asians and Pacific Islanders compared to black Protestants. Whereas specific religious beliefs only influenced white and black students' entering views of racial inequality, religiosity was more influential for all students regarding their views of racial outgroups and inequality. Religiosity increased Asian and Pacific Islander students' prejudice towards whites, blacks, and Latinos. More religious white students were found to have higher levels of support for individualistic explanations of racial inequality across all models, while religiosity increased Asian and Pacific Islander students' racial individualism when considering their own group. Given the higher socioeconomic positions held by whites since the founding of the United States, the fact that highly religious whites are strongly supportive of individualistic explanations for racial inequality for other groups' positions, building on their long-standing privileged positions, makes sense, as they likely had little discussion countering such perspectives in childhood as a result of a highly segregated society (Johnson 2015; Kozol 1991, 2005; Massey and Denton 1994). Considering the findings for Asian and Pacific Islander students, for these students to take a more critical stance toward members of their own ethnic groups regarding their individual efforts as their religiosity increases may result from a belief in the lack of structural barriers to equality following the civil rights movement similar to those views held by whites. However, the critical perspective of their own group may be used as a position of accountability for group members because their religious beliefs can buttress individualistic views in collaboration with a broader cultural frame about achievement and success reinforced by the highly competitive contexts of elite colleges orienting them to supporting particular "strategies of action."[10]

A common question asked by scholars is: How do precollege environments such as neighborhoods and schools influence students' attitudes toward various aspects of society? When we consider elite college students' precollege social environments, we find their neighborhoods and schools did not frequently influence their views of racial inequality. Regarding possible neighborhood influences, only one group was significantly impacted by these environments: Latino students from more segregated neighborhoods were less supportive of individualistic explanations of inequality for Asians and Pacific Islanders. School diversity was slightly more influential on students' views of racial inequality. White students who attended more segregated schools were more supportive of individualistic explanations of inequality for blacks, Asians and Pacific Islanders, and overall. Although the measure tapped into patterns of segregation in schools, in the case of white students, almost 75% of students attended predominantly white schools, 24% attended integrated schools, and only 2% attended what could be considered segregated schools prior to college. These findings may result from other segregation patterns that exist within schools in relation to tracking white students to more academically rigorous classes, while students of color are often tracked to general and remedial classes (see Harris 2011; Lewis and Diamond 2015; and Tyson 2011 for examinations of how racial segregation within schools continuously shapes discussions of racial achievement gaps, student efforts, and school policies). That is, the stronger support for individualistic explanations of racial inequality among white students entering elite colleges is the result of structured inequality around them, as the tracking patterns give them little basis to believe that students of color are working hard to achieve goals in school and life if they are rarely in the advanced classes with them. This ultimately creates an additional layer of availability bias among affluent white students, as not only are fewer students of color in their schools, but when they are, they are less likely to be in the same classes with them (Khan 2015). This allows white students to use the ultimate attribution error to explain away larger patterns of educational inequality surrounding them (for example, if only one or two black students were in their advanced chemistry class, it is taken as evidence that if you work hard, then you will succeed; thus, since most black students in their schools are in general tracks, they must not be working hard enough) (Pettigrew 1979). These findings point to the importance of the school context in influencing how white students develop their understanding of race and the causes of inequality, similar to the findings of other studies (Khan 2011, 194–199; also Lewis 2003; Lewis and Diamond 2015; Lewis-McCoy 2014; Van Ausdale and Feagin 2001).

Attending more racially diverse (not necessarily integrated) schools for white students entering elite colleges also relates to a possible subversive aspect of racial socialization: family decisions and socialization. As recent research by Hagerman and Johnson indicates, where affluent white students go to school is influenced by the neighborhoods their parents move to early in their childhood, often with the intention of immersing themselves and their children in both whiteness and socioeconomic privilege, which go hand in hand given patterns of residential segregation (Hagerman 2014; Johnson 2015; also Massey and Denton 1994). The complexities of how affluent backgrounds influence not only whites, but students of color entering elite colleges, were found throughout the analyses above. A somewhat liberalizing influence of higher education levels among fathers was found for white, Asian and Pacific Islander, and Latino students, particularly in relation to their views of racial inequality. However, how much income parents earned rarely influenced the views of students, while parental homeownership also had limited influence on students' views of race and inequality. Nonetheless, these analyses are limited in identifying how racial socialization takes place within the home and around family life for students of all races and ethnicities, and more research is needed to identify how affluent students are socialized beyond their lives at elite boarding schools (see Hagerman 2014).

In relation to exclusive experiences in precollege environments of young elites, attending a private school only influenced white students' views of racial inequality. White students were less supportive of individualistic explanations of racial inequality for each specific racial and ethnic minority group as well as overall. These results contrast with Khan's assertion that young elites hold highly individualistic views of racial inequality given that they live in almost exclusively elite social spaces, as white students from private schools were less likely to hold these views although attending such schools did not influence views of racial inequality among students of color (Khan 2011, 194–199; also Khan 2015; Khan and Jerolmack 2013). Here again, these findings suggest elite college students may view issues of race and inequality apathetically despite their educational opportunities at these well-resourced private schools (see Forman 2004).

Although the regional dynamics elite college students experienced prior to college were less influential on their views of racial inequality than found previously on their views of race, these experiences dramatically shaped Asian and Pacific Islander students' views of racial inequality. In this case, Asian and Pacific Islander students from outside of the South were less supportive of individualistic views of racial inequality. A similar finding existed among whites, but only from the West region. As mentioned earlier, a more nuanced picture develops concerning how regional context informs elite college students' racial ideology. Though not as influential on their racial inequality views, students' experiences or knowledge of racial inequality varies by region beyond the North-South dichotomy often used to discuss aspects of race and inequality in the United States.

When the possible influence of young elites' friendship networks formed prior to college on their views of racial inequality was considered, findings similar to those for their views of racial prejudice were discovered. That is, elite college students' friendships had limited effects on their views of racial inequality. Black students were the most influenced by their friendships whereas Asian and Pacific Islander students were only influenced in one model by one group of friendships. More friendships with white, black, and Asian and Pacific Islander peers reduced black students' support for individualistic views of racial inequality in all models except when considering their own racial group. Among Asian and Pacific Islander students, more friendships with white peers reduced their support for such views of racial inequality when considering Latinos. As these early friendships can lead to students' learning more about different racial and ethnic groups as well as the prevalence of racial inequality in society, it appears that the least affluent among students entering elite colleges benefit the most from such interactions. These initial findings do not bode well for the power of cross-race interactions among elite college students for broadening their understanding of racial inequality in society. However, the lack of influence of friendships at this stage of life should be interpreted with caution, as little is known about how long students had had friendships that they reported at the beginning of college, which can influence how impactful these friendships can be on students' beliefs.[11] What is certain from these analyses is the rigidity of students' views of race and inequality, which are not easily influenced by cross-race inter-actions despite their powerful effects such as those found among interracial friendships (Pettigrew and Tropp 2011, 115–129; also Pettigrew 1998). This rigid-ity in race and inequality views is reinforced by the fairly segregated friendship networks and precollege environments that students originate from before they arrive at elite colleges and universities.

Again, a complicated picture is presented when we consider how students' racialized social identities influence their views of racial inequality, with partial support as well as contrasting findings for social identity theory. The importance of racialized social identity takes on new meaning beyond the findings discussed earlier concerning elite college students' views of race. The degree of closeness toward whites was the major influence on students' views of inequality among the racialized social identity measures, while closeness toward blacks was also an important influence in these models, but specifically for Latino and Asian and Pacific Islander students. With only one exception (black students' support for individualistic explanations of racial inequality in relation to Asians and Pacific Islanders), students who had higher levels of closeness toward whites were also more supportive of individualistic explanations for racial inequality. These find-ings indicate the power of post–civil rights movement narratives centering on the importance of the American dream and its associated values of hard work and individual contributions to social mobility simultaneously buttressing whites' higher socioeconomic position as the result of holding the "appropri-ate" cultural values. Simultaneously, these narratives downplay the importance of structural barriers to social mobility, and buoy the belief that racial and eth-nic minorities must "be like whites" to achieve higher socioeconomic positions in society, as they are assumed to hold inferior cultural values and are more individually accountable for their successes and failures (see DiTomaso 2013; Hochschild 1995; Johnson 2015). That is, the "bar of whiteness" becomes the comparison for all groups, and these comparisons of racial and ethnic minorities with whites are instilled prior to students entering college.

Ingroup closeness was less influential for students of color at elite colleges. For each group, ingroup closeness did not impact their support for individualistic explanations of racial inequality. Closeness toward other racial and ethnic groups did influence these students' views of racial inequality more readily than ingroup closeness, but not as consistently as their closeness toward whites. Among black students, higher levels of closeness toward Latinos corresponded with less sup-port for such explanations for racial inequality specifically for their own group members. Higher closeness toward Asians and Pacific Islanders increased Latino students' support for individualistic explanations of racial inequality overall and toward blacks. For both Asian and Pacific Islander and Latino students, their closeness toward blacks influenced their views of racial inequality. With the exception of the Asian and Pacific Islander student model for racial individualism toward their own group, higher levels of closeness toward blacks reduced Asian and Pacific Islander students' as well as Latino students' support for individualistic explanations of racial inequality. Again, these findings indicate how students are drawing on their connections to multiple racial and ethnic groups at one time to understand whom they identify with in their ideas about life and society. This is critical as students are not simply considering their connection with their racial or ethnic ingroup with a general racial outgroup, but are linked to racial and ethnic outgroups in different ways that inform their understanding of themselves as well as others, all of which influences their views of race and inequality. Further, the fact that students do not carry a common ingroup identity with them also counters the aforementioned beliefs in a postracial society (Gaertner and Dovidio 2000). If students believed race did not matter, then they would arguably indicate they felt similarly close to all groups, yet students noted that they were closer to their own group compared to other racial and ethnic groups when they entered college.

CONCLUSION

The analyses in this chapter paint a complex picture of what elite college students bring with them to campus regarding their views of race and inequality. Students do not readily interact across racial and ethnic lines prior to attending college, particularly white and Asian and Pacific Islander students. Moreover, students do not view each other equally, as they hold varying levels of stereotypes toward racial and ethnic outgroups, and hold racial and ethnic minorities differentially accountable for the impact of individual efforts on their socioeconomic positions. Thus, students' nearly 18 years of socialization and experience in relation to race and inequality establish a strong component of their ideology that four years of college are expected to significantly influence. Above and beyond the influences of social characteristics and precollege experiences on students' views of race and inequality are how they identify with their own and other racial and ethnic groups. These early conceptions of race and identity can have lasting influences throughout their college years. However, college campuses often offer students varying opportunities to interact across racial and ethnic lines, impacting their early conceptions of identity and their views of race and inequality. Unfortunately, as we will see in the succeeding chapters, the assumption that cross-race interactions among friends and roommates, while dating, and when participating in racially diverse student organizations in college will positively influence students' views of race and inequality and better equip them to understand how racial inequality functions in society, is not only arguably misstated but also quite dangerous when we consider the influential positions these students go on to hold once they graduate from college.

3 · MIXING IT UP ON CAMPUS
Patterns of and Influences
on Student Interactions

Once students arrive on campus, their ability to expand what they know about the world, and whom they learn different histories and information from, can also expand throughout their college years. There is, however, an important difference between the opportunity to interact and learn from people different from oneself, and actually forming relationships with those people. A "sincere fiction" distorts our view of social interaction in college, which prominently reinforces whiteness and elitism.[1] Specifically, this narrative suggests that student bodies at colleges and universities are overwhelmingly populated with people dissimilar from each other who have ample opportunities to form meaningful relationships and learn new information from those supposedly different people on campus. The belief in a plethora of diversity on campus is fueled by the continued increase in racial and ethnic diversity of student bodies and the large number of first-generation college students (i.e., first students in a family to attend college). As noted in previous chapters, the likelihood that this sincere fiction reflects reality is limited at elite colleges and universities because these institutions predominantly admit and foster relationships with a limited group of socioeconomically advantaged students, mainly from the white elite of the United States.[2] A strongly held belief in the ability to form diverse relationships as well as learn from diverse interactions during college continues to frame the college-going experience of students as they step onto campus despite these limitations. Thus, whether elite college students form these relationships is the point of departure for the current chapter.

Although the sincere fiction continues today of meeting and forming meaningful relationships with peers different from themselves, which may possibly transform students' views on issues such as race and inequality, new cohorts of students arguably do not see this possibility in diverse interactions. For example, students entering college for the first time in the recent era have lower desires and expectations of interacting with peers from racial and ethnic backgrounds different from their own (Espenshade and Radford 2009, 389; see also Pryor et al. 2007). These lower expectations may result from the precollege environments and experiences of students, framed by beliefs in individualistic explanations of racial inequality, and growing beliefs in postracism (see Bonilla-Silva 2014). Further, the different experiences students have once on campus and their perceptions of the college environment can also shape whom they interact with during college. However, when we consider whom students interact with on campus, the sincere fiction quickly begins to fall apart.

MY FRIENDS, YOUR FRIENDS, AND OUR FRIENDS: RACE AND SOCIAL INTERACTION PATTERNS

The patterns of social interactions among elite college students can present important information about which students are likely to discuss issues such as race and inequality in their daily lives while pursuing their degrees. Disturbingly, previous research has uncovered distinct patterns of inter- and intraracial interaction that exist on college campuses, which somewhat conform to a black-nonblack divide noted by Herbert Gans (1999). In these studies, white students are the most isolated group on college campuses, mostly interacting with other whites and the least likely to interact across racial and ethnic lines (see the following for discussions of the general patterns of social interactions among college students by race and ethnicity: Bowman and Park 2014; Chang, Astin, and Kim 2004; Espenshade and Radford 2009; Saenz 2010; Stearns, Buchmann, and Bonneau 2009). White and Asian and Pacific Islander students are most likely to interact with each other during college, and black students are segregated from most students on campus. Latino students appear to be a bridge between whites and Asian and Pacific Islanders and blacks on campus, as they are the most integrated into students' social networks. Of utmost concern for the current study is that similar patterns of social interaction were found among elite college students.

The students at 28 of the most selective colleges and universities in the United States had vastly different social networks while on campus. Each student group exhibited a different pattern of social interaction spanning whom they were friends with, dated, and roomed with, and who were the majority of members of the student organizations they joined during college. These patterns present a particular racial hierarchy of social interaction at elite colleges (discussed further at the end of this chapter) that mimics other studies of societal-level racial hierarchy such as the black-nonblack divide (Gans 1999), but what is also referred to as the Latin Americanization perspective (Bonilla-Silva 2014, 225–245; Bonilla-Silva 2004; Bonilla-Silva and Dietrich 2009). Table 3.1 presents these patterns of interactions among elite college students and displays the proportions of each

TABLE 3.1   Comparison of elite college student interactions across four years of college attendance

Variable	Whites	Blacks	Latinos	Asians & Pacific Islanders	Means Tests
Friendships					
Whites	.73	.20	.49	.40	a,b,c,d,e,f
Blacks	.03	.56	.07	.04	a,b,c,d,e,f
Latinos	.03	.04	.20	.03	a,b,d,e,f
Asians & Pacific Islanders	.09	.06	.10	.38	a,c,d,e,f
Romantic relationships					
Whites	.73	.40	.44	.41	a,c
Blacks	.18	.40	.43	.21	a,b,e,f
Latinos	.12	.17	.29	.23	b,c
Asians & Pacific Islanders	.26	.14	.47	.35	a,b,c,d,e,f
Roommates					
Whites	.77	.29	.56	.47	a,b,c,d,e,f
Blacks	.02	.35	.04	.03	a,b,d,e
Latinos	.02	.05	.15	.03	a,b,d,e,f
Asians & Pacific Islanders	.09	.09	.11	.31	c,e,f
Memberships in student organizations					
Mostly whites	.65	.31	.46	.43	a,b,c,d,e
Mostly blacks	.01	.34	.03	.01	a,b,d,e,f
Mostly Latinos	.00	.01	.12	.01	a,b,d,f
Mostly Asians & Pacific Islanders	.02	.02	.03	.22	c,e,f

NOTE: Means calculated using nonimputed NLSF data.
[a] Significant difference ($p < .05$) between white and black students.
[b] Significant difference ($p < .05$) between white and Latino students.
[c] Significant difference ($p < .05$) between white and Asian and Pacific Islander students.
[d] Significant difference ($p < .05$) between black and Latino students.
[e] Significant difference ($p < .05$) between black and Asian and Pacific Islander students.
[f] Significant difference ($p < .05$) between Latino and Asian and Pacific Islander students.

group that students had friendships and romantic relationships with during college as well as whom they roomed with and who were the majority of members in their student organizations. In this table, means tests indicate the significant differences between each student group for the four forms of social interaction. Figures 3.1 through 3.4 display these patterns on elite college campuses for each form of social interaction among students.

Students at elite colleges often held the majority of friendships with similar-race peers, but this is not the whole story. White students held the most homophilous friendship networks, with 73% of their friendships in college being with other whites (see also McPherson, Smith-Lovin, and Cook 2001). Only 9% of white

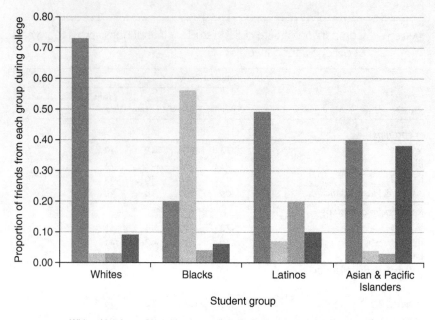

FIGURE 3.1. Proportion of friendships across racial and ethnic lines among elite college students

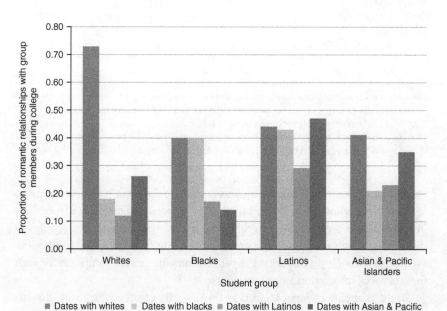

FIGURE 3.2. Proportion of romantic relationships across racial and ethnic lines among elite college students

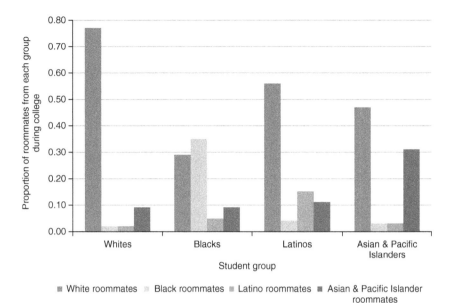

FIGURE 3.3. Proportion of roommates across racial and ethnic lines among elite college students

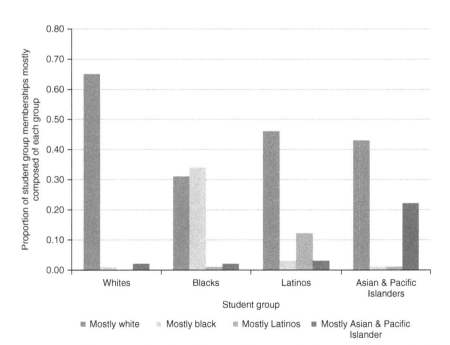

FIGURE 3.4. Proportion of memberships in student organizations composed mostly of particular racial and ethnic groups among elite college students

students' friendships during college were with Asians and Pacific Islanders, and only 3% of their friends were black or Latino. Black students' friendships were slightly dominated by same-race friendships (56% of their friendships were with other blacks). Twenty percent of black students' friends during college were whites, followed by 6% Asians and Pacific Islanders and 4% Latinos. Turning to Latino students, their friendships displayed much more racial diversity during college as 49% of their friendships were with whites, 20% with other Latinos, 10% with Asians and Pacific Islanders, and 7% with blacks. Among Asian and Pacific Islander students at elite colleges, these students predominantly split their friendships between their own ethnic group (38% of college friendships) and whites (40% of college friendships). Asians and Pacific Islanders had far fewer friendships with blacks (4%) and Latinos (3%) during college compared to their friendships with whites and among their own ethnic group. These patterns generally confirm previous studies of college students' friendship networks and suggest students' shift to slightly more homogenous friendships as they move past their first year in college (Charles et al. 2009, 71–98; Espenshade and Radford 2009, 176–225; Sidanius et al. 2008, 185–249).

In relation to whom elite college students dated, a similar pattern emerges among student groups to what is found in other studies (Charles et al. 2009; Espenshade and Radford 2009; Sidanius et al. 2008). Again, 73% of all people whom whites dated during college were white. These students were far less likely to date a person outside of their racial group, with Asians and Pacific Islanders (26%) the second most frequently dated group, followed by blacks (18%) and Latinos (12%). Black students, while less likely to date someone from their own racial group in comparison to white students, experienced same-race romantic relationships a slight majority of their time in college (40%). Following same-race romantic relationships, black students dated whites (37%) the second most frequently during college, then Latinos (17%), and Asians and Pacific Islanders (14%). Latino students reported the most diversity in their romantic relationships during college. Only slightly less than one-third (29%) of these students reported romantic relationships during college with other group members. Latino students reported dating Asians and Pacific Islanders (47%), whites (44%), and blacks (43%) at similar levels throughout their four years on campus. It is important to note that Latino students were the least likely to report dating members of their own ethnic group during college. Asian and Pacific Islander students displayed patterns in their romantic relationships that were similar to those in their friendships, with a larger experience dating whites (41%), followed by those dating members of their own ethnic group (35%), then Latinos (23%), and lastly blacks (21%).

The predominantly white student bodies composing elite college students are seen in the data on roommates among these students. White students were most likely to room with other whites during college (77%), and less likely to room with any other racial or ethnic group. The second group white students were likely to room with during college was Asians and Pacific Islanders (9%), followed by blacks and Latinos (2% each). Among black students, their roommates during college were somewhat split between their own racial group (35%) and whites (29%). These students were less likely to room with Asians and Pacific Islanders (9%) or Latinos (5%) during college. Latino students were mostly likely to room with whites during college (56%), followed by members of their own ethnic group (15%), Asians and Pacific Islanders (11%), and blacks (4%). Asian and Pacific Islander students were split in their social interactions regarding their roommates, as they were most likely to room with either whites (47%) or members of their own ethnic group (31%), and much less likely to room with either blacks or Latinos (3% each) during these years. Again, these patterns generally support previous studies of whom college students room with while pursuing their degrees (Espenshade and Radford 2009, 176–225).

Lastly, the organizations joined by students during college can influence their social interactions and possibly their views of race and inequality. Previous research (Park 2014b, Park and Kim 2013, Sidanius et al. 2008) suggests students gravitate towards organizations supporting their racial or ethnic identities, as students of color are more likely to join ethnic-related student organizations while white students are more likely to join Greek fraternities and sororities.[3] Similar patterns of social interaction are found in the composition of the student organizations students joined at elite colleges. White students were overwhelmingly members of predominantly white student organizations during college (65%), and rarely joined organizations that were mostly Asian and Pacific Islander (2%), black (1%), or Latino (less than 1%). Black students mostly likely joined student organizations that were mostly composed of members of their own race (34%) or whites (31%) during college. Black students were less likely to join organizations that were mostly composed of either Asians and Pacific Islanders (2%) or Latinos (1%). Latino students experienced more diversity in the student organizations they joined during college, but were mostly members of organizations composed predominantly of white students (46%). Next, Latino students joined organizations mostly composed of members of their own ethnic group (12%), and organizations mostly composed of either Asians and Pacific Islanders or blacks (2%). Finally, Asian and Pacific Islander students often joined student organizations composed mostly of white students (43%), followed by members of their own ethnic group (22%). They were far less likely to join student organizations that were either mostly black or Latino in their composition (1% each).

As helpful as these percentages are for understanding the composition of elite college students' social interactions during college, what is the likelihood that students would interact in some form with peers of different races and ethnicities? Figure 3.5 presents the average odds ratios across the four forms of social interactions for each student group pairing.[4] A few important points emerge

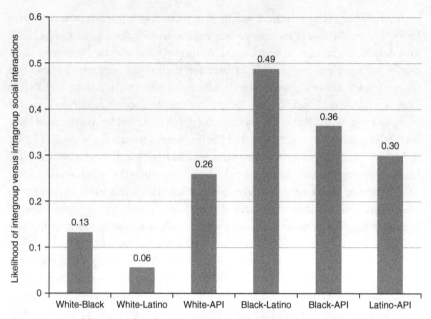

FIGURE 3.5. Odds ratios of student groups interacting during college

from these calculations. First, students of color are more likely to interact with each other during college than with whites. Black and Latino students are almost half as likely to interact with one another as they are with their ingroup members on campus. Black and Asian and Pacific Islander students are the next likeliest to interact with each other. On average, the likelihood of these students interacting with each other is approximately 64% lower than interacting with other ingroup members. Latino and Asian and Pacific Islander students are 70% less likely to interact with each other than with other ingroup members as well. Second, as noted above, white students are much less likely to interact with students of color. White students are 75% less likely to interact with Asian and Pacific Islanders, 87% less likely to interact with blacks, and nearly 95% less likely to interact with Latinos than with other whites while on campus. These calculations are in stark contrast to previous studies of elite college students' interactions, showing far fewer interactions between whites and students of color on campus (see Espenshade and Radford 2009, 215–216).

The patterns of social interactions on campus can influence not only whom students interact with during college and later in life, but also what types of experiences they may have as well as what they take away from diverse college interactions in relation to their views of race and inequality. What we see is that white students exhibited the most homophilous relationships during college regardless of what form of social interaction is considered. White students were almost exclusively interacting with other whites, and were least likely to interact with students of color regardless of social interaction form. Asian and Pacific Islander students reported slightly more interactions with whites during college as compared to same-group interactions, though these students were more likely to interact with blacks and Latinos compared to whites on campus in general. Latino students displayed the most diversity of and experience with interracial interactions during college. Although a majority of Latino students' interactions were with whites, they experienced much higher levels of friendships, romantic relationships, roommates, and group memberships with other students of color, and were more likely to interact with blacks and Asians and Pacific Islanders during college than with whites. Black students, on the other hand, displayed the most segregated social interactions in college. These students were mostly likely to interact with members of their own group, followed closely by interactions with whites. Black students were less likely to have cross-race interactions with Asians and Pacific Islanders and Latinos. What makes black students the most segregated at elite colleges is not their level of interactions with other racial and ethnic groups, nor their higher likelihood than other student groups to experience cross-race interactions in some form, but the level of interactions of those groups with them. Black students were frequently the least reported group of friends, romantic relationships, roommates, or majority members of student organizations among the other three racial and ethnic student groups during college. Thus, elite college students experience college quite differently regarding the social environment and those who compose their social networks. However, the question remains: What factors contribute to these patterns of social interaction among elite college students? In the next section, a series of analyses pull back the curtain on how these patterns unfold on college campuses.

SHAPING THE SOCIAL INTERACTIONS AMONG ELITE COLLEGE STUDENTS

The reasons behind the social interaction patterns among elite college students vary by not only the group of students examined, but also which form of social interaction is considered. In order to identify possible explanations for these patterns among elite college students, a series of regressions models examined how students' social characteristics and precollege experiences, entering racialized social identity, college experiences and perceptions related to race, and other campus characteristics such as the number of students of color on campus and college type influenced their social interactions across their four years of college and for each form of interaction.[5] The current study uses many measures similar to those used in previous research, with several differences to examine the wide range of whom students interact with across racial and ethnic lines, and in what ways they interact with others.[6] Similar analyses were conducted to examine the factors shaping the social interactions of whites (Tables 3.2–3.5), blacks

TABLE 3.2   Influences on white students' college friendship network

	Friendships			
Variable	White	Black	Latino	Asian & Pacific Islander
Prejudice at college entrance				
Anti-black	——	.008	——	——
Anti-Latino	——	——	−.068*	——
Anti-Asian	——	——	——	.018
Closeness to (first-year)				
Whites	.011	.014	.015	−.098**
Blacks	−.020	.139*	−.073	−.010
Latinos	.040	−.118	.128	−.135*
Asians & Pacific Islanders	−.083	.010	−.010	.193***
Entering college friendships				
Whites	.301*	−.384**	−.029	−.117
Blacks	.066	.136*	.049	.001
Latinos	.020	−.113	.297***	.038
Asians & Pacific Islanders	.019	−.240**	.019	.162*
College experiences and perceptions				
Campus racial climate	−.092**	.112**	.003	.049
College diversity commitment	−.018	.074*	−.013	−.028
Ethnic and Gender studies courses	.067*	.050	−.027	.026
Black student visibility[a]	.033	−.082	.044	.023
Latino student visibility[a]	−.036	.096	.034	−.116*
Asian & Pacific Islander student visibility[a]	.067	−.025	−.157**	.070
Campus characteristics				
Black students[b]	−.028	.099**	−.039	.041
Latino students[b]	−.117*	.080	.068	.068
Asian & Pacific Islander students[b]	−.174**	−.091	.062	.265***
Private research university	.005	−.024	.056	.051
Liberal arts college	.091*	.023	.033	.014
Precollege environments				
Private high school	.025	.005	.020	−.061
School segregation level	.028	−.042	.046	−.024
Neighborhood segregation level	−.029	.067*	−.043	.006
Social characteristics				
Female	.017	.053	−.071*	−.035
Darker skin color	−.037	.025	.019	.056
International student	−.085**	.061	.025	.067*
Mother's education	.043	−.013	−.030	−.019
Father's education	−.037	.033	.015	−.028
Family income	.040	−.093**	−.021	−.005
Parental homeownership	.003	.008	.039	.050
Catholic	−.061	.009	−.029	.014

(continued)

TABLE 3.2   (CONTINUED)

| Variable | Friendships | | | |
	White	Black	Latino	Asian & Pacific Islander
Other religious beliefs	.009	−.015	−.056	−.089**
Religiosity	.004	−.041	.002	−.004
Northeast	.026	.041	−.050	.015
Midwest	.029	.012	−.036	−.013
West	.077	.015	−.083	.039
Constant	.705***	.038	.028	.029
Adjusted R^2	.205***	.159***	.185***	.329***

NOTE: Models estimated with imputed NLSF data; standardized coefficients (β) displayed. Reference categories include: male, US citizen, Protestant, South resident, attended public high school, attended public research university.
[a] Visibility of each student group is relative to [specific racial or ethnic group]'s visibility on campus.
[b] Proportion of student group entered into models.
*$p < .05$, **$p < .01$, ***$p < .001$.

TABLE 3.3   Influences on white students' romantic relationships during college

| Variable | Romantic relationships | | | |
	White	Black	Latino	Asian & Pacific Islander
Prejudice at college entrance				
Anti-black	——	−.101**	——	——
Anti-Latino	——	——	−.114***	——
Anti-Asian	——	——	——	−.023
Closeness to (first-year)				
Whites	.065	.090*	.028	.000
Blacks	−.026	−.001	.051	−.077
Latinos	−.075	.124	.108	.078
Asians & Pacific Islanders	−.030	.053	.094	.180**
Precollege college friendships				
Whites	.278*	−.557***	−.576***	−.439***
Blacks	.036	−.084	−.126*	−.033
Latinos	.032	−.160**	−.050	−.113*
Asians & Pacific Islanders	.037	−.276**	−.279***	−.208*
College experiences and perceptions				
Campus racial climate	−.121***	.152***	.147***	.185***
College diversity commitment	−.058	.027	−.006	.015
Ethnic and Gender studies courses	−.030	.072*	.104***	.121***
Black student visibility[a]	−.019	−.102*	−.093*	−.079
Latino student visibility[a]	.085	.192***	.079	.103*
Asian & Pacific Islander student visibility[a]	−.015	−.010	.048	.014

(continued)

TABLE 3.3   (CONTINUED)

	Romantic relationships			
Variable	White	Black	Latino	Asian & Pacific Islander
Campus characteristics				
Black students[b]	.040	.034	−.009	.003
Latino students[b]	−.067	.153**	.095*	.020
Asian & Pacific Islander students[b]	.013	.072	.041	.166**
Private research university	−.066	.030	.124***	.163***
Liberal arts college	−.005	−.019	.046	.024
Precollege environments				
Private high school	.082*	.050	.070*	−.036
School segregation level	−.019	.079*	.136***	.043
Neighborhood segregation level	.034	−.036	−.087**	−.053
Social characteristics				
Female	−.026	.029	−.081**	−.122***
Darker skin color	.008	−.012	.009	−.008
International student	.014	−.034	−.063*	−.003
Mother's education	−.008	.064	.028	−.008
Father's education	−.027	−.116**	−.034	.004
Family income	.038	−.098**	−.118***	−.087**
Parental homeownership	−.016	.057	.095**	.063*
Catholic	−.008	−.065	−.117***	−.061
Other religious beliefs	.066	−.084*	−.138***	−.083*
Religiosity	.179***	−.131***	−.138***	−.106**
Northeast	−.129**	.261***	.314***	.298***
Midwest	−.057	.186***	.244***	.139**
West	−.072	.161***	.234***	.218***
Constant	.676***	.247*	.223*	.163
Adjusted R^2	.150***	.276***	.375***	.293***

NOTE: Models estimated with imputed NLSF data; standardized coefficients (β) displayed. Reference categories include: male, US citizen, Protestant, South resident, attended public high school, attended public research university.
[a] Visibility of each student group is relative to [specific racial or ethnic group]'s visibility on campus.
[b] Proportion of student group entered into models.
*$p < .05$, **$p < .01$, ***$p < .001$.

(Tables 3.6–3.9), Latinos (Tables 3.10–3.13), and Asians and Pacific Islanders (Tables 3.14–3.17) on elite college campuses. Although cumbersome, these many models uncover how students' patterns of social interaction develop throughout college. Rather than tediously work through each table, I summarize the general findings garnered from these analyses to note common themes and unique circumstances shaping how elite college students interact with one another on campus.

TABLE 3.4   Influences on white students' roommate diversity during college

Variable	White	Black	Latino	Asian & Pacific Islander
	Roommates			
Prejudice at college entrance				
Anti-black	——	.024	——	——
Anti-Latino	——	——	−.046	——
Anti-Asian	——	——	——	.008
Closeness to (first year)				
Whites	.040	.036	.068	−.010
Blacks	.000	.079	.010	.007
Latinos	−.068	.020	.166*	−.057
Asians & Pacific Islanders	.055	−.174**	−.187**	.112*
Precollege college friendships				
Whites	.228*	−.160	.254*	−.302**
Blacks	.103	−.025	.120	−.109
Latinos	.086	−.038	.145*	−.072
Asians & Pacific Islanders	−.048	−.103	.223*	.006
College experiences and perceptions				
Campus racial climate	.001	.074*	.001	.038
College diversity commitment	−.015	.059	.012	−.013
Ethnic and Gender studies courses	.024	.019	−.064	.016
Black student visibility[a]	−.001	−.100	−.097	.072
Latino student visibility[a]	−.032	.212***	.121*	−.099*
Asian & Pacific Islander student visibility[a]	.051	−.105*	−.104*	.026
Campus characteristics				
Black students[b]	−.136***	.124**	−.016	.025
Latino students[b]	−.320***	−.079	.246***	.122*
Asian & Pacific Islander students[b]	−.135*	.243***	.054	.137*
Private research university	−.060	.066	.019	−.087*
Liberal arts college	−.098**	−.036	.007	−.163***
Precollege environments				
Private high school	.046	−.031	−.054	.021
School segregation level	.061	−.071	.002	−.059
Neighborhood segregation level	.009	.033	.091**	−.006
Social characteristics				
Female	−.052	−.048	.062	.050
Darker skin color	−.012	−.021	.002	.029
International student	−.149***	.046	.032	.026
Mother's education	.018	.048	−.025	−.010
Father's education	−.024	.019	.000	.033
Family income	.134***	−.136***	−.013	−.083*
Parental homeownership	−.040	−.024	−.023	.066*
Catholic	.044	.018	−.054	−.049

(continued)

TABLE 3.4   (CONTINUED)

Variable	Roommates			
	White	Black	Latino	Asian & Pacific Islander
Other religious beliefs	.073*	.006	.031	−.073*
Religiosity	−.010	−.020	.013	.042
Northeast	.037	.147**	−.043	−.036
Midwest	.041	.005	−.027	−.026
West	.029	.045	−.042	.057
Constant	.668***	.017	−.090*	.165
Adjusted R^2	.297***	.085***	.116***	.262***

NOTE: Models estimated with imputed NLSF data; standardized coefficients (β) displayed. Reference categories include: male, US citizen, Protestant, South resident, attended public high school, attended public research university.
[a] Visibility of each student group is relative to [specific racial or ethnic group]'s visibility on campus.
[b] Proportion of student group entered into models.
*$p < .05$, **$p < .01$, ***$p < .001$.

TABLE 3.5   Influences on white students' involvement in racially diverse college student organizations

Variable	Memberships in student organizations			
	Mostly White	Mostly Black	Mostly Latino	Mostly Asian & Pacific Islander
Prejudice at college entrance				
Anti-black	——	−.012	——	——
Anti-Latino	——	——	−.015	——
Anti-Asian	——	——	——	−.034
Closeness to (first-year)				
Whites	.005	−.006	.092*	−.025
Blacks	−.011	.136	−.003	−.039
Latinos	.109	−.112	.050	.023
Asian & Pacific Islanders	−.082	−.040	−.095	.065
Precollege college friendships				
Whites	.031	.116	−.301*	.058
Blacks	−.010	.229**	−.153*	.018
Latinos	−.026	.039	.089	.103
Asians & Pacific Islanders	−.050	.058	−.170	.099
College experiences and perceptions				
Campus racial climate	.005	−.035	.063	.073*
College diversity commitment	.001	−.051	−.049	−.022
Ethnic and Gender studies courses	.106**	.059	.021	−.008
Black student visibility[a]	.015	−.049	−.005	.036
Latino student visibility[a]	−.084	−.026	−.004	−.033
Asian & Pacific Islander student visibility[a]	.079	.008	−.042	.047

(continued)

TABLE 3.5   (CONTINUED)

Variable	Memberships in student organizations			
	Mostly White	Mostly Black	Mostly Latino	Mostly Asian & Pacific Islander
Campus characteristics				
Black students[b]	.065	−.055	.049	−.034
Latino students[b]	−.072	.001	.011	.131*
Asian & Pacific Islander students[b]	−.109	−.008	−.005	.142*
Private research university	.079	.020	.056	−.042
Liberal arts college	.117**	−.018	−.005	−.034
Precollege environments				
Private high school	.005	−.057	.011	−.034
School segregation level	.029	−.025	.055	−.037
Neighborhood segregation level	−.007	.105**	−.039	.037
Social characteristics				
Female	.008	−.007	−.029	−.024
Darker skin color	.050	.027	−.001	.003
International student	−.020	−.011	.053	.007
Mother's education	.086*	−.010	.046	−.061
Father's education	−.002	.077	.035	−.031
Family income	−.061	−.021	−.019	−.006
Parental homeownership	−.003	.014	.040	.069*
Catholic	−.056	.027	.005	−.035
Other religious beliefs	−.044	−.002	−.087*	−.105**
Religiosity	.090**	.035	.038	−.012
Northeast	.133**	−.043	.068	−.025
Midwest	.093*	−.050	.035	−.028
West	.055	.015	.018	.028
Constant	.339	−.028	.007	−.062
Adjusted R²	.072***	.034**	.059***	.124***

NOTE: Models estimated with imputed NLSF data; standardized coefficients (β) displayed. Reference categories include: male, US citizen, Protestant, South resident, attended public high school, attended public research university.
[a] Visibility of each student group is relative to [specific racial or ethnic group]'s visibility on campus.
[b] Proportion of student group entered into models.
*p < .05, **p < .01, ***p < .001.

Several important trends exist in relation to the groups of variables included in these models, and specifically, in relation to what factors prominently influenced students' different forms of social interactions during college. Students' social characteristics were an important contextual aspect of their social interactions across the four forms. A majority of the effects found among the social characteristics of elite college students related to their dating and romantic

TABLE 3.6   Influences on black students' college friendship network

| Variable | Friendships | | | |
	White	Black	Latino	Asian & Pacific Islander
Prejudice at college entrance				
Anti-white	.031	——	——	——
Anti-Latino	——	——	.039	——
Anti-Asian	——	——	——	.032
Closeness to (first-year)				
Whites	.140***	−.059	.044	−.064
Blacks	−.160***	.150***	−.131**	−.076
Latinos	−.015	−.018	.218***	.013
Asian & Pacific Islanders	.001	−.004	−.091	.125*
Precollege college friendships				
Whites	.397***	−.070	−.126	.028
Blacks	−.100	.404***	−.219	−.175
Latinos	.004	.012	.030	−.029
Asians & Pacific Islanders	.038	−.030	.035	.257***
College experiences and perceptions				
Campus racial climate	−.063*	.060*	−.011	−.001
College diversity commitment	−.098***	.001	−.067	.054
Ethnic and Gender studies courses	−.004	.104***	−.051	−.040
White student visibility[a]	.026	−.116*	.008	.134*
Latino student visibility[a]	.006	.034	−.095	−.079
Asian & Pacific Islander student visibility[a]	−.040	.010	−.072	.105*
Campus characteristics				
Black students[b]	−.117**	.106**	.002	.000
Latino students[b]	.069	−.160**	.177**	.090
Asian & Pacific Islander students[b]	−.120*	−.011	−.006	.136*
Private research university	.005	−.019	.049	.058
Liberal arts college	.034	−.112***	.134**	.040
Precollege environments				
Private high school	−.010	.015	−.006	−.117**
School segregation level	.065	−.057	.106*	.017
Neighborhood segregation level	−.021	.023	.016	.033
Social characteristics				
Female	−.079**	.087**	.025	−.023
Darker skin color	−.098***	.074**	−.039	.010
International student	.035	−.003	−.036	.011
Mother's education	.055	−.024	−.017	.011
Father's education	.032	.019	−.013	−.027
Family income	−.020	.059	−.045	−.057
Parental homeownership	−.019	.017	−.004	.050
Catholic	.046	−.018	−.023	.005

(continued)

TABLE 3.6   (CONTINUED)

| Variable | Friendships | | | |
	White	Black	Latino	Asian & Pacific Islander
Other religious beliefs	.035	−.043	.031	.030
Religiosity	−.020	.033	−.025	.015
Northeast	.000	.082*	.040	−.032
Midwest	.049	−.026	.020	.066
West	−.008	.031	−.034	−.020
Constant	.375***	.066	.067	.036
Adjusted R^2	.483***	.485***	.142***	.282***

NOTE: Models estimated with imputed NLSF data; standardized coefficients (β) displayed. Reference categories include: male, US citizen, Protestant, South resident, attended public high school, attended public research university.
[a] Visibility of each student group is relative to [specific racial or ethnic group]'s visibility on campus.
[b] Proportion of student group entered into models.
$*p < .05, **p < .01, ***p < .001.$

TABLE 3.7   Influences on black students' romantic relationships during college

| Variable | Romantic relationships | | | |
	White	Black	Latino	Asian & Pacific Islander
Prejudice at college entrance				
Anti-white	.122***	——	——	——
Anti-Latino	——	——	−.093***	——
Anti-Asian	——	——	——	−.007
Closeness to (first-year)				
Whites	.153***	.100*	.044	.044
Blacks	.003	.100**	.012	−.158***
Latinos	−.228***	.129**	.132**	.100*
Asians & Pacific Islanders	.016	.003	.074	.171***
Precollege college friendships				
Whites	.489***	−.606***	−.571***	−.391***
Blacks	.486***	−.388**	−.780***	−.537***
Latinos	.092	−.094	−.020	−.134**
Asians & Pacific Islanders	.085	−.208***	−.186***	−.115*
College experiences and perceptions				
Campus racial climate	−.265***	.309***	.242***	.277***
College diversity commitment	.029	.014	−.074**	−.039
Ethnic and Gender studies courses	.053	.042	−.027	.018
White student visibility[a]	−.180**	−.135**	.039**	.058
Latino student visibility[a]	.019	.320***	.156**	.155**

(continued)

TABLE 3.7 (CONTINUED)

Variable	Romantic relationships			
	White	Black	Latino	Asian & Pacific Islander
Asian & Pacific Islander student visibility[a]	−.118**	.089*	.100**	.094*
Campus characteristics				
Black students[b]	.029	.082*	−.059	−.027
Latino students[b]	−.136*	.145**	.173***	.132***
Asian & Pacific Islander students[b]	−.061	.045	.043	.132*
Private research university	−.122**	.036	.123***	.164***
Liberal arts college	−.173***	.064	.152***	.150***
Precollege environments				
Private high school	.086*	.091**	.074*	−.060
School segregation level	−.001	.161***	.250***	.135***
Neighborhood segregation level	.109**	−.094**	−.205***	−.142***
Social characteristics				
Female	−.010	−.009	−.155***	−.217***
Darker skin color	−.043	.029	−.021	−.036
International student	.062	−.061*	−.063*	.004
Mother's education	.012	.066	.022	−.010
Father's education	−.028	−.054	.019	.079*
Family income	.048	−.097*	−.130***	−.102**
Parental homeownership	−.094**	.077*	.150***	.061*
Catholic	.067*	−.102**	−.099***	−.039
Other religious beliefs	.035	−.084**	−.107***	−.037
Religiosity	.163***	−.077*	−.124***	−.088**
Northeast	−.049	.111**	.225***	.198***
Midwest	−.074*	.057	.158***	.091**
West	−.026	.109**	.165***	.131***
Constant	.364***	.187**	.248***	.264**
Adjusted R^2	.313***	.388***	.523***	.459***

NOTE: Models estimated with imputed NLSF data; standardized coefficients (β) displayed. Reference categories include: male, US citizen, Protestant, South resident, attended public high school, attended public research university.
[a] Visibility of each student group is relative to [specific racial or ethnic group]'s visibility on campus.
[b] Proportion of student group entered into models.
*$p < .05$, **$p < .01$, ***$p < .001$.

relationships while on campus. When we consider the other three forms of social interaction, students' social characteristics take a backseat to campus-related experiences. The perceptions of the campus environment were the most powerful influences on elite college students' social interactions, followed closely by the characteristics of their campus. These findings support previous research

TABLE 3.8   Influences on black students' roommate diversity during college

| | Roommates | | | |
Variable	White	Black	Latino	Asian & Pacific Islander
Prejudice at college entrance				
Anti-white	−.006	——	——	——
Anti-Latino	——	——	.021	——
Anti-Asian	——	——	——	−.062
Closeness to (first-year)				
Whites	.065	−.037	.147**	−.074
Blacks	−.136***	.142***	−.045	−.036
Latinos	−.044	−.034	.096	−.053
Asians & Pacific Islanders	.067	−.032	−.106	.190***
Precollege college friendships				
Whites	.268*	−.049	.167	−.133
Blacks	−.069	.279*	.195	−.324*
Latinos	.029	−.016	.076	.031
Asians & Pacific Islanders	−.016	−.038	.128*	.085
College experiences and perceptions				
Campus racial climate	−.068*	.104**	.034	−.051
College diversity commitment	−.006	.004	−.048	.019
Ethnic and Gender studies courses	−.072*	.051	−.187***	−.044
White student visibility[a]	−.032	−.094	.062	.053
Latino student visibility[a]	−.024	.198**	−.024	−.166*
Asian & Pacific Islander student visibility[a]	−.056	.039	−.096	−.015
Campus characteristics				
Black students[b]	−.278***	.209***	−.103*	−.039
Latino students[b]	−.040	−.237***	.269***	−.099
Asian & Pacific Islander students[b]	−.122*	.211***	−.009	.200*
Private research university	−.044	.006	.021	−.028
Liberal arts college	.018	−.127***	.022	−.141***
Precollege environments				
Private high school	.053	.011	−.053	.056
School segregation level	.135**	−.072	.051	−.048
Neighborhood segregation level	−.024	.047	.020	.087*
Social characteristics				
Female	−.136***	.050	.114**	.050
Darker skin color	−.056	.046	−.037	.034
International student	−.084**	.058	−.050	−.035
Mother's education	−.030	.021	−.036	.113**
Father's education	.014	.004	.013	−.064
Family income	.090*	.030	−.075	−.084
Parental homeownership	−.031	−.041	.027	.056
Catholic	.092**	−.041	−.033	−.047

(continued)

TABLE 3.8   (CONTINUED)

	Roommates			
Variable	White	Black	Latino	Asian & Pacific Islander
Other religious beliefs	.016	−.037	.033	−.014
Religiosity	−.038	.012	−.014	.013
Northeast	−.049	.081*	.057	.003
Midwest	−.029	−.058	−.034	.051
West	−.008	.012	−.024	.105*
Constant	.573***	−.040	−.043	.131
Adjusted R^2	.366***	.406***	.138***	.260***

NOTE: Models estimated with imputed NLSF data; standardized coefficients (β) displayed. Reference categories include: male, US citizen, Protestant, South resident, attended public high school, attended public research university.
[a] Visibility of each student group is relative to [specific racial or ethnic group]'s visibility on campus.
[b] Proportion of student group entered into models.
*$p < .05$, **$p < .01$, ***$p < .001$.

TABLE 3.9   Influences on black students' involvement in racially diverse college student organizations

	Memberships in student organizations			
Variable	Mostly White	Mostly Black	Mostly Latino	Mostly Asian & Pacific Islander
Prejudice at college entrance				
Anti-white	−.050	———	———	———
Anti-Latino	———	———	.012	———
Anti-Asian	———	———	———	−.020
Closeness to (first-year)				
Whites	.119*	.045	.014	−.076
Blacks	−.102*	.096*	−.022	.074
Latinos	−.057	.089	.089	−.055
Asians & Pacific Islanders	.031	−.090	−.034	.056
Precollege college friendships				
Whites	−.078	.057	−.134	.054
Blacks	−.242	.322*	−.118	−.066
Latinos	−.118*	.022	.016	−.041
Asians & Pacific Islanders	−.049	.073	−.029	.117
College experiences and perceptions				
Campus racial climate	.043	.110**	.065	−.006
College diversity commitment	−.034	.008	−.050	.028
Ethnic and Gender studies courses	−.015	.113**	−.057	−.015
White student visibility[a]	.109	−.018	.012	.020
Latino student visibility[a]	−.109	.083	−.043	.000
Asian & Pacific Islander student visibility[a]	−.024	.048	−.065	.118

(continued)

TABLE 3.9 (CONTINUED)

Variable	Memberships in student organizations			
	Mostly White	Mostly Black	Mostly Latino	Mostly Asian & Pacific Islander
Campus characteristics				
Black students[b]	−.186***	.187***	.012	.039
Latino students[b]	.004	−.003	−.073	.026
Asian & Pacific Islander students[b]	−.130*	−.019	.153*	.130
Private research university	.057	.026	.039	.071
Liberal arts college	.000	−.010	.019	.057
Precollege environments				
Private high school	−.040	−.024	−.036	−.043
School segregation level	−.044	−.006	−.062	−.045
Neighborhood segregation level	−.017	−.007	.021	.021
Social characteristics				
Female	−.077*	.055	.001	−.003
Darker skin color	−.037	.034	−.001	.028
International student	−.044	.068*	−.033	.004
Mother's education	.080	−.060	−.004	−.003
Father's education	−.022	.027	.025	−.023
Family income	−.075	.045	−.024	−.058
Parental homeownership	−.002	−.036	.033	.032
Catholic	.066	−.065	.025	−.038
Other religious beliefs	.000	−.049	.004	.037
Religiosity	−.003	.091**	.005	.080*
Northeast	.045	−.008	.074	.040
Midwest	.065	−.045	−.002	.042
West	−.009	.027	.000	.037
Constant	.730***	−.398*	.010	−.037
Adjusted R^2	.147***	.234***	.003	.058***

NOTE: Models estimated with imputed NLSF data; standardized coefficients (β) displayed. Reference categories include: male, US citizen, Protestant, South resident, attended public high school, attended public research university.
[a] Visibility of each student group is relative to [specific racial or ethnic group]'s visibility on campus.
[b] Proportion of student group entered into models.
*$p < .05$, **$p < .01$, ***$p < .001$.

(Harper and Hurtado 2007; Hurtado et al. 1999; Locks et al. 2008; Sidanius et al. 2008), noting the importance of campus climates for understanding students' interactions. Further, it becomes quite clear that representation and visibility are mutually reinforcing aspects of the campus racial climate. A larger proportion of students of color on campus offer more opportunities to interact across racial and ethnic lines and ultimately reduce students' racial prejudice (see also

TABLE 3.10 Influences on Latino students' college friendship network

	Friendships			
Variable	White	Black	Latino	Asian & Pacific Islander
Prejudice at college entrance				
Anti-white	−.051	——	——	——
Anti-black	——	−.027	——	——
Anti-Asian	——	——	——	.047
Closeness to (first-year)				
Whites	.160***	−.111*	−.158***	−.050
Blacks	−.026	.204**	.010	−.182**
Latinos	−.082	.011	.125**	−.015
Asians & Pacific Islanders	−.026	−.098*	−.008	.146**
Precollege college friendships				
Whites	.341**	−.128	−.017	−.068
Blacks	−.041	.264***	.013	.076
Latinos	.012	−.079	.343**	−.030
Asians & Pacific Islanders	.057	−.039	.022	.115
College experiences and perceptions				
Campus racial climate	−.131***	.075*	.093**	−.038
College diversity commitment	.001	−.056	−.051	.015
Ethnic and Gender studies courses	−.012	.043	−.014	.120**
White student visibility[a]	−.088*	.008	.081*	.055
Black student visibility[a]	.005	.033	.040	.029
Asian & Pacific Islander student visibility[a]	−.004	.080*	.020	−.045
Campus characteristics				
Black students[b]	−.007	.129***	−.013	.016
Latino students[b]	−.167**	.078	.088	.061
Asian & Pacific Islander students[b]	−.032	−.147*	−.011	.210**
Private research university	.025	−.037	.008	.074
Liberal arts college	.014	.054	−.009	.016
Precollege environments				
Private high school	−.040	−.054	.014	−.016
School segregation level	.037	−.063	−.015	−.030
Neighborhood segregation level	−.008	−.018	.024	−.011
Social characteristics				
Female	−.029	.003	.057	−.078*
Darker skin color	−.089**	.071*	.047	−.015
International student	−.026	.001	.018	.008
Mother's education	.046	.009	−.047	.024
Father's education	.020	−.027	−.046	.026
Family income	.101**	−.130**	−.009	−.103*
Parental homeownership	−.005	.038	−.035	.034

(continued)

TABLE 3.10   (CONTINUED)

	Friendships			
Variable	White	Black	Latino	Asian & Pacific Islander
Catholic	−.031	.038	.107**	−.068
Other religious beliefs	.030	−.007	.028	−.056
Religiosity	−.060*	.003	.072*	.019
Northeast	−.051	.057	.047	−.006
Midwest	−.023	−.036	.052	−.038
West	.022	.015	−.003	.013
Constant	.542***	.048	.107	.134
Adjusted R²	.441***	.268***	.376***	.221***

NOTE: Models estimated with imputed NLSF data; standardized coefficients (β) displayed. Reference categories include: male, US citizen, Protestant, South resident, attended public high school, attended public research university.
[a] Visibility of each student group is relative to [specific racial or ethnic group]'s visibility on campus.
[b] Proportion of student group entered into models.
*$p < .05$, **$p < .01$, ***$p < .001$.

TABLE 3.11   Influences on Latino students' romantic relationships during college

	Romantic relationships			
Variable	White	Black	Latino	Asian & Pacific Islander
Prejudice at college entrance				
Anti-white	.049	——	——	——
Anti-black	——	.009	——	——
Anti-Asian	——	——	——	.044
Closeness to (first-year)				
Whites	.176***	.051	−.054	−.034
Blacks	.054	.069	.047	−.132**
Latinos	−.348***	.142**	.227***	.206***
Asians & Pacific Islanders	.059	.009	.011	.115**
Precollege college friendships				
Whites	.322*	−.521***	−.470***	−.282*
Blacks	.037	−.040	−.166***	−.017
Latinos	.208	−.363**	.047	−.275*
Asians & Pacific Islanders	.110	−.224***	−.149**	−.105
College experiences and perceptions				
Campus racial climate	−.152***	.185***	.170***	.180***
College diversity commitment	−.033	.006	−.023	.029
Ethnic and Gender studies courses	−.017	.085**	.074**	.148***

(continued)

TABLE 3.11   (CONTINUED)

Variable	Romantic relationships			
	White	Black	Latino	Asian & Pacific Islander
White student visibility[a]	−.031	−.094**	−.010	−.052
Black student visibility[a]	−.030	−.140**	−.075*	−.102*
Asian & Pacific Islander student visibility[a]	−.042	−.029	.019	−.019
Campus characteristics				
Black students[b]	−.028	.051	.012	.007
Latino students[b]	−.183**	.188***	.154***	.104
Asian & Pacific Islander students[b]	.043	.072	.028	.211***
Private research university	−.028	.023	.127***	.188***
Liberal arts college	−.024	.068	.073*	.057
Precollege environments				
Private high school	.040	.087**	.095***	−.018
School segregation level	−.031	.121**	.185***	.075
Neighborhood segregation level	.131**	−.027	−.150***	−.101*
Social characteristics				
Female	−.096**	.020	−.070**	−.172***
Darker skin color	.012	.009	−.009	−.028
International student	−.021	−.018	.003	.118***
Mother's education	.064	.125**	.026	.006
Father's education	−.014	−.139***	.015	.111**
Family income	.030	−.158**	−.130***	−.155***
Parental homeownership	−.030	.088**	.137***	.085*
Catholic	.030	−.072	−.094**	−.074
Other religious beliefs	.113*	−.128**	−.153***	−.140**
Religiosity	.075*	−.101**	−.089***	−.057
Northeast	−.212***	.267***	.306***	.344***
Midwest	−.078	.100**	.165***	.079*
West	−.074	.127**	.196***	.197***
Constant	.506***	.229*	.168*	.234**
Adjusted R²	.256***	.398***	.609***	.353***

NOTE: Models estimated with imputed NLSF data; standardized coefficients (β) displayed. Reference categories include: male, US citizen, Protestant, South resident, attended public high school, attended public research university.
[a] Visibility of each student group is relative to [specific racial or ethnic group]'s visibility on campus.
[b] Proportion of student group entered into models.
*$p < .05$, **$p < .01$, ***$p < .001$.

Wagner et al. 2006). Chang and colleagues (2006) found students on campuses with high levels of cross-race interaction occurring benefited from these interactions without having high levels of cross-race interactions themselves. Specifically, students who are part of such campuses are more open to diversity than

TABLE 3.12   Influences on Latino students' roommate diversity during college

| Variable | Roommates | | | |
	White	Black	Latino	Asian & Pacific Islander
Prejudice at college entrance				
Anti-white	−.064*	——	——	——
Anti-black	——	−.008	——	——
Anti-Asian	——	——	——	−.001
Closeness to (first-year)				
Whites	.078	−.017	−.123**	.022
Blacks	.095*	.177**	.039	−.089
Latinos	−.135**	−.031	.168**	−.106*
Asians & Pacific Islanders	−.039	−.145**	−.059	.132**
Precollege college friendships				
Whites	.507***	−.334*	.102	−.571***
Blacks	.020	.038	.024	−.145*
Latinos	.273*	−.336*	.255	−.393**
Asians & Pacific Islanders	.159**	−.135	.068	−.173*
College experiences and perceptions				
Campus racial climate	−.089**	.165***	.095*	.000
College diversity commitment	.050	−.041	−.050	.001
Ethnic and Gender studies courses	−.006	.032	−.053	.026
White student visibility[a]	−.106**	.017	.094*	.006
Black student visibility[a]	−.022	−.071	−.003	.071
Asian & Pacific Islander student visibility[a]	−.062	.055	.087*	−.035
Campus characteristics				
Black students[b]	−.085**	.127**	−.026	−.033
Latino students[b]	−.346***	.022	.289***	−.048
Asian & Pacific Islander students[b]	−.048	.076	−.075	.329***
Private research university	−.067	.063	.000	−.042
Liberal arts college	−.135***	−.015	−.015	−.124**
Precollege environments				
Private high school	.035	−.053	−.046	.068
School segregation level	.098*	−.052	−.033	−.016
Neighborhood segregation level	.042	.021	.022	−.002
Social characteristics				
Female	−.078**	−.081*	.120***	−.005
Darker skin color	−.048	.022	.039	−.010
International student	−.105***	.041	.030	.021
Mother's education	−.006	.056	−.030	.056
Father's education	.063	−.002	−.038	.005
Family income	.125**	−.139**	−.009	−.051
Parental homeownership	.028	.027	−.030	.014
Catholic	−.031	−.042	.120**	−.152**

(continued)

TABLE 3.12   (CONTINUED)

Variable	Roommates			
	White	Black	Latino	Asian & Pacific Islander
Other religious beliefs	−.032	−.065	.052	−.101*
Religiosity	−.060*	−.057	.057	.017
Northeast	−.002	.170***	−.003	−.015
Midwest	.011	−.010	−.007	.007
West	.061	−.018	−.047	.005
Constant	.493**	.043	−.114	.368***
Adjusted R²	.432***	.172***	.250***	.198***

NOTE: Models estimated with imputed NLSF data; standardized coefficients (β) displayed. Reference categories include: male, US citizen, Protestant, South resident, attended public high school, attended public research university.
[a] Visibility of each student group is relative to [specific racial or ethnic group]'s visibility on campus.
[b] Proportion of student group entered into models.
*p < .05, **p < .01, ***p < .001.

TABLE 3.13   Influences on Latino students' involvement in racially diverse college student organizations

Variable	Memberships in student organizations			
	Mostly White	Mostly Black	Mostly Latino	Mostly Asian & Pacific Islander
Prejudice at college entrance				
Anti-white	−.026	——	——	——
Anti-black	——	.074	——	——
Anti-Asian	——	——	——	.049
Closeness to (first-year)				
Whites	.015	.027	−.071	−.068
Blacks	−.043	.109	−.014	−.026
Latinos	−.003	.022	.090	.054
Asians & Pacific Islanders	.010	−.086	.037	.032
Precollege college friendships				
Whites	.467**	.089	−.187	−.404*
Blacks	.095	.103	−.062	−.157*
Latinos	.326*	.050	.039	−.496**
Asians & Pacific Islanders	.123	.062	−.024	−.150
College experiences and perceptions				
Campus racial climate	.006	.056	.201***	.027
College diversity commitment	−.029	−.053	−.071*	−.001
Ethnic and Gender studies courses	.044	.033	.024	−.031
White student visibility[a]	.033	−.071	.090*	−.024

(continued)

TABLE 3.13 (CONTINUED)

Variable	Memberships in student organizations			
	Mostly White	Mostly Black	Mostly Latino	Mostly Asian & Pacific Islander
Black student visibility[a]	−.022	−.014	.023	.073
Asian & Pacific Islander student visibility[a]	.011	−.012	.046	−.041
Campus characteristics				
Black students[b]	−.006	.066	.049	−.027
Latino students[b]	−.135*	−.044	.063	−.020
Asian & Pacific Islander students[b]	−.056	−.030	−.075	.185*
Private research university	.177***	.022	.048	.010
Liberal arts college	.059	.130**	.019	−.033
Precollege environments				
Private high school	−.007	−.001	−.060	−.003
School segregation level	.010	.150**	−.074	−.011
Neighborhood segregation level	−.102	−.107	.083	.061
Social characteristics				
Female	−.040	−.013	.016	.036
Darker skin color	−.026	.064	.033	.024
International student	−.038	−.004	−.015	.009
Mother's education	.140**	−.059	−.076	−.035
Father's education	.002	.051	.004	−.041
Family income	.077	−.074	−.046	.047
Parental homeownership	.024	.042	−.019	.044
Catholic	.033	−.025	.078	−.097
Other religious beliefs	.055	−.046	−.003	−.063
Religiosity	.023	−.005	.058	−.042
Northeast	.045	.041	.084	−.058
Midwest	−.007	−.004	.072	−.095*
West	.132**	.039	−.034	−.071
Constant	−.081	−.080	−.058	.176*
Adjusted R^2	.153***	.055***	.207***	.045**

NOTE: Models estimated with imputed NLSF data; standardized coefficients (β) displayed. Reference categories include: male, US citizen, Protestant, South resident, attended public high school, attended public research university.
[a] Visibility of each student group is relative to [specific racial or ethnic group]'s visibility on campus.
[b] Proportion of student group entered into models.
*$p < .05$, **$p < .01$, ***$p < .001$.

students with similar levels of cross-race interactions on campuses with fewer students interacting across racial and ethnic lines. An extension of this research by Denson and Chang (2009) suggests students on campuses with peers more frequently engaged in interacting across racial and ethnic lines may also benefit. The current study, coupled with previous research (Bowman and Park 2014;

TABLE 3.14 Influences on Asian and Pacific Islander students' college friendship network

| Variable | Friendships | | | |
	White	Black	Latino	Asian & Pacific Islander
Prejudice at college entrance				
Anti-white	.029	——	——	——
Anti-black	——	.020	——	——
Anti-Latino	——	——	.041	——
Closeness to (first-year)				
Whites	.251***	−.130**	−.021	−.114**
Blacks	−.090	.278***	.078	−.099
Latinos	.108*	−.079	.017	−.052
Asians & Pacific Islanders	−.200***	−.076	−.067	.233***
Precollege college friendships				
Whites	.284**	.015	.164	.043
Blacks	.039	.313***	.074	.001
Latinos	.040	.007	.271***	−.002
Asians & Pacific Islanders	−.020	.022	.191	.306**
College experiences and perceptions				
Campus racial climate	−.091**	.153***	.054	.050
College diversity commitment	.007	−.047	.016	−.073**
Ethnic and Gender studies courses	−.061*	.015	.072	.119***
White student visibility[a]	−.080	.036	.047	.085*
Black student visibility[a]	.034	−.102*	−.020	.053
Latino student visibility[a]	−.016	.008	.050	−.083
Campus characteristics				
Black students[b]	−.042	.007	−.103**	.008
Latino students[b]	.037	.123*	.355***	−.073
Asian & Pacific Islander students[b]	−.288***	−.113	−.180**	.238***
Private research university	−.038	.084*	−.005	−.034
Liberal arts college	.041	.093*	.040	−.105**
Precollege environments				
Private high school	−.013	−.007	−.021	.016
School segregation level	−.038	.037	.006	.023
Neighborhood segregation level	.002	.078*	−.001	−.032
Social characteristics				
Female	−.032	−.007	.006	.016
Darker skin color	.014	.010	−.021	.012
International student	−.060*	.016	−.040	.054
Mother's education	−.050	.046	−.007	−.015
Father's education	.088*	.058	−.030	−.062
Family income	.020	−.033	−.056	−.030

(continued)

TABLE 3.14 (CONTINUED)

	Friendships			
Variable	White	Black	Latino	Asian & Pacific Islander
Parental homeownership	.017	−.007	.045	−.026
Catholic	.041	−.031	.060	−.059
Other religious beliefs	−.023	−.010	.086*	.007
Religiosity	−.137***	−.045	−.024	.123**
Northeast	.022	−.054	−.131**	−.038
Midwest	.052	−.031	−.072	−.066
West	.104**	−.009	−.144**	−.108**
Constant	.501***	−.066	−.004	.255
Adjusted R^2	.424***	.214***	.141***	.416***

NOTE: Models estimated with imputed NLSF data; standardized coefficients (β) displayed. Reference categories include: male, US citizen, Protestant, South resident, attended public high school, attended public research university.
[a] Visibility of each student group is relative to [specific racial or ethnic group]'s visibility on campus.
[b] Proportion of student group entered into models.
*p < .05, **p < .01, ***p < .001.

TABLE 3.15 Influences on Asian and Pacific Islander students' romantic relationships during college

	Romantic relationships			
Variable	White	Black	Latino	Asian & Pacific Islander
Prejudice at college entrance				
Anti-white	.153***	——	——	——
Anti-black	——	−.160***	——	——
Anti-Latino	——	——	−.205***	——
Closeness to (first-year)				
Whites	.234***	−.060	−.032	−.078
Blacks	−.095	.192**	.115*	−.066
Latinos	−.076	.021	.080	.045
Asians & Pacific Islanders	−.082*	.078*	.124***	.244***
Precollege college friendships				
Whites	.462***	−.762***	−.686***	−.407***
Blacks	.123*	−.160**	−.225***	−.114*
Latinos	.028	−.118**	.024	−.072
Asians & Pacific Islanders	.290*	−.671***	−.553***	−.299**

(continued)

TABLE 3.15 (CONTINUED)

Variable	Romantic relationships			
	White	Black	Latino	Asian & Pacific Islander
College experiences and perceptions				
Campus racial climate	−.111**	.171***	.163***	.185***
College diversity commitment	.013	.007	−.014	−.033
Ethnic and Gender studies courses	−.055	.118***	.151***	.212***
White student visibility[a]	−.057	−.071	−.013	.013
Black student visibility[a]	.016	−.151***	−.111**	−.050
Latino student visibility[a]	−.007	.286***	.090*	.077
Campus characteristics				
Black students[b]	−.026	.020	−.052	−.016
Latino students[b]	−.020	.116*	.104*	−.024
Asian & Pacific Islander students[b]	−.059	.087	−.021	.182**
Private research university	−.025	.079*	.117***	.112**
Liberal arts college	−.006	.072*	.059*	−.009
Precollege environments				
Private high school	.038	.057	.122***	−.005
School segregation level	−.036	.116***	.197***	.080*
Neighborhood segregation level	.053	−.034	−.116***	−.087**
Social characteristics				
Female	−.058	.044	−.102***	−.126***
Darker skin color	−.036	.003	.008	.030
International student	.001	−.081**	−.062*	.084**
Mother's education	−.024	.106**	.009	−.027
Father's education	.009	−.168***	−.051	−.010
Family income	.108**	−.120**	−.135***	−.135***
Parental homeownership	−.131***	.127***	.183***	.092**
Catholic	.056	−.061	−.138***	−.066*
Other religious beliefs	.135***	−.139***	−.272***	−.135***
Religiosity	.127***	−.116***	−.164***	−.047
Northeast	−.168***	.237***	.290***	.259***
Midwest	−.063	.131***	.199***	.067
West	−.117*	.224***	.288***	.196***
Constant	.301***	.332***	.283***	.328***
Adjusted R^2	.226***	.386***	.498***	.411***

NOTE: Models estimated with imputed NLSF data; standardized coefficients (β) displayed. Reference categories include: male, US citizen, Protestant, South resident, attended public high school, attended public research university.

[a] Visibility of each student group is relative to [specific racial or ethnic group]'s visibility on campus.

[b] Proportion of student group entered into models.

*$p < .05$, **$p < .01$, ***$p < .001$.

TABLE 3.16 Influences on Asian and Pacific Islander students' roommate diversity during college

	Roommates			
Variable	White	Black	Latino	Asian & Pacific Islander
Prejudice at college entrance				
Anti-white	.017	——	——	——
Anti-black	——	−.046	——	——
Anti-Latino	——	——	.035	——
Closeness to (first-year)				
Whites	.132**	−.090	.045	−.130**
Blacks	.073	.149*	.040	−.052
Latinos	.012	−.046	−.011	−.043
Asians & Pacific Islanders	−.120**	−.080	−.033	.213***
Precollege college friendships				
Whites	.269*	−.061	.353**	−.027
Blacks	.051	.141*	.125*	−.045
Latinos	.035	−.096*	.154**	.040
Asians & Pacific Islanders	.006	−.106	.302*	.189
College experiences and perceptions				
Campus racial climate	−.067*	.151***	.051	.028
College diversity commitment	.037	−.048	.017	−.040
Ethnic and Gender studies courses	−.071*	.024	−.083*	.078**
White student visibility[a]	−.012	.045	−.024	.004
Black student visibility[a]	−.038	−.141**	−.126*	.109*
Latino student visibility[a]	−.040	.101	.152*	−.062
Campus characteristics				
Black students[b]	−.094**	.085*	−.040	−.005
Latino students[b]	−.052	−.018	.484***	−.198***
Asian & Pacific Islander students[b]	−.277***	.100	−.142*	.308***
Private research university	−.041	.189***	−.030	−.109**
Liberal arts college	−.031	−.004	.013	−.194***
Precollege environments				
Private high school	−.005	−.036	−.086*	.100**
School segregation level	.007	.020	−.042	.007
Neighborhood segregation level	−.002	.142***	−.036	−.027
Social characteristics				
Female	−.057*	−.011	.101**	.006
Darker skin color	.029	−.025	−.017	−.059
International student	−.139***	.082*	−.001	.060*
Mother's education	−.066	.078	.038	.041
Father's education	.024	.040	−.065	−.025
Family income	.116***	−.082*	−.012	−.078*
Parental homeownership	.031	−.019	.004	−.031

(continued)

TABLE 3.16   (CONTINUED)

| Variable | Roommates | | | |
	White	Black	Latino	Asian & Pacific Islander
Catholic	.131**	−.044	−.044	−.124***
Other religious beliefs	.022	−.095*	.022	−.034
Religiosity	−.112***	−.054	−.009	.117***
Northeast	.052	.075	−.112*	−.028
Midwest	.059	.054	−.102*	−.037
West	.112**	.060	−.106*	−.052
Constant	.502**	−.052	−.085*	.308*
Adjusted R²	.411***	.156***	.137***	.368***

NOTE: Models estimated with imputed NLSF data; standardized coefficients (β) displayed. Reference categories include: male, US citizen, Protestant, South resident, attended public high school, attended public research university.
ᵃ Visibility of each student group is relative to [specific racial or ethnic group]'s visibility on campus.
ᵇ Proportion of student group entered into models.
*p < .05, **p < .01, ***p < .001.

TABLE 3.17   Influences on Asian and Pacific Islander students' involvement in racially diverse college student organizations

| Variable | Memberships in student organizations | | | |
	Mostly White	Mostly Black	Mostly Latino	Mostly Asian & Pacific Islander
Prejudice at college entrance				
Anti-white	−.005	—	—	—
Anti-black	—	−.016	—	—
Anti-Latino	—	—	.045	—
Closeness to (first-year)				
Whites	.186***	.051	−.044	−.149**
Blacks	−.097	.137**	−.017	.078
Latinos	.030	−.032	.060	−.069
Asians & Pacific Islanders	−.117**	−.154	−.018	.156***
Precollege college friendships				
Whites	.156	−.039	.060	.065
Blacks	.015	.144*	.040	.037
Latinos	.018	−.014	.141**	.003
Asians & Pacific Islanders	−.049	.038	.046	.292*
College experiences and perceptions				
Campus racial climate	−.004	.023	.041	.131***
College diversity commitment	−.029	−.065	−.031	−.019

(continued)

TABLE 3.17   (CONTINUED)

Variable	Memberships in student organizations			
	Mostly White	Mostly Black	Mostly Latino	Mostly Asian & Pacific Islander
Ethnic and Gender studies courses	.049	.006	.038	.078*
White student visibility[a]	.038	−.090	.029	.019
Black student visibility[a]	.030	−.035	−.113*	−.073
Latino student visibility[a]	−.064	.091	.037	.040
Campus characteristics				
Black students[b]	−.029	.009	.002	−.014
Latino students[b]	.036	.045	.095	−.049
Asian & Pacific Islander students[b]	−.288***	−.002	−.008	.216**
Private research university	.049	.037	.027	.002
Liberal arts college	.037	−.008	−.033	.006
Precollege environments				
Private high school	−.014	.019	−.027	−.040
School segregation level	.011	.052	−.017	−.016
Neighborhood segregation level	.039	−.019	.063	−.090*
Social characteristics				
Female	−.038	−.031	.078*	.006
Darker skin color	.016	.016	−.077*	−.028
International student	−.060	.039	−.008	.013
Mother's education	−.005	−.001	.004	−.027
Father's education	.080	.059	−.013	−.026
Family income	.043	.019	.051	−.048
Parental homeownership	−.017	−.065	−.025	.002
Catholic	.026	−.053	.024	.004
Other religious beliefs	−.020	−.028	−.023	−.046
Religiosity	−.038	−.001	.024	.135***
Northeast	.006	.045	−.049	−.010
Midwest	−.005	−.004	−.044	.012
West	.064	.014	−.022	−.105*
Constant	.408	−.005	−.023	−.079
Adjusted R²	.155***	.040**	.029**	.228***

NOTE: Models estimated with imputed NLSF data; standardized coefficients (β) displayed. Reference categories include: male, US citizen, Protestant, South resident, attended public high school, attended public research university.
[a] Visibility of each student group is relative to [specific racial or ethnic group]'s visibility on campus.
[b] Proportion of student group entered into models.
*$p < .05$, **$p < .01$, ***$p < .001$.

Chang et al. 2006; Park and Kim 2013) suggests that a "compositional effect" may be present on some campuses. Additionally, Bahns and colleagues' (2012) research cautions us from using a simplistic view that more diversity in schools and colleges leads to more diverse friendships or influences students' views in particular positive ways; they found such institutions allow students more of an opportunity to create racial ingroup friendships rather than diversifying their networks.[7] As found above, greater representation of students of color affected elite college students' social interactions differently, as more representation did not neatly correspond with greater diversity in the social interactions of students (considered further below).

An aspect closely related to the diversity of colleges and universities is the institutional type, which was found to influence students' interactions in varying ways. Partially supporting previous research (Bowman and Park 2014), students at public research universities had somewhat fewer cross-race friendships and social interactions on the whole compared to their peers at liberal arts colleges and private research universities. However, the general trend masks variations that are campus- and group-specific whereby we must fully consider who is interacting with whom, in what situation they are interacting, and where they are interacting because these contexts can indicate, as the analyses above do, that liberal arts and private research institutions can be toxic social environments for students.

The precollege friendships and social environments of elite college students were the next greatest influence on their social interactions during college. These findings (discussed further below) support previous research on the importance of precollege experiences with interacting with diverse peers and the context of those experiences for influencing students' social interactions (see Hall, Cabrera, and Milem 2011; Levin, Taylor, and Caudle 2007; Park and Chang 2015; Park and Kim 2013; Sidanius et al. 2008; Stearns, Buchmann, and Bonneau 2009). In particular, precollege friendships impacted whom elite college students interacted with during college more frequently than students' schools or the neighborhoods they experienced prior to college. As these relationships are integral to learning new information about and possibly breaking down stereotypes of other groups, these precollege social interactions appear to increase students' willingness to interact with peers across racial and ethnic lines. Lastly, in relation to stereotypes of other groups, students' entering levels of prejudice were less likely than other factors to shape their social interactions during college. However, students' prejudice predominantly influenced one form of social interactions: romantic relationships. With the exception of one finding for Asian and Pacific Islander students (discussed further below), students with more prejudice toward one group or another were less likely to date members of that particular group during college. Next, we turn to findings about how these students' social interactions arguably form a racial hierarchy on elite college campuses.

The Shape of Racial Hierarchy and Campus Climates among Students

The social interaction patterns presented above are similar to those found in other studies of college students.[8] These patterns among elite college students arguably support the Latin Americanization perspective in the racial hierarchy literature despite little agreement on where new immigrants to the United States fall on the black-white continuum of privilege (see Lee and Bean 2007). That is, students appear to be moving toward a triracial stratification system of race with three groups: white students, honorary white students (Asian and Pacific Islander more so than Latino students), and black students. White and Asian and Pacific Islander students, when not interacting with ingroup members, interacted mostly with each other during college. Latinos interacted mostly with whites and Asians and Pacific Islanders, although they had a bit more interaction with blacks than either white or Asian and Pacific Islander students. However, when forms of interracial interactions are considered, white, Asian and Pacific Islander, and Latino students interact with black students the least at elite colleges. The notable lack of interaction with blacks by the other student groups, who have more interactions with whites, supports their movement toward an "honorary white" status on campus. Furthermore, although students' skin color was not used to distinguish lighter- and darker-skinned Asian and Pacific Islander and Latino students, as is often done in studies of the Latin Americanization of race (see Bonilla-Silva 2014, 225–245; also Bonilla-Silva 2004; Bonilla-Silva and Dietrich 2009), the average skin color of students was a fairly light complexion and suggests lighter-skinned members of these two ethnic groups may be more likely to enter elite colleges and universities than darker-skinned members of the same groups. However, although Asian and Pacific Islander and Latino students inhabit a similar position in the racial hierarchy on elite college campuses, they do not view each other as equals, given the different levels of prejudice toward each other found in the current study.

The Latin Americanization of race on elite college campuses may be part of a longer process of racial stratification leading to Gans's (1999) black-nonblack divide, whereby nonblack minority groups merge with whites in distinction to blacks. With the exception of Latino students, white and Asian and Pacific Islander students had fewer friendships with blacks during college than they did with members of other racial and ethnic groups. Asian and Pacific Islander students as well as Latino students associated more with whites and each other than with blacks during college as well. What is certain is that black students are segregated on elite college campuses. Privileged white students remain at the top of the hierarchy, and Asian and Pacific Islander and Latino students occupy a "racial middle" (O'Brien 2008) in relation to their social interactions on campus. Importantly, the need to frame the conversation of elite college students' social interactions as one of racial hierarchy relates to resources and opportunities on campus. As noted at the outset of this volume, the institutions included in this study as well as many others were created for a wealthy, white elite student body to support their interests, studies, and career pursuits. These orientations and the privileging of white students continues today, particularly in relation to elite college students' career opportunities, and extends to the campus racial climate (see

Binder, Davis, and Bloom 2016; Rivera 2015). These patterns of social interactions are shaped by competitive, career-driven orientations of elite colleges and their students, which also are shaped by privileging of white students on campus in everyday life, while students of color must navigate racially contentious grounds. The hierarchy, then, is not simply a question of who is preferred in social interactions, but reflects how these interactions are framed within racialized organizations that syphon resources and opportunities predominantly to one group over the others. (An elaboration of this point is presented in Chapter Five).

Scholars should not misinterpret the racial hierarchy on elite college campuses as "cut-and-dry," as if the relations between all groups were well-defined. Although Asians and Pacific Islanders and Latinos interact more with whites than other groups and have similar positions above blacks in the racial hierarchy on elite college campuses, these students are not immune to racial discrimination.[9] Whites may continue to interact with these groups more than blacks during college, but such interactions do not indicate they necessarily see them as "equals" or do not discriminate against them. White students have more positive attitudes toward Asians and Pacific Islanders than any other group including their own, yet they continue to have limited interactions with them during college. Though this reality may result from the representation of Asian and Pacific Islander and Latino students on campus, it gives rise to the following question: If Asians and Pacific Islanders are perceived as "equals" or even somewhat more favorably than whites as a group, why don't white students interact more with these students? As Bonilla-Silva (2014, 241–246; also Bonilla-Silva and Dietrich 2009) and colleagues note, a conditional status as an "honorary white" does not guarantee that people of color experience fair treatment from whites.

The above point about the malleability of the favorable or "honorary white" status some groups are afforded on campus compared to black students is found in measures examining the impact of particular race-related perceptions and experiences among students during college. The campus racial climate scale indicated that all student groups, including white students, are affected by their perceptions of racial hostility on campuses. Among elite college students, perceiving campuses as more racially hostile influenced whom students interacted with during college. Importantly, the campus racial climate measure taps into student views of "racial hostility towards whom?" on campus, framed by the black-white comparison of the traditional racial hierarchy. Oftentimes, students who perceived a more racially hostile campus had fewer social interactions with whites, but more with blacks, during college. The degree to which these perceptions influenced students' social interactions depended on what form of interaction was considered, because the campus racial climate influenced students' romantic relationships the most, followed by their friendships, while their roommate and student organization situations were the least influenced by the campus climate.

In relation to the campus climate at elite colleges, students perceiving their institutions as strongly committed to diversity generally experienced more cross-race interactions during college, but these effects predominantly influenced students' interactions with whites and blacks. These findings may relate to the sociohistorical context of "diversity" in higher education relating to the increase of black students on campus during and immediately following the civil rights movement in the mid-twentieth century. This shift in both the student body's composition, but also the institutional support for aspects of racial diversity and inclusion, has reverberated across the nation as a contentious point on campus and in society as we move further away from the rights movements and into an era of supposed equal opportunity and postracism.[10] Thus, a more racially hostile climate, though it can influence all students, is concretely anchored in the discriminatory experiences of black students and the historical hostility of white students to such campus diversification.

Ethnic and gender studies courses influenced students' social interactions across racial and ethnic lines, which relates to the campus racial climate and their precollege social interactions as well. White students who took more courses discussing race and inequality had more white friendships as well as more memberships in mostly white organizations, but were also more likely to form diverse romantic relationships during college. Although the former results could be seen as a negative reaction by these students, progressive views of race and inequality do not always increase in a linear fashion, and the formation of more ingroup connections by white students may result from discomfort with an increased awareness of racism and racial inequality combined with more exposure to and experience with racially diverse peers (Astin 1993; Bowman 2012; Bowman and Denson 2012; Hurtado 2005). However, it is also likely these students do not agree with perspectives and discussions in these courses because they do not align with their racial ideologies, and thus they seek out other students who they feel support their views, which frequently are other white students on campus given their similar precollege experiences. Further, these findings may result from the limited experience most white students have with diverse peers, and if a classroom confrontation arises, students may recoil given their lack of experience with and knowledge of issues of race and inequality.

Different effects of taking ethnic and gender studies courses existed for black students as they formed more ingroup relationships during college, particularly having more black friends and joining more predominantly black student organizations. Black students who took more ethnic and gender studies courses were also less likely to room with whites or Latinos. Among Latino students as well as Asian and Pacific Islander students, ethnic and gender studies courses increased their interactions with each other and increasingly with blacks during college. However, for both student groups, enrolling in these courses also decreased many of their interactions with whites. It should be noted that this measure did not disaggregate what the specific courses were or what programs they fall under in the academic structure and curriculum of these colleges, which could account for their varying effects on students. For example, the differences found in these analyses may relate to students taking courses focusing on black women's experiences and epistemologies rather than taking a course on Japanese history, and may also relate to electing to take courses in an American Indian and Indigenous Studies program compared to an Africana Studies program on campus. These findings somewhat complicate previous findings of similar courses' increasing cross-race interactions among college students, but also do not necessarily indicate students are not, in fact, learning important information from these courses (see Denson and Chang 2009).

Another important aspect of the racial hierarchy existing on elite college campuses is the perceived visibility and representation of students of color. These measures indicate how fragile students perceive their group position to be while having more opportunity to interact across racial and ethnic lines compared to their precollege experiences (for more on group positioning and group threat perspectives, see Blalock 1967; Blumer 1958; Bobo 1988; and Bobo and Tuan 2006). These group visibility measures suggest that if white students perceive another racial or ethnic group as comparable or more visible on campus—a position historically held, and arguably expected or entitled, by white students—this may push those white students to seek out other cross-race relationships with students of color who are not of the supposedly more visible group, often to decrease their interactions with the more visible group on campus. Such actions by white students may be a coping mechanism to solidify their group position, and as in Bonacich's (1973) "middle man minority" perspective and Bonilla-Silva's description of the Latin Americanization of race (Bonilla-Silva 2014, 225–254), they may use other racial and ethnic groups to "buffer" themselves from perceived outgroup threats to resources and opportunities. The greater representation of students of color on campus generally increased whites' cross-race interactions during college. These measures point to the influence of greater exposure to racial diversity on campus found in previous research (Bowman and Park 2014; Chang et al. 2006; Park and Kim 2013), but also somewhat support the contention that, depending on the perceived visibility and size of student groups on campus, white students form relationships to buffer themselves and their positions on campus.

When we consider the visibility and representation measures among students of color, different pictures come to light. Among black students, many of the effects of students' visibility perceptions were related to interactions with other students of color, and were not limited to direct considerations of that specific group but extended to indirect connections to other student groups. Oftentimes, black students who viewed other groups as more visible than their own experienced increasing interactions with students of color, with sporadic reductions in their interactions with whites. For Asian and Pacific Islander students, their perceptions of group visibility had fewer influences on their cross-race interactions, but those influences are telling. There appears to be a link drawn between black and Latino students on campus for Asian and Pacific Islander students, as perceptions of each student group corresponded with extended interaction effects with other groups. Somewhat similar to "extended" or "secondary contact" effects whereby cross-race interactions with one group can influence the beliefs about other groups (see Pettigrew 2009; Wright et al. 1997), the perceptions of both black and Latino students seem linked in the minds of Asian and Pacific Islander students. Among Latino students, again, the impact of their perceptions of group visibility was limited, but indicates that perceiving their visibility on campus as less than that of other student groups corresponded to having fewer interactions with more visible groups and increasing ingroup interactions during college.

Greater representation of students of color on campus consistently increased elite college students' cross-race interactions with students of color during college, but less so with whites among black students. These effects of student representation were explicitly found for each racial and ethnic minority student group, leading to more interactions of various forms during college. Similar to the case for black students, greater representation of students of color on campus generally increased Asian and Pacific Islander students' cross-race interactions with other students of color, but led to fewer interactions with whites. These greater representations of different racial and ethnic groups on campus often led to cross-race interactions being constrained for Asian and Pacific Islander students, as increases in representation for one group corresponded to fewer interactions with another group. Greater representation of students of color on campus generally increased Latino students' cross-race interactions, but reduced their interactions with whites during college overall. These findings indicate students' social interactions are impacted by multiple aspects of the college environment from academic structures such as courses available to the representation of students of color on campus coupled with the perceptions of racial hostility and group representation. Thus, it is not simply how diversity influences elite college students' social interactions with one another, but also how diversity is situated within the culture and structures of colleges influencing these social interactions.

Roommate Diversity and Solidifying Residential Preferences on Campus

A common discussion in social science and popular circles concerns the perpetuation of racial residential segregation in society. College presents people with some of their first opportunities to exercise choice in the residential arrangements after childhood. In the current study, the examination of factors influencing whom elite college students roomed with during college found much less explanatory power from the models compared to the analyses of other social interactions. These findings may relate to the generally low levels of racial and ethnic diversity at these institutions in addition to the limited data collected concerning this particular form of social interaction." Another possible explanation for the lower explanatory power of these models is the consistent preference among whites for residentially segregated communities, while people of color more often identify racially integrated communities as their residential preference (Charles 2003). The findings from the current study provide general support for past research, and extend our understanding of how younger generations choose their residential environments. Among white students, their overwhelming preference was for same-race roommates. However, social class, considering both family income and homeownership, made a difference by increasing their same-race roommates while corresponding to somewhat higher numbers of roommates they had with Asians and Pacific Islanders during college. Their previous experiences in more integrated or segregated schools and neighborhoods had little influence on who their roommates were in college, though they did have more Latino roommates if they were from more segregated neighborhoods. Black students were less influenced by social class, but it is worth noting that students from higher-income families had more white roommates in college, which provides partial support for previous research on residential patterns and preferences (Charles 2003). Black students' school and neighborhood experiences also weakly influenced their roommate situations during college; coming from a more segregated school or neighborhood increased the number of roommates they had with whites and Asian and Pacific Islanders.

Asian and Pacific Islander students were moderately influenced by social class and precollege environments, but more influenced by racialized social identity. These students were pushed or pulled between rooming with other Asians and Pacific Islanders and rooming with whites depending on how close they were to each group and the financial situation of their families. Also notable, living in a more segregated neighborhood increased Asian and Pacific Islander students' number of black roommates in college, which corresponds with previous research suggesting that having more black residents in one's neighborhood increases one's preference for black neighbors in their ideal neighborhoods (see Charles 2007). Latino students, while exhibiting the most racially integrated pattern of roommates during college, were less influenced by social class compared to other student groups. Students from higher-income families had more white but fewer black roommates during college. Latino students who had higher levels of prejudice toward whites had fewer white roommates as well. Each of these findings is consistent with previous research on neighborhood preferences among Latinos (Charles 2003, 2007). Together, these findings suggest residential segregation found prominently across the U.S. (see Logan, Stults, and Farley 2004; Massey and Denton 1994) forms early on college campuses through students' roommate decisions. These decision-making opportunities represent students' first chance to exercise some sort of autonomy in making residential decisions. With this in mind, although this study does not explore where these students lived in relation to the cost and amenities of their residences, or what the compositions of the apartment complexes and neighborhoods were, the findings above as well as the neighborhood preference literature suggests students are aligning themselves with general patterns perpetuating racial residential segregation across the United States, structured by race and class.

Precollege Friendships and Other Influential Characteristics and Experiences

As important as the campus context is to shaping the racial hierarchy of interactions among elite college students, their social interactions prior to college are critical to understanding their interactions during college as well. These findings support previous studies of the importance of prior social interactions, specifically interracial friendships, in predicting whom students interact with across racial and ethnic lines during college (Hall, Cabrera, and Milem 2011; Levin, Van Laar, and Sidanius 2003; Park and Kim 2013; Pettigrew and Tropp 2011; Sidanius et al. 2008; Stearns, Buchmann, and Bonneau 2009). White students with more diverse friendships prior to college often had correspondingly higher levels of friendships with those same groups during college. However, it appears their experience with diverse precollege friendships influenced their interactions with Latinos slightly more across all forms of social interactions. The importance of exposure to precollege diversity for white students was prominently found when considering romantic relationships with Latinos during college. Similarly, more precollege friendships with different racial and ethnic groups generally corresponded to higher levels of cross-race interactions with those particular groups during college for students of color in this study. Despite such findings, the influence of precollege friendships on these students' social interactions during college varied in terms of their presence as well as the direction of influence. What is consistent even among students of color is the impact of precollege friendships and environments on students' interactions with Latinos. These findings suggest that the patterns of social interactions on elite college campuses are influenced by a variety of aspects of students' precollege lives in relation to their exposure to people of different races and ethnicities from their own, but also that the degree to which they relate to people such as forming friendships early in life can have lasting influences on their relationships during college.

How connected a student is to multiple racial and ethnic groups, as measured by their racialized social identities, also played an important role in shaping their social interactions during college. These findings point to the influence of group connections dissimilar to traditional social identity and intergroup relations approaches using a distinct racial ingroup-outgroup framing.[12] Here, students used a multidimensional approach to understand their connection with a specific racial or ethnic group as well as their specific ingroup's connection with other racial and ethnic groups. Further, these connections do not allow a distinct ingroup-outgroup designation to be reached, as it appears not to be a matter of "which group are you a part of," but more of "how much of a connection with each group do you have?" In relation to these multiple considerations of group connections, the different experiences students had prior to college as well as their relationship to each group history and relation to one another complicates how students decide whom they interact with during college. Further, one could argue that these initial levels of closeness to each racial and ethnic group are shaped by the history and context of race on elite college campuses and manifest in the racial hierarchy pattern of social interaction among these students. Thus, although there is fairly strong support for social identity theory's perspective of ingroup and outgroup bias, these biases take on multiple layers as they are not distinct, but interrelated in how students relate to groups and interact with one another on campus.

Overall, more measures were significant in the romantic relationship models compared to any other models of social interactions among elite college students. These findings suggest, although the campus context is important, that the intimate connections students find with each other are more of a driving force in whom they date during college. These romantic relationships were frequently influenced by students' religion and religiosity, which supports previous research on the powerful influences of these social characteristics on students' social interactions (see Bowman and Park 2014; Park 2012, 2014b; Park and Chang 2015; Park and Kim 2013; Sidanius et al. 2008). Additionally, the regional place of origin for students influenced whom they did and did not form romantic relationships with during college, which points to the greater complexity of understanding how students' regional location connects to different histories of racial and ethnic relations of those places they may use in shaping whom they pursue romantic interests with during college.

The subtle, but potent influence of colorism is evident across elite college students' social interactions. Colorism is the discrimination of people based on skin complexions and physiological features such that preference is given to individuals with lighter skin complexions and European-associated physiological features, which correspond with higher social status within and across racial and ethnic groups (for more research on colorism, see Blair et al. 2002; Bonilla-Silva 2014; Bonilla-Silva and Dietrich 2009; Gomez 2000; Herring, Keith, and Horton 2004; Ross 1997). Consistent with this research, black students with darker skin complexions had more black friends but fewer white friends during college. Thus, colorism assists with differentiating those stereotypically identified as black from people of different races and ethnicities. In this situation, whites are distancing themselves from darker skinned black students at elite colleges. The inter- and intra-ethnic distancing of colorism is seen prominently among Asian and Pacific Islander students. For students with darker skin complexions, they had fewer memberships in student organizations mostly composed of Latino students. These findings point out how Asian and Pacific Islander students with darker skin complexions are negotiating the "racial middle" (O'Brien) with their comparisons and interactions with other Asians and Pacific Islanders with lighter complexions as well as other people of color. Friendship patterns similar to those found among black students existed among Latino students. Those students with darker skin complexions had fewer white friends but more black friends during college, which suggests some distancing of "noticeable" Latinos on campus by whites. Taken together, these findings suggest colorism works in subtle ways to shape how students interact with each other.

One perplexing set of findings was that black and Asian and Pacific Islander students who had more prejudice toward whites had more romantic relationships with whites during college. Additionally, those students who had higher levels of closeness toward whites had more romantic relationships with whites. These findings may relate to the lower representation of each group on campus as well as a differentiation between white partners they formed romantic relationships with in comparison to other whites, particularly on more racially hostile campuses. Thus, as these students are closer to whites in their everyday lives in college, they may distinguish between compatible partners on campuses where they view fewer whites as accepting of interracial romantic relationships, and those sustaining a more hostile campus setting for black and Asian and Pacific Islander students.

A few limitations to the examination of social interactions among elite college students deserve a degree of explanation. One limitation expressed in the language of this chapter is the inability to clearly identify in the data whom exactly students are interacting with during college. That is, the NLSF does not allow for clear identification of whether the people students report as friends and roommates, or whom they form romantic relationships with, are students on campus, students at other institutions, or not students at all. Therefore, these analyses cannot indicate that increases or decreases in social interactions during college for students were solely college-related increases, meaning they had increases or decreases with their fellow students at their institution. Despite this limitation, that most of these social interactions during college are with other students at their respective institutions seems certain given the important influence that campus characteristics such as the climate, visibility, and representation measures had in each of the models shaping the patterns of social interactions among students.

An additional limitation is the focus on the composition of organizations that students joined during college. The types of organizations students join such as racial and ethnic-oriented organizations and Greek fraternities and sororities

suggests students often join organizations based on the similarities and interests they have with other student members of these groups (Park 2014a, 2014b;
Pascarella and Terenzini 1991, 2005; Sidanius et al. 2008). The type of student
organization is not what is of concern here despite the importance of, for
example, who joins Greek fraternities in comparison to ethnic organizations
or religious organizations. Across organizations, most white students joined
predominantly white organizations, black students were evenly split with most
of their memberships in predominantly white and black organizations, Latino
students mostly joined predominantly white organizations with more diversity in their memberships across other organizations, and Asian and Pacific
Islander students joined predominantly white and Asian and Pacific Islander
student organizations. This pattern of student organization membership is in
line with the larger racial hierarchy across the different forms of social interactions on campus. Thus, the composition of organizations complicates how we
understand who joins what beyond the often compared Greek-ethnic student
organization comparison hinging on similar interests among students. What
is arguably influencing these patterns more is the overall pattern of student
interaction spanning the entire social environment of elite colleges. These patterns have existed for many years and are part of the racial structure of colleges
with a collective memory component influencing students' views of whether
they would be welcome or included in organizations even if they shared similar interests with students in the group who are predominantly of a different
racial or ethnic group from their own. Lastly, all the forms of social interaction
examined in this chapter are interrelated and not easily or completely disconnected from one another. It is clear from previous research (Bowman and Park
2014; Park 2014a; Park and Kim 2013; Sidanius et al. 2008) that different forms
of social interactions can influence one another simultaneously, and this likelihood is considered in later chapters.

CONCLUSION

The students at elite colleges and universities display a racial hierarchy structuring their social interactions throughout college. This hierarchy of social interaction did not influence one form of their social experiences on campus, but cut
across four forms of social interactions to impact these students' friendships and
romantic relationships, their roommate situations, and who were most likely to
be members of their student organizations. Further, these analyses indicate the
prominence of many student characteristics and experiences prior to and during college that create this racial hierarchy on campus. Similar to the analyses of
entering views of race and inequality in the previous chapter, students' racialized social identities continue to shape their lives beyond their views on race
and inequality to whom they interacted with during college. Importantly, this

pattern held across students' four years of college and was highly influenced by the institutions they were enrolled in throughout this time. Elite college students' social interaction patterns can profoundly impact their views of race and inequality in unexpected ways as they graduate college and enter the workforce. In the next chapter, I explore how students' social interactions do or do not influence their views of each other and the importance of racial individualism in sustaining racial inequality.

4 · GRADUATING RACIAL IDEOLOGIES

The College Impact on Views
of Race and Inequality

A college education is often discussed as having academic and social components of student experiences forming the "impact" of college attendance (see overviews of the college impact literature in Astin 1968, 1993; Hurtado 2007; Pascarella and Terenizini 1991, 2005). That is, students' education involves not just their classroom experiences, but also social interactions on and around campus. As argued throughout this volume and the intergroup relations literature as a whole, social interaction can modify college students' views of race and inequality (see Allport 1954; Hewstone and Brown 1986; Pettigrew 1998; Pettigrew and Tropp 2011; also Sidanius et al. 2008). Generally speaking, this literature finds that cross-group interactions reduce prejudicial views of outgroups and their societal circumstances. However, what of the purported "best and brightest" college students in America? Do interracial and intraracial interactions during college influence elite students' racial ideology (i.e., their views of race and inequality) before they graduate and enter the workforce?

At first glance, elite college students may appear to be less prone to changing their views of race and inequality than the general population. As shown in Chapter Two, cross-race friendships that were developed during childhood did not influence elite college students' entering levels of racial prejudice toward different groups, and they rarely influenced views of racial inequality. As influential as childhood experiences are on shaping students' foundational views of race and inequality (see Hagerman 2014; Johnson 2015; Lewis 2003), the current examination of elite college students somewhat contradicts these findings, as precollege friendships had little influence on students' racial ideology before they stepped onto campus. Despite these disappointing findings, college attendance can greatly shape how people consider race and inequality later in life. This means the limited influence of childhood friendships on elite college students' entering views are not the end of the story for understanding how America's future leaders think about race and inequality after college. However, how influential social interactions are on elite college students' racial ideology is not without another cautionary note regarding the racial hierarchy of these social interactions existing on campus. The fairly infrequent amount of cross-race interactions among elite college students suggests such experiences may not correspond to prejudice reduction or modification of students' views of racial inequality.

As noted earlier, social scientific studies conducted over nearly a century on the dynamics of intergroup relations find cross-group interactions under particular circumstances have prejudice-reducing effects (Pettigrew and Tropp 2011, 13–27). The mechanisms of these intergroup situations indicate friendships can influence people somewhat differently compared to other forms of interaction such as romantic relationships or whom a person rooms with during college. As Pettigrew and Tropp's extensive meta-analysis of these studies indicates, not all cross-group interactions reduce prejudice, and they can sometimes increase prejudice among people. Importantly, Pettigrew and Tropp's volume addresses a critical point that the current study explores more thoroughly in this and other chapters: how individual-level interactions and attitudes can and are shaped by the culture and structure of their institutions (see Pettigrew and Tropp 2011, 201–216). Although I am not generalizing to all college students and the influence of their interactions nationwide, the analyses of elite college students below show that their interactions provide another cautionary tale about how restricted cross-race interactions are even on diverse college campuses (see Bahns et al. 2012). In addition, the analyses show how people mistakenly assume that because students may experience some prejudice-reducing effects and decrease their reliance on views that individual efforts shape racial inequality, it does not mean that the campus as a whole reflects these findings of progressive views. Even though cross-race interactions often reduce elite college students' prejudice toward one another and limit their reliance on individualistic views of racial inequality, the context of these interactions can amplify negative cross-race interactions as well as hinder prejudice-reducing effects of such interactions.

In response to a question presented at the outset of this volume, the analyses below clarify the relationships between whom elite college students interact with, in what circumstances they interact across racial and ethnic lines, and how these interactions influence their views of race and inequality. That is, this chapter answers the question: What is the relationship between elite college students' social interactions and their racial attitudes? Simultaneously, these analyses provide a tentative answer to the question of how students' racialized social identities influence their views of race and inequality. Three sets of analyses are presented below. First, I explore the views of race and inequality that elite college students carry with them when they graduate from college, and I detail how these views have changed since they first stepped onto campus four years earlier. Second, a series of models examines how social interactions influence students' view of racial and ethnic outgroups. Finally, I explore how social interactions can influence elite college students' views of individual efforts shaping racial inequality in society. Following these analyses I discuss several key patterns and findings extending our knowledge of how social interactions influence people, particularly the budding young elites at these highly selective institutions, and I examine how the context of these colleges can and cannot shape students' racial ideology as they leave and enter the workforce.

END-OF-COLLEGE VIEWS OF RACE AND INEQUALITY

The graduating elite college students in this study carried with them broader views of race and inequality as well as their racialized social identities than they displayed when they entered college four years earlier. Although their views appeared similar at first, many changes influenced students during college. This section identifies the patterns of racial prejudice, racial individualism, and racialized social identity among each elite college student group. Then, these patterns are compared to those displayed by the students when they entered college to examine how students' views of race, inequality, and identity evolved during college.

As Table 4.1 shows, students generally do not see one another as equals when they consider their racial prejudice toward each other, but these differences shrunk over four years of college. In this table, positive scores indicate more ingroup bias and negative scores indicate less ingroup bias. White students had slightly negative views toward both blacks and Latinos at the end of college, but carried more positive views of Asians and Pacific Islanders when compared to their own group. Black students at these institutions held slightly negative views of whites, but more positive views of both Latinos and Asians and Pacific Islanders. Latino students viewed Asians and Pacific Islanders more positively than their own group as well, but they also slightly viewed whites in a similar positive vein, while having slight negative bias toward blacks. In contrast, Asian and Pacific Islander students thought negatively of each racial and ethnic outgroup compared to their own.

Turning to elite college students' views of individual efforts shaping racial inequality, a slightly different pattern existed than was present when students entered college. Across all four groups, students generally disagreed that people of color had only themselves to blame for not doing better in life. Although students consistently disagreed that individual efforts alone dictate socioeconomic positions in life, a few patterns are apparent in the table. Asian and Pacific Islander students had the highest levels of agreement on the racial individualism

TABLE 4.1   Exiting racial prejudice, racial individualism, and closeness among elite college students

Variable	Whites	Blacks	Latinos	Asians & Pacific Islanders	Group Means Tests
		Student Group			
Traditional racial prejudice					
Anti-white	———	.05	−.05	.51	d,e,f
Anti-black	.06	———	.08	.66	c,f
Anti-Latino	.07	−.04	———	.62	a,c,e
Anti-Asian	−.48	−.59	−.62	———	a,b
Racial individualism toward					
Blacks	2.50	2.81	2.52	2.99	a,c,f
Latinos	2.14	2.46	2.48	2.64	a,b,c
Asians & Pacific Islanders	2.00	2.60	2.29	2.99	a,b,c,d,e,f
All three groups	2.22	2.63	2.42	2.88	a,c,f
Closeness to					
Whites	5.61	4.33	5.65	5.69	a,d,e
Blacks	4.95	6.25	5.34	5.26	a,b,c,d,e
Latinos	4.77	5.10	6.27	5.09	a,b,c,d,f
Asians & Pacific Islanders	4.95	4.14	4.87	6.43	a,c,d,e,f

NOTE: Means calculated using nonimputed NLSF data.
[a] Significant difference ($p < .05$) between white and black students.
[b] Significant difference ($p < .05$) between white and Latino students.
[c] Significant difference ($p < .05$) between white and Asian and Pacific Islander students.
[d] Significant difference ($p < .05$) between black and Latino students.
[e] Significant difference ($p < .05$) between black and Asian and Pacific Islander students.
[f] Significant difference ($p < .05$) between Latino and Asian and Pacific Islander students.

measures, followed by black students, Latino students, and then white students. This interesting pattern somewhat contradicts earlier research (see Hunt 2007) noting that whites in general subscribe more to racial individualism and individualistic views of racial inequality compared to racial and ethnic minority groups. Additionally, a subtle pattern is indicated in the group-specific measures. Students agreed slightly more that blacks' positions in society were more individually determined. For white students as well as Latino students, the second highest agreement on these items was for Asians and Pacific Islanders, while black and Asian and Pacific Islander students had higher agreement levels for Latinos as their second highest levels on these items. In general, students of color held strong support for individualistic explanations for racial inequality for their own groups. These slight variations indicate students do not hold the same individualistic view for racial and ethnic groups. Nevertheless, all the means indicate disagreement that individualistic efforts solely determine racial and ethnic minorities' societal positions. But it is important to recall that less support for individualistic explanations of racial inequality does not simultaneously indicate more support for structural explanations (see Hunt 2007 for additional discussion of the relationship between individualistic and structural explanations for racial inequality over time.). This finding is further discussed later in the chapter.

On level of closeness toward each racial and ethnic group, students were closest to members of their own group at the end of college. White students felt equally close to blacks and Asians and Pacific Islanders, while they were slightly less close to Latinos. Black students at these institutions were closest to Latinos, then whites, and least close to Asians and Pacific Islanders. Latino students were closest to whites, then blacks, and lastly Asians and Pacific Islanders. Asian and Pacific Islander students felt closest to whites and then blacks, and least close to Latinos. All of these closeness scores were within one point of the midpoint score on these scales, meaning although students were closest to their own racial or ethnic group members, they did not feel wholly distant from outgroup members either. Similar to findings in previous chapters, these scores indicate students are not necessarily forming singular ingroup-outgroup comparisons in relation to their racialized social identity (similar to an "us" versus "them" mentality) but are similarly close to all groups.

We learn several interesting things when we compare elite college students' views of race and inequality in addition to their racialized social identities at the end of college with such views when they first stepped onto campus. Table 4.2 provides such a comparative look for these measures. Negative scores indicate a decrease over time in students' scores, while a positive score indicates an increase over time. On the racial prejudice measures, students generally, but not completely, had less negative bias toward racial and ethnic outgroups. White students' views of each racial and ethnic outgroup grew more positive during college. Their views changed the most toward Asians and Pacific Islanders, while their views toward blacks and Latinos changed similarly during their four years on campus. Asian and Pacific Islander students similarly thought more positively of each racial and ethnic outgroup, particularly blacks and Latinos. Black students viewed Latinos more positively at the end of college, but viewed whites and Asians and Pacific Islanders more negatively. Latino students also viewed whites and Asians and Pacific Islanders more negatively, while their views of blacks did not significantly change across their four years of college. Despite these mostly positive changes, it is important to recall that elite college students did not view each other as complete equals on these measures. For example, despite the significant changes among Asian and Pacific Islander students, they still firmly held whites, blacks, and Latinos as inferior to their own group on these measures.

The racial individualism comparisons also provide an optimistic view of change among elite college students.[1] When comparing their entering views of

TABLE 4.2   Four-year changes in elite college students' racial prejudice, racial individualism, and racialized social identity

Variable	Student Group			
	Whites	Blacks	Latinos	Asians & Pacific Islanders
Traditional racial prejudice				
Anti-white	——	.12**	.11**	−.17***
Anti-black	−.21***	——	−.03	−.40***
Anti-Latino	−.25***	−.14***	——	−.49***
Anti-Asian	−.73***	.29***	.25***	——
Racial individualism toward[a]				
Blacks	−1.29***	−1.22***	−1.43***	−1.05***
Latinos	−1.40***	−1.46***	−1.58***	−1.38***
Asians & Pacific Islanders	−1.52***	−1.47***	−1.74***	−1.39***
All three groups	−1.39***	−1.38***	−1.58***	−1.28***
Closeness to				
Whites	−1.01***	−.31***	−.22**	−.22***
Blacks	−.47***	−.44***	.19*	.23***
Latinos	−.33***	−.17*	.07	.29***
Asians & Pacific Islanders	−.51***	−.22*	−.09	.10

NOTE: Means calculated using nonimputed NLSF data. Students' fourth-year scores for each measure were subtracted from their first-year scores to evaluate changes in their racial prejudice, racial individualism, and racialized social identity over four years of elite college attendance.
[a] Used first-year measure of group blame for racial individualism comparisons.
*$p < .05$, **$p < .01$, ***$p < .001$.

racial inequality and those same views four years later, we see decreases among all elite college students in their individualistic views of racial inequality. For each student group on each measure they were less likely to agree that individual efforts were the sole determinants of racial and ethnic minorities' societal positions than they were when they entered college. Latino students had the largest changes across the measures, followed by white and black students, and then Asian and Pacific Islander students. Similar to the patterns noted above, these changes varied among students depending on the group asked about in the measures. The largest decrease in individualistic views of racial inequality existed for Asians and Pacific Islanders, followed closely by Latinos. The least amount of change occurred when students considered the individual efforts of blacks.

A few interesting findings emerge when we turn our attention to the changes in students' racialized social identities. White and black students felt less close to each racial and ethnic group at the end of college than they did when they entered college. For these students, the largest decrease in closeness was toward their own group. White students had the greatest decrease in closeness toward their own racial group, while black students had the second-most decrease.

Neither Latino students nor Asian and Pacific Islander students were less close to their own group members at the end of college. In fact, their levels of closeness to ingroup members did not significantly change during college. However, both groups grew closer to blacks during this time, and Asians and Pacific Islanders also grew closer to Latinos. All student groups were less close to whites at the end of college than they were when they first stepped onto campus.

These findings at the end of college provide a tentative, optimistic conclusion for the influence of college on students' views of race and inequality. That each student group generally held less stereotypical views of each other, were less likely to view individual efforts as the sole determinant of racial inequality, and were similarly close to one another after four years on campus is an important finding. How did social interactions contribute to this finding? Below, I examine the impact of such interactions in changing elite college students' views of race and inequality in addition to that of other factors.

HOW SOCIAL INTERACTIONS SHAPE RACIAL IDEOLOGIES AT THE END OF COLLEGE

To examine how social interactions may change elite college students' views of race and inequality, models similar to the regression analyses in previous chapters were applied to clarify how and in what ways these interactions may influence students' racial ideology. These models include variables for students' precollege experiences, entering and exiting racialized social identity, college experiences and perceptions related to race, campus characteristics such as the number of students of color on campus and whether the college was a private research or a liberal arts college , and each form of social interaction during college. Each table below (Tables 4.3–4.6) displays the analyses for each college student group and each group's associated prejudice levels toward racial and ethnic outgroups. Although the social characteristics of students are included in the models reported below, the discussion does not explore these effects. At this point, noting the specific influences of social interactions on students' views of race provides a window into the complexity of how interaction shapes racial prejudice.

In general, elite college students' social interactions were a fairly consistent influence on their views of racial and ethnic outgroups during college. Students' romantic relationships were the most influential on their racial prejudice levels, followed closely by their friendship networks. Whom students roomed with during college was the third most influential form of social interaction on their views of race, followed lastly by who predominantly composed their student organizations. However, despite the influence of social interactions on students' views of race at the end of college, many of the possible effects of such interactions during college were not present across these analyses (discussed further below).

TABLE 4.3   Factors influencing exiting levels of prejudice among white students

Variable	Traditional Prejudice Form		
	Anti-black	Anti-Latino	Anti-Asian
Entering racial prejudice			
Anti-black	.360***	——	——
Anti-Latino	——	.398***	——
Anti-Asian	——	——	.431***
Closeness to (fourth-year)			
Whites	.197***	.133*	−.016
Blacks	−.109	.193*	.065
Latinos	−.011	−.269***	−.027
Asians & Pacific Islanders	−.062	.000	−.027
Closeness (first-year)			
Whites	.194***	.134**	.055
Blacks	−.176*	−.171*	−.273**
Latinos	.044	.139	.057
Asians & Pacific Islanders	−.076	−.104	−.016
College friendships			
White	−.214**	−.277***	.200***
Black	.016	.036	.016
Latino	−.099*	−.140**	.027
Asian & Pacific Islander	.007	−.151*	.356**
College romantic relationships			
White	.090	.235***	−.020
Black	−1.238***	−1.642***	.194
Latino	2.209***	1.764***	1.220***
Asian & Pacific Islander	−.857***	.088	−1.321***
College roommates			
White	−.394***	−.447***	−.091
Black	−.105**	−.041	−.046
Latino	−.155***	−.131**	−.053
Asian & Pacific Islander	−.252***	−.262***	−.048
Membership in student organizations			
Mostly white	−.245***	−.141**	−.189***
Mostly black	.013	.031	.001
Mostly Latino	−.044	−.045	−.074*
Mostly Asian & Pacific Islander	−.026	.027	.031
College experiences and perceptions			
Campus racial climate	.003	−.060	−.054
College diversity commitment	.108**	.039	−.066
Ethnic and Gender studies courses	−.034	−.034	.055
Black student visibility[a]	.092	.085	.013

(continued)

TABLE 4.3   (CONTINUED)

Variable	Traditional Prejudice Form		
	Anti-black	Anti-Latino	Anti-Asian
Latino student visibility[a]	.027	.050	.083
Asian & Pacific Islander student visibility[a]	−.029	−.055	−.175**
Campus characteristics			
Black students[b]	−.010	−.032	.006
Latino students[b]	−.068	.085	−.084
Asian & Pacific Islander students[b]	.009	−.129*	.027
Private research university	−.149***	−.204***	−.034
Liberal arts college	−.217***	−.192***	−.012
Precollege friendships			
Whites	.411**	.270*	.155
Blacks	.192**	.107	.097
Latinos	−.087	−.051	−.155*
Asians & Pacific Islanders	.153	.112	.023
Precollege environments			
Private high school	−.150***	−.069	−.180***
School segregation level	−.158***	−.106**	−.077
Neighborhood segregation level	.170***	.091**	.037
Social characteristics			
Female	.034	.127**	−.080
Darker skin color	.011	.006	.066
International student	−.013	−.012	.033
Mother's education	−.020	.002	−.074
Father's education	−.050	−.066	.150**
Family income	.130***	.085*	−.007
Parental homeownership	−.121***	−.064*	−.054
Catholic	.179***	.118**	.135**
Other religious beliefs	.178***	.140***	.145**
Religiosity	.114**	.051	.082*
Northeast region	−.136**	−.158**	.011
Midwest region	−.255***	−.152**	−.131*
West region	−.165**	−.173***	.014
Constant	.326	.701	−.033
Adjusted R^2	.417***	.426***	.255***

NOTE: Standardized coefficients (β) reported in table. Models estimated with imputed NLSF data. Reference categories include: male, US citizen, Protestant, South resident, attended public high school, attended public research university.
[a] Visibility of each student group is relative to [specific racial or ethnic group]'s visibility on campus.
[b] Proportion of student group entered into models.
*$p < .05$, **$p < .01$, ***$p < .001$.

TABLE 4.4   Factors influencing exiting levels of prejudice among black students

Variable	Traditional Prejudice Form		
	Anti-white	Anti-Latino	Anti-Asian
Entering racial prejudice			
Anti-white	.488***	——	——
Anti-Latino	——	.317***	——
Anti-Asian	——	——	.387***
Closeness to (fourth-year)			
Whites	−.109*	.010	−.135**
Blacks	−.004	.072	−.085
Latinos	−.002	−.173*	−.028
Asians & Pacific Islanders	−.010	.142*	.212**
Closeness to (first-year)			
Whites	.016	−.040	−.101
Blacks	−.326***	−.006	−.184**
Latinos	−.108	−.023	.060
Asians & Pacific Islanders	.192**	.015	.100
College friendships			
Whites	.505***	−.214*	.258**
Blacks	.326**	−.039	.144
Latinos	.200***	−.082	.161**
Asians & Pacific Islanders	.605***	.000	.292***
College romantic relationships			
Whites	−.223***	.336***	.134*
Blacks	.492***	−.514***	.569***
Latinos	2.275***	1.211***	1.020***
Asians & Pacific Islanders	−3.072***	−.182	−1.354***
College roommates			
Whites	.107	−.445***	−.017
Blacks	−.363***	−.280**	−.218*
Latinos	−.070	−.228***	−.041
Asians & Pacific Islanders	.003	−.206**	−.019
Membership in student organizations			
Mostly white	−.305***	−.146*	−.237***
Mostly black	−.308***	−.040	−.271***
Mostly Latino	−.185***	−.063	−.170***
Mostly Asian & Pacific Islander	−.010	−.051	−.061
College experiences and perceptions			
Campus racial climate	.162***	−.067	−.025
College diversity commitment	.044	−.039	.008
Ethnic and Gender studies courses	.156***	−.069	.090*

(continued)

TABLE 4.4   (CONTINUED)

Variable	Traditional Prejudice Form		
	Anti-white	Anti-Latino	Anti-Asian
White student visibility[a]	−.125*	−.004	.079
Latino student visibility[a]	.249***	−.009	.058
Asian & Pacific Islander student visibility[a]	−.030	−.047	−.011
Campus characteristics			
Black students[b]	.096	−.266***	−.119*
Latino students[b]	−.244***	−.008	−.167*
Asian & Pacific Islander students[b]	.285***	−.029	.113
Private research university	.198***	−.138**	.120*
Liberal arts college	.029	−.150**	.020
Precollege friendships			
Whites	.276	.352*	.305*
Blacks	.581**	.488*	.471*
Latinos	−.244***	−.023	−.013
Asians & Pacific Islanders	.078	.105	.151
Precollege environments			
Private high school	−.306***	−.075	−.173***
School segregation level	−.332***	−.134*	−.168**
Neighborhood segregation level	.041	.128*	.030
Social characteristics			
Female	−.122**	.103*	−.054
Darker skin color	.016	−.035	−.005
International student	.165***	−.064	.047
Mother's education	−.064	−.031	−.038
Father's education	.166***	−.003	.101*
Family income	.023	.046	.120*
Parental homeownership	−.250***	−.117*	−.190***
Catholic	.158***	.069	.072
Other religious beliefs	.070	.074	.091*
Religiosity	.092*	−.003	.008
Northeast region	.021	−.102	−.049
Midwest region	−.159***	−.167**	−.102*
West region	−.075	−.269***	−.065
Constant	.144	.238	−1.110*
Adjusted R^2	.400***	.207***	.304***

NOTE: Standardized coefficients (β) reported in table. Models estimated with imputed NLSF data. Reference categories include: male, US citizen, Protestant, South resident, attended public high school, attended public research university.
[a] Visibility of each student group is relative to [specific racial or ethnic group]'s visibility on campus.
[b] Proportion of student group entered into models.
*$p < .05$, **$p < .01$, ***$p < .001$.

TABLE 4.5 Factors influencing exiting levels of prejudice among Latino students

	Traditional Prejudice Form		
Variable	Anti-white	Anti-black	Anti-Asian
Entering racial prejudice			
Anti-white	.443***	——	——
Anti-black	——	.385***	——
Anti-Asian	——	——	.374***
Closeness to (fourth-year)			
Whites	−.254***	.076	−.104
Blacks	−.018	−.170*	.000
Latinos	.123*	−.014	−.097
Asian & Pacific Islanders	−.004	.124*	.121
Closeness to (first-year)			
Whites	.065	.144**	−.162**
Blacks	−.301***	−.094	−.199**
Latinos	−.026	−.051	.026
Asians & Pacific Islanders	.130*	−.024	.178**
College friendships			
Whites	.506***	−.159	.354***
Blacks	.159**	.089	.027
Latinos	.360***	−.025	.445***
Asians & Pacific Islanders	.775***	.185*	.428***
College romantic relationships			
Whites	−.250***	.100	.096
Blacks	.710***	−.991***	.775***
Latinos	2.137***	2.773***	1.148***
Asians & Pacific Islanders	−2.488***	−1.118***	−1.417***
College roommates			
Whites	.200*	−.370***	.142
Blacks	−.213**	−.038	−.095
Latinos	−.017	−.531***	−.139
Asians & Pacific Islanders	−.031	−.242***	.006
Membership in student organizations			
Mostly white	−.357***	−.415***	−.237***
Mostly black	−.116**	−.064	−.073
Mostly Latino	−.587***	−.569***	−.403***
Mostly Asian & Pacific Islander	−.031	.005	−.072*
College experiences and perceptions			
Campus racial climate	.136**	.091*	.072
College diversity commitment	−.075*	.036	−.099**
Ethnic and Gender studies courses	.173***	.067	.143***
White student visibility[a]	.142**	.000	.174***

(continued)

TABLE 4.5   (CONTINUED)

Variable	Traditional Prejudice Form		
	Anti-white	Anti-black	Anti-Asian
Black student visibility[a]	−.231***	−.020	−.203***
Asian & Pacific Islander student visibility[a]	−.113**	−.162***	−.123**
Campus characteristics			
Black students[b]	.018	.096*	−.003
Latino students[b]	−.194**	−.212**	−.011
Asian & Pacific Islander students[b]	.236**	.066	.003
Private research university	.234***	−.064	.126**
Liberal arts college	−.048	−.107*	−.057
Precollege friendships			
Whites	.436*	.684***	.321
Blacks	.163*	.293***	.126
Latinos	−.731***	−.587***	−.349*
Asians & Pacific Islanders	.086	.142	.078
Precollege environments			
Private high school	−.313***	−.192***	−.209***
School segregation level	−.299***	−.193**	−.183**
Neighborhood segregation level	.088	.178**	.024
Social characteristics			
Female	−.264***	−.021	−.142**
Darker skin color	.007	.000	.031
International student	.305***	.182***	.180***
Mother's education	−.194***	−.035	−.093*
Father's education	.368***	−.095	.200***
Family income	.012	.218***	.050
Parental homeownership	−.159***	−.194***	−.047
Catholic	.142**	.204***	.015
Other religious beliefs	.133**	.141**	.088
Religiosity	.096*	.077*	.014
Northeast region	.061	−.155**	−.013
Midwest region	−.152**	−.203***	−.046
West region	.011	−.073	.030
Constant	−.030	.117	−1.214
Adjusted R^2	.384***	.387***	.357***

NOTE: Standardized coefficients (β) reported in table. Models estimated with imputed NLSF data. Reference categories include: male, US citizen, Protestant, South resident, attended public high school, attended public research university.

[a] Visibility of each student group is relative to [specific racial or ethnic group]'s visibility on campus.

[b] Proportion of student group entered into models.

*$p < .05$, **$p < .01$, ***$p < .001$.

TABLE 4.6   Factors influencing exiting levels of prejudice among Asian and
Pacific Islander students

Variable	Traditional Prejudice Form		
	Anti-white	Anti-black	Anti-Latino
Entering racial prejudice			
Anti-white	.614***	——	——
Anti-black	——	.514***	——
Anti-Latino	——	——	.530***
Closeness to (fourth-year)			
Whites	−.028	.035	.036
Blacks	−.134*	−.220***	−.030
Latinos	.001	.000	−.123*
Asians & Pacific Islanders	.084*	.150***	.120***
Closeness to (first-year)			
Whites	.290***	.207***	.200***
Blacks	−.294***	−.087	−.145**
Latinos	−.217***	−.181***	−.078
Asians & Pacific Islanders	.095*	−.020	−.096**
College friendships			
Whites	.288**	−.160*	−.400***
Blacks	.121**	.061	.049
Latinos	.062	.012	−.109***
Asians & Pacific Islanders	1.293***	.390**	−.172
College romantic relationships			
Whites	−.174**	.073	.242***
Blacks	−.534***	−1.047***	−1.246***
Latinos	2.782***	2.466***	2.210***
Asians & Pacific Islanders	−2.647***	−1.486***	−.692***
College roommates			
Whites	−.312***	−.556***	−.693***
Blacks	−.140**	−.066*	−.086**
Latinos	−.195***	−.255***	−.200***
Asians & Pacific Islanders	−.533***	−.580***	−.630***
Membership in student organizations			
Mostly white	−.515***	−.395***	−.373***
Mostly black	−.095**	−.029	−.003
Mostly Latino	−.085**	−.092***	−.084**
Mostly Asian & Pacific Islander	−.014	.041	.052
College experiences and perceptions			
Campus racial climate	.226***	.135***	.044
College diversity commitment	.089**	.097***	.069**
Ethnic and gender studies courses	.029	.015	−.043
White student visibility[a]	−.109*	−.113**	−.109**

(continued)

TABLE 4.6   (CONTINUED)

Variable	Traditional Prejudice Form		
	Anti-white	Anti-black	Anti-Latino
Black student visibility[a]	−.093*	.030	.004
Latino student visibility[a]	.229***	.101*	.111**
Campus characteristics			
Black students[b]	.033	−.001	−.009
Latino students[b]	−.266***	−.154**	−.126**
Asian & Pacific Islander students[b]	.350***	.090	.039
Private research university	.029	−.063*	−.172***
Liberal arts college	−.177***	−.185***	−.216***
Precollege friendships			
Whites	.714***	.599***	.667***
Blacks	.461***	.362***	.362***
Latinos	−.236***	−.163***	−.101*
Asians & Pacific Islanders	.360**	.276*	.387***
Precollege environments			
Private high school	−.239***	−.196***	−.132***
School segregation level	−.263***	−.190***	−.176***
Neighborhood segregation level	.117**	.118***	.151***
Social characteristics			
Woman	−.104**	.066*	.126***
Darker skin color	.006	−.002	−.022
International student	.216***	.101**	.007
Mother's education	.007	.037	.094**
Father's education	.105*	−.027	−.063
Family income	.041	.129***	.114***
Parental homeownership	−.177***	−.180***	−.159***
Catholic	.135***	.121***	.133***
Other religious beliefs	.217***	.178***	.193***
Religiosity	.107**	.048	.035
Northeast region	−.052	−.137***	−.158***
Midwest region	−.304***	−.270***	−.198***
West region	−.136**	−.164***	−.169***
Constant	−.239	.812	1.043**
Adjusted R^2	.532***	.694***	.695***

NOTE: Standardized coefficients (β) reported in table. Models estimated with imputed NLSF data. Reference categories include: men, U.S. citizen; Protestants, South residents, public high school attendance, public research university attendance.
[a] Visibility of each student group is relative to [specific racial or ethnic group]'s visibility on campus.
[b] Proportion of student group entered into models.
*p < .05, **p < .01, ***p < .001.

When we note specific influences of different forms of social interaction among student groups, a nuanced picture comes into view of how interacting across racial and ethnic lines does not always lead to prejudice reduction because it could increase prejudice as well. Among white students, those with more ingroup friendships during college were less prejudiced toward blacks and Latinos, but more prejudiced toward Asians and Pacific Islanders. Those students with more Latino friendships also had less prejudice toward blacks and Latinos at the end of college. White students who had more Asian and Pacific Islander friends during college were less prejudiced toward Latinos, but more prejudiced toward Asians and Pacific Islanders.

As noted above, white students' romantic relationships had powerful effects on their racial prejudice at the end of college. Dating more whites during college led to higher prejudice toward Latinos at the end of college for white students, while students with more romantic relationships with black partners during college were less prejudiced toward both blacks and Latinos. However, more romantic relationships with Latinos increased prejudice toward all three racial and ethnic minority groups. Somewhat contrary to this finding, white students who more frequently dated Asian and Pacific Islander partners were less prejudiced toward both blacks and Asians and Pacific Islanders at the end of college.

Roommate diversity among white students generally reduced their prejudice toward blacks and Latinos, but did not do so for their prejudice toward Asians and Pacific Islanders. Rooming with more roommates of each racial and ethnic group reduced white students' prejudice toward blacks, while those students with more non-black roommates had less prejudice toward Latinos at the end of college. The influence of the composition of organizations that students joined displayed the least influence of these four forms of social interaction on their racial prejudice. Interestingly, white students with more memberships in predominantly white student organizations held less prejudice toward each racial and ethnic minority group. Also, white students with more memberships in mostly Latino student organizations during college held less prejudice toward Asians and Pacific Islanders.

Black students' social interactions during college had a variety of influences on their racial prejudice. For these students, more friendship diversity did not always correspond to better views of different races and ethnicities. Black students with more friendships with each racial and ethnic group during college had higher levels of prejudice toward whites at the end of college. Similarly, more friendships with whites, Latinos, and Asians and Pacific Islanders during college increased black students' prejudice toward Asians and Pacific Islanders. Black students who had more friendships with whites had less prejudice toward Latinos at the end of college as well.

Consistent with other elite college students, black students' romantic relationships strongly influenced their racial prejudice. Black students with more romantic relationships with whites and Asians and Pacific Islanders during college were less prejudiced toward whites, but those with more romantic relationships with other blacks and Latinos had higher levels of prejudice toward whites at the end of college. Romantic relationships formed with whites and Latinos during college increased black students' prejudice toward Latinos at the end of college, while more relationships formed with ingroup members decreased prejudice toward Latinos. Black students with more romantic relationships with Asians and Pacific Islanders during college had lower levels of prejudice toward that specific group, while forming more romantic relationships with all other groups increased their prejudice by the end of college toward Asians and Pacific Islanders.

In terms of black students' living situations, roommate effects almost exclusively impacted black students' prejudice toward Latinos, but in positive ways. More roommates of each racial and ethnic group corresponded with less prejudice toward Latinos at the end of college for black students. Additionally, more roommates who were also black had less prejudice toward whites and Asians and Pacific Islanders. Unlike the roommate findings, the student organizations black students joined during college rarely influenced their prejudice toward Latinos, but did influence their views of whites and Asians and Pacific Islanders. Black students who had more memberships in predominantly white, black, or Latino student organizations had less prejudice toward whites and Asians and Pacific Islanders at the end of college. Black students who had more memberships in mostly white student organizations were also less prejudiced toward Latinos.

Many of Latino students' social interactions during college actually increased these students' prejudice toward other racial and ethnic groups by the end of college. More friendships with each racial and ethnic group during college corresponded to higher levels of prejudice toward whites among Latino students. Similarly, more friendships with each group except blacks during college increased these students' prejudice toward Asians and Pacific Islanders. Latino students who had more Asian and Pacific Islander friends during college also were more prejudiced toward blacks at the end of college.

More romantic relationships with other Latinos during college increased students' prejudice toward each racial and ethnic outgroup, while the opposite effect was found for Latino students who had more romantic relationships with Asians and Pacific Islanders. Latino students who had more romantic relationships with whites during college were less prejudiced toward whites at the end of college. More romantic relationships with black partners corresponded with less prejudice toward blacks at the end of college for Latino students, but more prejudice toward both whites and Asians and Pacific Islanders.

College roommates only influenced Latino students' prejudice toward whites and blacks by the end of college. Those students who had more white, Latino, and Asian and Pacific Islander roommates in college were less prejudiced toward blacks. Latino students who had more white roommates during college were more prejudiced toward whites, but those with more black roommates were less so. Student organizations had a variety of influences on Latino students' racial prejudice, in all cases reducing their prejudice. More memberships in mostly white and Latino student organizations during college reduced Latino students' prejudice toward all three racial and ethnic outgroups. Latino students who had more memberships in predominantly black student organizations were less prejudiced toward whites, while those with more memberships in mostly Asian and Pacific Islander student organizations were less prejudiced toward that specific ethnic group at the end of college.

Asian and Pacific Islander students' social interactions during college varied in influence on each form of end-of-college prejudice, with romantic relationships and roommates exerting fairly strong influences on students' racial prejudice. Asian and Pacific Islander students who had more white friends during college were more prejudiced toward whites, but less so towards blacks and Latinos. More black friendships during college also increased Asian and Pacific Islander students' prejudice toward whites. Asian and Pacific Islander students who had more Latino friends were less prejudiced toward that specific ethnic group, while more ingroup friends increased prejudice toward both whites and blacks at the end of college.

Romantic relationships often led to less prejudice for Asians and Pacific Islanders toward racial and ethnic outgroups. More romantic relationships with Latinos during college increased Asian and Pacific Islander students' prejudice toward all three groups, while more romantic relationships with both blacks and other Asians and Pacific Islanders decreased prejudice toward each group by the end of college. Similarly, more romantic relationships during college with whites decreased Asian and Pacific Islander students' prejudice toward whites and Latinos.

Surprisingly, more racial diversity among the roommates of Asian and Pacific Islander students decreased their prejudice toward all three racial and ethnic outgroups by the end of college. Moreover, more roommates with each racial and ethnic group decreased these students' prejudice toward each outgroup. Although the influence of student organization memberships was not as robust as that found for roommates, they still had a powerful reduction influence on Asian and Pacific Islander students' prejudice. Those students who had more memberships in mostly white and mostly Latino student organizations during college had lower levels of prejudice toward all three racial and ethnic outgroups. Asian and Pacific Islander students who had more memberships in predominantly black student organizations had lower levels of prejudice toward whites at the end of college. The findings above point to various ways social interactions during college influence elite college students' prejudice toward one another's racial and ethnic groups when they leave campus. The influences of these interactions are not uniformly progressive, meaning cross-race interactions do not always correspond to reduced prejudice for elite college students.

When we turn to how social interactions may influence students' views of racial inequality, the models examining elite college students' individualistic views of racial inequality included similar measures of students' precollege experiences, entering and exiting racialized social identity, college experiences and perceptions related to race, campus characteristics such as the number of students of color on campus and college type, and each form of social interaction during college. Again, the social characteristics of students are displayed in the models, but are not considered in forthcoming discussions to provide an overview of how social interaction influenced elite college students' support for individualistic views of racial inequality. Below, each table (Tables 4.7–4.10) displays the analyses for each college student group for group-specific as well as overall levels of racial individualism at the end of college.

Social interactions, in general, were even less influential on elite college students' racial individualism levels compared to their racial prejudice at the end of college. White students' college friendships with other whites and Latinos often reduced their individualistic views of racial inequality. More white friendships during college corresponded to less racial individualism on all measures except for the specific Latino measure, while white students who had more Latino friends during college held less individualistic views of racial inequality in all four models. White students' romantic relationships influenced their racial inequality views, particularly those they had with blacks and Latinos. More romantic relationships with blacks during college corresponded to less racial individualism regardless of the group considered, while more romantic relationships with Latinos had opposite effects on their views of racial inequality. Additionally, white students who had more romantic relationships with Asians and Pacific Islanders during college were more individualistic in their views of inequality toward Asians and Pacific Islanders. Turning to college roommates, those students with more white and Asian and Pacific Islander roommates had less individualistic views of racial inequality, except when specifically considering Latinos. The student organizations that white students joined during college had limited influence on their support for individualistic views of racial inequality. White students who belonged to more mostly white student organizations had less racial individualism toward blacks at the end of college, but those who belonged to more mostly Asian and Pacific Islander student organizations held more individualistic views of racial inequality overall as well as specifically toward blacks.

Among black students at elite colleges, romantic relationships were the predominant form of social interaction shaping their views of racial inequality. Only one college friendship measure influenced students' racial inequality views, as black students who had more white friends during college held less

TABLE 4.7   Factors influencing individualistic views of racial inequality among white students at college exit

| Variable | Racial individualism toward | | | |
	Black	Latino	Asian & Pacific Islander	All Three Groups
Racial individualism toward (first-year)				
Blacks	.242***	————	————	————
Latinos	————	.168***	————	————
Asians & Pacific Islanders	————	————	.120**	————
All three groups	————	————	————	.208***
Closeness to (fourth-year)				
Whites	.189**	.124*	.109	.154**
Blacks	−.171*	−.070	−.111	−.133
Latinos	.129	.066	.096	.109
Asians & Pacific Islanders	−.141	−.127	−.065	−.119
Closeness to (first-year)				
Whites	.098*	.039	.068	.066
Blacks	−.008	−.006	.040	.015
Latinos	−.013	−.054	.088	.010
Asians & Pacific Islanders	−.082	.011	−.131	−.076
College friendships				
Whites	−.333***	−.142	−.298***	−.278***
Blacks	−.037	−.040	−.040	−.043
Latinos	−.127**	−.117*	−.179***	−.151**
Asians & Pacific Islanders	−.117	.102	−.099	−.051
College romantic relationships				
Whites	.012	−.075	−.004	−.022
Blacks	−1.183***	−.639***	−.965***	−1.009***
Latinos	.858***	.691**	.351	.666**
Asians & Pacific Islanders	.093	−.370	.440*	.088
College roommates				
Whites	−.173**	−.056	−.167*	−.146*
Blacks	.003	−.008	−.048	−.016
Latinos	−.078	.012	−.018	−.032
Asians & Pacific Islanders	−.159**	−.110	−.161*	−.153*
Membership in student organizations				
Mostly white	−.094*	−.069	−.030	−.067
Mostly black	.016	−.008	.005	.004
Mostly Latino	−.009	−.030	−.037	−.026
Mostly Asian & Pacific Islander	.076*	.058	.078	.077*
College experiences and perceptions				
Campus racial climate	.094**	.063	.019	.062
College diversity commitment	.151***	.175***	.124**	.156***

(continued)

TABLE 4.7   (CONTINUED)

Variable	Racial individualism toward			
	Black	Latino	Asian & Pacific Islander	All Three Groups
Ethnic and Gender studies courses	−.057	−.016	−.051	−.043
Black student visibility[a]	−.066	−.057	−.062	−.065
Latino student visibility[a]	.165**	.068	.100	.122*
Asian & Pacific Islander student visibility[a]	−.043	.034	−.016	−.013
Campus characteristics				
Black students[b]	−.035	−.072	−.093*	−.071
Latino students[b]	−.062	−.038	−.050	−.056
Asian & Pacific Islander students[b]	.110	.051	.020	.065
Private research university	−.024	.014	−.035	−.019
Liberal arts college	−.041	−.060	−.064	−.057
Precollege friendships				
Whites	.058	.007	−.058	.003
Blacks	.037	.023	−.008	.019
Latinos	.034	.028	.004	.025
Asians & Pacific Islanders	.022	.028	−.003	.016
Precollege environments				
Private high school	.043	.037	.101*	.069
School segregation level	−.011	−.028	−.002	−.015
Neighborhood segregation level	−.009	−.029	−.035	−.026
Social characteristics				
Female	−.061	−.168***	−.103*	−.113**
Darker skin color	.040	.017	.008	.022
International student	−.073*	−.010	−.074**	−.061**
Mother's education	−.010	−.034	.029	−.004
Father's education	−.118**	−.085	−.127	−.117
Family income	.027	.026	−.026	.009
Parental homeownership	−.021	−.001	−.011	−.012
Catholic	.050	.086*	.071	.071
Other religious beliefs	.066	.046	.020	.049
Religiosity	.066	.051	.054	.058
Northeast region	−.031	.074	.017	.020
Midwest region	−.028	−.022	−.011	−.018
West region	−.047	.024	.023	.002
Constant	5.630**	4.443*	7.600**	5.801**
Adjusted R^2	.325***	.216***	.191***	.271***

NOTE: Standardized coefficients (β) reported in table. Models estimated with imputed NLSF data. Reference categories include: male, US citizen, Protestant, South resident, attended public high school, attended public research university.

[a] Visibility of each student group is relative to [specific racial or ethnic group]'s visibility on campus.
[b] Proportion of student group entered into models.

*$p < .05$, **$p < .01$, ***$p < .001$.

TABLE 4.8   Factors influencing individualistic views of racial inequality among black students at college exit

	Racial individualism toward			
Variable	Black	Latino	Asian & Pacific Islander	All Three Groups
Racial individualism toward (first-year)				
Blacks	.150***	——	——	——
Latinos	——	.197***.	——	——
Asians & Pacific Islanders	——	——	.185***.	——
All three groups	——	——	——	.204***
Closeness to (fourth-year)				
Whites	.095	.084	.095	.096***
Blacks	−.072	−.003	.021	−.023
Latinos	−.046	−.099	−.034	−.061
Asians & Pacific Islanders	−.056	−.045	−.058	−.056
Closeness to (first-year)				
Whites	.197***	.116*	.106	.143*
Blacks	−.147*	−.139*	−.115	−.141*
Latinos	−.058	−.018	.044	−.010
Asians & Pacific Islanders	.077	.114	.062	.086
College friendships				
Whites	−.152	−.118	−.246*	−.186
Blacks	.133	.103	.028	.097
Latinos	.049	.011	−.037	.007
Asians & Pacific Islanders	.118	.166	−.108	.058
College romantic relationships				
Whites	−.075	−.052	.033	−.037
Blacks	−.703***	−.430***	−.716***	−.668***
Latinos	1.033***	.661**	.185	.670**
Asians & Pacific Islanders	−.655**	−.678**	.319	−.347
College roommates				
Whites	.040	.086	−.038	.030
Blacks	.150	.071	.133	.128
Latinos	−.065	.020	−.035	−.031
Asians & Pacific Islanders	−.118	−.130	−.125	−.136
Membership in student organizations				
Mostly white	−.157**	−.086	.017	−.079
Mostly black	−.077	−.063	.104	−.013
Mostly Latino	−.099*	−.095*	−.020	−.076
Mostly Asian & Pacific Islander	.080*	.066	.106*	.089
College experiences and perceptions				
Campus racial climate	.140**	.121*	.040	.107*
College diversity commitment	.009	.008	−.027	−.005
Ethnic and Gender studies courses	−.068	−.038	−.079	−.063

(continued)

TABLE 4.8 (CONTINUED)

Variable	Racial individualism toward			
	Black	Latino	Asian & Pacific Islander	All Three Groups
White student visibility[a]	.032	.114	.084	.083
Latino student visibility[a]	.027	−.085	−.003	−.017
Asian & Pacific Islander student visibility[a]	−.035	−.071	−.066	−.060
Campus characteristics				
Black students[b]	.002	.028	−.058	−.014
Latino students[b]	.023	.026	.077	.044
Asian & Pacific Islander students[b]	.028	.039	−.012	.024
Private research university	−.114*	−.064	−.082	−.094
Liberal arts college	−.085	−.025	−.036	−.048
Precollege friendships				
Whites	−.285	−.301	−.274	−.303
Blacks	−.278	−.298	−.288	−.307
Latinos	−.316***	−.215**	−.101	−.225**
Asians & Pacific Islanders	−.268**	−.231**	−.182*	−.239**
Precollege environments				
Private high school	−.018	−.049	.011	−.019
School segregation level	−.092	−.087	.011	−.062
Neighborhood segregation level	.110*	.101*	.109*	.114*
Social characteristics				
Female	−.120**	−.144**	−.040	−.107*
Darker skin color	−.035	−.039	−.037	−.039
International student	.028	.060	−.054	.012
Mother's education	.084	.116*	.108*	.111*
Father's education	−.102*	−.080	−.175**	−.128*
Family income	−.045	−.090	−.050	−.063
Parental homeownership	−.034	−.015	.006	−.017
Catholic	.026	−.018	.001	.004
Other religious beliefs	−.002	−.020	−.021	−.011
Religiosity	.019	−.024	−.034	−.013
Northeast region	.062	.105	.010	.058
Midwest region	−.112*	−.039	.030	−.044
West region	.004	.035	.028	.022
Constant	10.217***	7.771***	7.420***	8.296***
Adjusted R^2	.258***	.212***	.190***	.245***

NOTE: Standardized coefficients (β) reported in table. Models estimated with imputed NLSF data. Reference categories include: male, US citizen, Protestant, South resident, attended public high school, attended public research university.
[a] Visibility of each student group is relative to [specific racial or ethnic group]'s visibility on campus.
[b] Proportion of student group entered into models.
*p < .05, **p < .01, ***p < .001.

TABLE 4.9   Factors influencing individualistic views of racial inequality among Latino students at college exit

| Variable | Racial individualism toward | | | |
	Black	Latino	Asian & Pacific Islander	All Three Groups
Racial individualism toward (first-year)				
Blacks	.248***	——	——	——
Latinos	——	.238***	——	——
Asians & Pacific Islanders	——	——	.194***	——
All three groups	——	——	——	.259***
Closeness to (fourth-year)				
Whites	.137*	.155*	.157**	.158**
Blacks	−.012	.024	.088	.039
Latinos	−.132*	−.145*	−.108	−.139*
Asians & Pacific Islanders	.054	.042	.045	.047
Closeness to (first-year)				
Whites	.178**	.152**	.175**	.173**
Blacks	−.151*	−.149*	−.059	−.115
Latinos	.025	.085	.120*	.081
Asians & Pacific Islanders	−.071	−.063	−.148*	−.105
College friendships				
Whites	−.198*	.041	−.327**	−.181
Blacks	−.034	.040	.054	.018
Latinos	.120	.215*	−.150	.058
Asians & Pacific Islanders	.054	.255**	−.117	.060
College romantic relationships				
Whites	.019	−.128*	−.019	−.043
Blacks	−.908***	−.468***	−1.150***	−.903***
Latinos	1.100***	.703**	.367	.749***
Asians & Pacific Islanders	−.234	−.552**	.513**	−.069
College roommates				
Whites	−.076	.137	−.066	−.005
Blacks	.149**	.122*	.142**	.149**
Latinos	−.332***	−.123	−.265**	−.253**
Asians & Pacific Islanders	−.194**	−.156*	−.228***	−.202**
Membership in student organizations				
Mostly white	−.148**	−.123*	−.061	−.113*
Mostly black	−.077	−.135**	−.092*	−.107**
Mostly Latino	−.160*	−.089	.048	−.065
Mostly Asian & Pacific Islander	.021	.019	.028	.023
College experiences and perceptions				
Campus racial climate	.077	.107*	.041	.079
College diversity commitment	.172***	.133**	.107**	.143***

(continued)

TABLE 4.9   (CONTINUED)

Variable	Racial individualism toward			
	Black	Latino	Asian & Pacific Islander	All Three Groups
Ethnic and Gender studies courses	−.044	−.032	−.048	−.042
White student visibility[a]	−.084	−.015	−.051	−.052
Black student visibility[a]	−.074	−.136**	−.120*	−.120*
Asian & Pacific Islander student visibility[a]	−.017	.001	−.051	−.023
Campus characteristics				
Black students[b]	−.061	−.051	−.104**	−.077*
Latino students[b]	−.086	−.056	.036	−.035
Asian & Pacific Islander students[b]	.204**	.223**	.105	.187*
Private research university	.024	.115*	.005	.051
Liberal arts college	−.013	.047	.017	.025
Precollege friendships				
Whites	.178	−.099	−.122	−.019
Blacks	.190*	.060	−.015	.083
Latinos	−.333*	−.403*	−.268	−.354*
Asians & Pacific Islanders	.041	−.023	−.077	−.022
Precollege environments				
Private high school	−.135**	−.086	.011	−.071
School segregation level	−.046	−.043	.060	−.010
Neighborhood segregation level	.113*	.038	.112	.095
Social characteristics				
Female	−.036	−.127**	.020	−.046
Darker skin color	.017	.014	.058	.030
International student	.008	.071	−.083	−.004
Mother's education	.078	−.018	.041	.036
Father's education	−.128*	−.013	−.180**	−.114*
Family income	.034	−.046	−.018	−.008
Parental homeownership	−.036	−.019	.034	−.006
Catholic	.143**	.095	.082	.110*
Other religious beliefs	.101*	.045	.072	.075
Religiosity	.012	.016	−.027	−.001
Northeast region	−.107*	.029	−.095	−.066
Midwest region	−.128**	−.078	−.049	−.089
West region	−.131	−.046	−.070	−.088
Constant	1.980	2.325	3.819	2.541
Adjusted R²	.350***	.311***	.328***	.355***

NOTE: Standardized coefficients (β) reported in table. Models estimated with imputed NLSF data. Reference categories include: male, US citizen, Protestant, South resident, attended public high school, attended public research university.
[a] Visibility of each student group is relative to [specific racial or ethnic group]'s visibility on campus.
[b] Proportion of student group entered into models.
*p < .05, **p < .01, ***p < .001.

TABLE 4.10 Factors influencing individualistic views of racial inequality among Asian & Pacific Islander students at college exit

| | Racial individualism toward | | | |
Variable	Black	Latino	Asian & Pacific Islander	All Three Groups
Racial individualism toward (first-year)				
Blacks	.246***	——	——	——
Latinos	——	.202***	——	——
Asians & Pacific Islanders	——	——	.154***	——
All three groups	——	——	——	.227***
Closeness to (fourth-year)				
Whites	.137**	.103	.121*	.127*
Blacks	−.051	.018	.114	.030
Latinos	.011	−.051	−.110	−.052
Asians & Pacific Islanders	−.087	−.063	−.030	−.068
Closeness to (first-year)				
Whites	.136**	.188**	.200***	.180**
Blacks	−.164*	−.194*	−.033	−.128
Latinos	.095	.096	.164**	.125*
Asians & Pacific Islanders	.074	.022	−.116*	−.010
College friendships				
Whites	−.516***	−.279**	−.611***	−.503***
Blacks	−.057	−.047	−.055	−.059
Latinos	−.084*	−.047	−.082	−.077
Asians & Pacific Islanders	.018	.485***	−.583***	−.051
College romantic relationships				
Whites	−.357***	−.434***	−.223**	−.360***
Blacks	−.935***	−.645***	−1.115***	−.974***
Latinos	.548***	.505**	−.204	.290*
Asians & Pacific Islanders	−.434*	−.891***	.852**	−.133
College roommates				
Whites	.129	.196*	−.046	.093
Blacks	.107*	.069	.112*	.108*
Latinos	−.005	.059	−.063	−.005
Asians & Pacific Islanders	−.086	−.091	−.134	−.108
Membership in student organizations				
Mostly white	.019	−.015	.120*	.047
Mostly black	−.015	.002	.061	.017
Mostly Latino	.063	.034	.097**	.070
Mostly Asian & Pacific Islander	.096*	.070	.091	.091*
College experiences and perceptions				
Campus racial climate	.105**	.148***	.056	.110**
College diversity commitment	.057	.061	.014	.045

(continued)

TABLE 4.10 (CONTINUED)

Variable	Racial individualism toward			
	Black	Latino	Asian & Pacific Islander	All Three Groups
Ethnic and Gender studies courses	.027	.071	−.035	.020
White student visibility[a]	−.011	−.020	−.052	−.028
Black student visibility[a]	−.069	−.073	−.021	−.055
Latino student visibility[a]	.095	.151*	.145*	.136*
Campus characteristics				
Black students[b]	−.013	−.043	−.052	−.038
Latino students[b]	.102	.025	.084	.076
Asian & Pacific Islander students[b]	−.078	.041	−.022	−.025
Private research university	.033	.062	−.052	.014
Liberal arts college	.047	.058	.056	.062
Precollege friendships				
Whites	−.432**	−.303	−.361*	−.387*
Blacks	−.134*	−.027	−.140*	−.108
Latinos	−.153**	−.100	−.040	−.101
Asians & Pacific Islanders	−.437**	−.313	−.311*	−.374*
Precollege environments				
Private high school	.008	.026	.165***	.073
School segregation level	.047	.072	.165***	.102*
Neighborhood segregation level	−.011	−.008	−.035	−.020
Social characteristics				
Female	−.116**	−.200***	−.038	−.120**
Darker skin color	.010	.041	.036	.029
International student	.017	.069	−.140**	−.027
Mother's education	−.031	−.019	.063	.007
Father's education	−.108*	−.049	−.220***	−.136**
Family income	−.042	−.098*	−.093*	−.083*
Parental homeownership	.064	.072	.138***	.098**
Catholic	−.023	−.046	−.058	−.045
Other religious beliefs	−.042	−.077	−.107*	−.081
Religiosity	−.049	−.050	−.096*	−.073
Northeast region	.034	.124*	.005	.058
Midwest region	−.030	−.014	.040	.002
West region	−.024	.036	−.029	−.003
Constant	11.859***	8.802***	10.478***	10.237***
Adjusted R[2]	.406***	.329***	.365***	.400***

NOTE: Standardized coefficients (β) reported in table. Models estimated with imputed NLSF data. Reference categories include: male, US citizen, Protestant, South resident, attended public high school, attended public research university.
[a] Visibility of each student group is relative to [specific racial or ethnic group]'s visibility on campus.
[b] Proportion of student group entered into models.
*p < .05, **p < .01, ***p < .001.

individualistic views of inequality toward Asians and Pacific Islanders. Black students who had more romantic relationships during college with other blacks held less individualistic views of racial inequality regardless of the group considered, while those students who had more romantic relationships with Asians and Pacific Islanders were less supportive of such views when specifically considering blacks and Latinos. However, black students who had more romantic relationships with Latinos during college held higher levels of racial individualism except toward Asians and Pacific Islanders. The college roommates of black students did not influence their views of racial inequality, while their student organizations had limited influence on such views. Black students who had more memberships in predominantly white and Latino student organizations held less individualistic views of racial inequality for blacks, but those who joined mostly Asian and Pacific Islander student organizations were more supportive of such views. Blacks who had more memberships in mostly Latino student organizations during college also held lessened individualistic views of racial inequality toward Latinos, and black students who joined mostly Asian and Pacific Islander student organizations held higher levels of racial individualism toward Asians and Pacific Islanders.

Latino students' views of racial inequality were predominantly influenced by their experiences in romantic relationships and with college roommates. Latino students who had more white friends during college held less individualistic views of racial inequality for whites and Asians and Pacific Islanders. Those students with more ingroup and Asian and Pacific Islander friends during college were more supportive of such views when specifically considering blacks. Latino students who had more romantic relationships with blacks during college held less individualistic views of racial inequality in all four models, while those students with more ingroup romantic relationships during this time were more supportive of such views in each model except when specifically considering Asians and Pacific Islanders. Latino students who had more romantic relationships with whites and Asians and Pacific Islanders held lower levels of racial individualism toward their own ethnic group. Additionally, those students who had more romantic relationships with Asians and Pacific Islanders during college held higher levels of racial individualism toward Asians and Pacific Islanders at the end of college. Among college roommate effects, Latino students who had more black roommates during college held more individualistic views of racial inequality regardless of the group considered. Those students with more ingroup roommates during college were less supportive of such views in each model except when considering their own ethnic group, while Latino students with more Asian and Pacific Islander roommates during college were less supportive of such views overall. Latino students who had more memberships in mostly white student organizations held lower levels of racial individualism in each model except when considering Asians and Pacific Islanders. Those students with more memberships in mostly black student organizations also had lower levels of racial individualism in three models except when considering blacks, while Latino students who had more memberships in mostly Latino student organizations held lower levels of racial individualism toward blacks.

Similar to the findings for black and Latino students, the influence of social interactions during college for Asians and Pacific Islanders was predominantly found among the romantic relationship experiences. Asian and Pacific Islander students who had more white friends during college held less individualistic views of racial inequality regardless of the group considered. Asian and Pacific Islander students who had more Latino friends during college held less individualistic views of inequality, particularly toward blacks. However, those students who had more friendships with other Asians and Pacific Islanders during college were more supportive of such views of both Latinos as well as their own group. Romantic relationships generally reduced Asian and Pacific Islander students' individualistic views of racial inequality, but not completely. Asian and Pacific Islander students who had more white and black romantic relationships during college held lower levels of racial individualism overall. Those students who had more romantic relationships with Latinos in college held higher levels of racial individualism except when considering their own group. Although Asian and Pacific Islander students who had more ingroup romantic relationships during college held less individualistic views of racial inequality for blacks and Latinos at the end of college, they were more supportive of such views when considering their own group. Among college roommate effects, those students who had more white college roommates were more supportive of highly individualistic views of racial inequality for Latinos. Asian and Pacific Islander students who had more black roommates during college held higher levels of racial individualism except when specifically considering Latinos. Those students who had more memberships in mostly white and Latino student organizations held more individualistic views of racial inequality for their own ethnic group. Lastly, Asian and Pacific Islander students who had more memberships in student organizations composed of mostly other ingroup members were more supportive of such views for blacks and overall.

Despite the general reduction in elite college students' individualistic views of racial inequality noted earlier in this chapter, the analyses in this section paint a complicated picture of what factors shape such views of inequality. Although students' social interactions during college influenced their views of how individual efforts shape racial inequality in society, these effects were not always reducing individualistic views nor were they consistently increasing such views of racial inequality. What we find is that some interactions with people of different races and ethnicities could increase or decrease their individualistic views even within the same group of interactions. For example, white students who belonged to more mostly white student organizations held less individualistic views for blacks' social positions, while their peers who belonged to more mostly Asian and Pacific Islander student organizations held more individualistic views toward blacks at the end of college. Thus, even though elite college students' views were shaped by their social interactions across racial and ethnic lines, these interactions' influence was less than uniform in direction and in what perspectives of racial and ethnic outgroups they influenced by the end of college. In the next section, I discuss the tentative conclusions gathered from these analyses of how social interactions across race and ethnicity influence (or not) elite college students' racial ideology.

PATTERNS OF INTER- AND INTRARACIAL INTERACTION EFFECTS

The examination of elite college students' racial ideology, particularly their views of specific racial and ethnic groups and the influence of individual efforts on racial inequality, found that whom students interact with and in what context they interact with someone during college can impact their views. However, there are apparent limited and sometimes conflicting effects that social interactions can have on students' views. Generally speaking, elite college students' racial prejudice was influenced more than their racial individualism by their interactions during college. A few patterns emerged of how students' inter- and intraracial interactions shape their racial ideology. Table 4.11 summarizes these findings, with those interactions increasing prejudice or individualistic views of inequality receiving a plus sign (+), those decreasing such views receiving a minus sign (−), and those interactions not significantly influencing students' views of race and inequality having an "ns" inserted in the column.

Overall, students' inter- and intraracial interactions had little effect on their racial ideology, regardless of where students fell within the racial hierarchy on campus (as noted in the previous chapter). On the whole, half of all possible social interactions tested across all four student groups were not significant in the models. Approximately one-third of social interactions examined were significant and reduced students' prejudice or their individualistic views of racial inequality. The remaining one-sixth of social interactions increased students' prejudice or their racial individualism by the end of college.

On average, elite college students did not experience specific positive or negative influences with students of their own group or other groups. However, interactions with whites during college exhibited fairly stable racial prejudice and racial individualism–reducing effects across all four groups. The racial composition of the organizations students joined during college had the fewest effects on students' racial ideology. Although Pettigrew and Tropp (2011, 115–129) note the powerful influence of cross-group friendships in their meta-analysis of intergroup relations research, such friendships exhibited the second-fewest effects

TABLE 4.11   Summary of cross-race interaction effects on elite college students' racial ideology

	Prejudice				Racial individualism toward			
Interaction	AW	AB	AH	AA	B	H/L	A/PI	All
White students								
Friendships								
Whites	——	−	−	−	−	ns	−	−
Blacks	——	ns	ns	ns	ns	ns	ns	ns
Latinos	——	−	−	ns	−	−	−	−
Asians & Pacific Islanders	——	ns	−	+	ns	ns	ns	ns
Romantic relationships								
Whites	——	ns	+	ns	ns	ns	ns	ns
Blacks	——	−	−	ns	−	−	−	−
Latinos	——	+	+	+	+	+	ns	+
Asians & Pacific Islanders	——	−	ns	−	ns	ns	+	ns
Roommates								
Whites	——	−	−	ns	−	ns	−	−
Blacks	——	−	ns	ns	ns	ns	ns	ns
Latinos	——	−	−	ns	ns	ns	ns	ns
Asians & Pacific Islanders	——	−	−	ns	−	ns	−	−
Membership in student organizations								
Mostly white	——	−	−	−	−	ns	ns	ns
Mostly black	——	ns	ns	ns	ns	ns	ns	ns
Mostly Latino	——	ns	ns	−	ns	ns	ns	ns
Mostly Asian & Pacific Islander	——	ns	ns	ns	−	ns	ns	−
Black students								
Friendships								
Whites	+	——	−	+	ns	ns	−	ns
Blacks	+	——	ns	ns	ns	ns	ns	ns
Latinos	+	——	ns	+	ns	ns	ns	ns
Asians & Pacific Islanders	+	——	ns	+	ns	ns	ns	ns
Romantic relationships								
Whites	−	——	+	+	ns	ns	ns	ns
Blacks	+	——	−	+	−	−	−	−
Latinos	+	——	+	+	+	+	ns	+
Asians & Pacific Islanders	−	——	ns	−	−	−	ns	ns
Roommates								
Whites	ns	——	−	ns	ns	ns	ns	ns
Blacks	−	——	−	−	ns	ns	ns	ns
Latinos	ns	——	−	ns	ns	ns	ns	ns
Asians & Pacific Islanders	ns	——	−	ns	ns	ns	ns	ns

(continued)

TABLE 4.11   (CONTINUED)

Interaction	Prejudice				Racial individualism toward			
	AW	AB	AH	AA	B	H/L	A/PI	All
Membership in student organizations								
Mostly white	−	——	−	−	−	ns	ns	ns
Mostly black	−	——	ns	−	ns	ns	ns	ns
Mostly Latino	−	——	ns	−	−	−	ns	ns
Mostly Asian & Pacific Islander	ns	——	ns	ns	ns	ns	+	ns
Latino students								
Friendships								
Whites	+	ns	——	+	−	ns	−	ns
Blacks	+	ns	——	ns	ns	ns	ns	ns
Latinos	+	ns	——	+	ns	+	ns	ns
Asians & Pacific Islanders	+	+	——	+	ns	+	ns	ns
Romantic relationships								
Whites	−	ns	——	ns	ns	ns	ns	ns
Blacks	+	−	——	+	−	−	−	−
Latinos	+	+	——	+	+	+	ns	+
Asians & Pacific Islanders	−	−	——	−	ns	−	+	ns
Roommates								
Whites	+	−	——	ns	ns	ns	ns	ns
Blacks	−	ns	——	ns	+	+	+	+
Latinos	ns	−	——	ns	−	ns	−	−
Asians & Pacific Islanders	ns	−	——	ns	−	−	−	−
Membership in student organizations								
Mostly white	−	−	——	−	−	−	ns	−
Mostly black	−	ns	——	ns	ns	ns	ns	−
Mostly Latino	−	−	——	−	−	ns	ns	ns
Mostly Asian & Pacific Islander	ns	ns	——	−	ns	ns	ns	ns
Asian and Pacific Islander students								
Friendships								
Whites	+	+	−	——	−	−	−	−
Blacks	+	ns	ns	——	ns	ns	ns	ns
Latinos	ns	−	−	——	−	ns	ns	ns
Asians & Pacific Islanders	+	ns	ns	——	ns	+	+	ns
Romantic Relationships								
Whites	−	ns	+	——	−	−	−	−
Blacks	−	−	−	——	−	−	−	−
Latinos	+	+	+	——	+	+	ns	+
Asians & Pacific Islanders	−	−	−	——	−	−	+	ns
Roommates								
Whites	−	−	−	——	ns	+	ns	ns

(continued)

TABLE 4.11   (CONTINUED)

Interaction	Prejudice				Racial individualism toward			
	AW	AB	AH	AA	B	H/L	A/PI	All
Blacks	–	–	–	——	+	ns	+	+
Latinos	–	–	–	——	ns	ns	ns	ns
Asians & Pacific Islanders	–	–	–	——	ns	ns	ns	ns
Membership in student organizations								
Mostly white	–	–	–	——	ns	ns	+	ns
Mostly black	–	ns	ns	——	ns	ns	ns	ns
Mostly Latino	–	–	–	——	ns	ns	+	ns
Mostly Asian & Pacific Islander	ns	ns	ns	——	+	ns	ns	+

NOTE: Prejudice abbreviations: AW—anti-white prejudice; AB—anti-black prejudice; AH—anti-Latino prejudice; AA—anti-Asian prejudice. Racial individualism abbreviations: B—specific focus on blacks; H/L—specific focus on Latinos; A/PI—specific focus on Asian and Pacific Islanders; All—all three groups' racial individualism. Table symbols: increased prejudice or racial individualism (+); decreased prejudice or racial individualism (–); not significant in model (ns).

on elite college students' racial prejudice and racial individualism. Closely following friendships' few effects, the influence of roommates on students' views of race and inequality was often inconsequential. Unlike the other forms of social interaction, students' romantic relationships more often influenced their racial ideology during college. Each form of social interaction, when it was significant in the models above, often reduced students' racial prejudice and individualistic views of racial inequality. This finding existed particularly for college roommates and the organizations that elite college students joined, and was to a lesser extent found for the impact of their romantic relationships during this time. College friendships were evenly split in how they influenced students' racial ideology during college. Additionally, not all ingroup interactions increased prejudice toward racial and ethnic outgroups or individualistic views of racial inequality. In fact, some ingroup interactions reduced prejudice and racial individualism among students, which contrasts with findings in Sidanius and colleagues' (2008) longitudinal study of students at UCLA.

The variety of patterns noted above for how social interactions influence elite college students' racial ideology provides findings that both support and contrast with those of previous studies of intergroup relations among college students. While some interactions reduced prejudice and reliance on individualistic views of racial inequality, others increased such views. What is clear is how social interactions across race and ethnicity oftentimes have no effect on students' views of race or racial inequality. As mentioned earlier, these findings present tentative conclusions about whether and how social interactions across race and ethnicity influence elite college students' racial ideology. Do inter- and intraracial interactions influence students' views of race and inequality? Although they may not reduce prejudice and individualistic views of racial inequality as often as one would hope, these college social interactions do influence students' views, which buttresses the long-standing importance of studying how people interact with one another across group lines. However, so do many other aspects of a student's life on and before campus, which indicates how tenuous inter- and intraracial contact effects are for these students. Below, I synthesize these analyses of elite college students' end-of-college racial ideology to describe other aspects of the college-going experience shaping students' views of race and inequality.

THE IMPACT OF THE COLLEGE YEARS BEYOND SOCIAL INTERACTIONS

A wealth of information about the college-going experiences of elite college students derives from the analyses concerning how social interactions shape their racial ideology after four years. Below, I discuss some of the more interesting findings and patterns emerging from the many models in this chapter, contextualizing these social interactions and their influences on students' racial ideology. First, I consider how students' racialized social identities shape their views of race and inequality. An important discussion relates these racialized social identities to how elite social worlds and whiteness impact students' identities, but also interact across group lines during college. Second, how the racial contexts of campuses influence views of race and inequality at the end of college is discussed further. Lastly, I examine the remaining precollege experiences of students that shape their racial ideology even after four years on campus.

Race, Social Identity, and Whiteness in Elite Social Worlds

Students' racialized social identities were malleable and somewhat influential on their racial ideology during college. Similar to the findings of how multiracial children identify among multiple groups (see Harris and Sim 2002; Lee and Bean 2007; Rockquemore and Brunsma 2002; Rockquemore, Brunsma, and Delgado 2009), elite college students' closeness with each racial and ethnic group was not solidified at college entrance and changed throughout college. White students reported the largest changes in their ingroup closeness compared to other student groups, and were less close to other whites at the end of college. Similarly, black students were less close to other blacks at the end of college, but Asian and Pacific Islander students as well as Latino students did not significantly differ in how close they were to their own groups. Students of color reported lower levels of closeness to whites at the end of college, while Latino and Asian and Pacific Islander students were closer to blacks after four years of college.

Given students were less close to multiple groups at the end of their college experience, which may indicate that these students are attempting to identify as "individuals" rather than with specific racial and ethnic groups. This desire to not be linked to stereotyped groups is arguably in line with the ideology crafted within elite social worlds around the importance of individualism in social positioning and inequality (see Khan 2011; Khan and Jerolmack 2013; Warikoo 2016). As this mindset increases the belief in individual agency and accountability for social positions, elite college students withdraw their connections to racial and ethnic groups to remove any deterministic logic of why they, as individuals, are in the positions they are currently in or could possibly find themselves in later in life. This fits the larger narrative of superiority that they, as elite college students, are the "best and brightest" and successfully competed in a meritocratic system. This narrative dilutes consideration of factors external to the individual influencing how they came to these campuses in the first place, which are rarely based solely on their individual efforts. However, this ability to rely on racial individualism to explain social positions is disproportionately shaped by and for whites in these elite social worlds. Parents' residential choices (Frankenberg and Orfield 2013; Johnson 2015; Lareau and Goyette 2014) and childrearing practices (Lareau 2003; Lewis-McCoy 2014) and the continual wealth gap privileging white families (Oliver and Shapiro 2006) are among many factors providing whites with a luxury of not seeing themselves as part of any specific group such as the category of "white" in general (for further discussion of how whites often detach themselves from racial identities, categories, and group membership, see Lewis 2004). White students were less likely to identify with the ingroup than any other student group, which I argue is because the elite conception of the "individual" is intertwined with the privileges of whiteness allowing these students to claim more responsibility for their successes and positions in life, while eschewing other factors directly shepherding them to such positions or causing people of color to fill lower positions in the racial hierarchy on campus and in the broader social world.[2]

The students of color on elite college campuses also support this form of racial individualism to a lesser extent, which may influence their closeness to their own groups in some ways, but more importantly to other people of color. The connection among these students as non-white in a white social world is present (as noted further below), which possibly influences how they identify with multiple racial and ethnic groups. Similar to the findings of Gaztambide-Fernandez and DiAquoi (2010), these elite social worlds can heighten students' understanding of their positions as non-white in varying ways. Thus, the less closeness toward whites at the end of college, but general higher levels of closeness of Latino and Asian and Pacific Islander students toward each minority group, suggests these students are not necessarily identifying with other groups, but other groups' experiences within these exclusive, elite, and white social worlds. Although black students were slightly less close to each group at the end of college, this may also reflect their understanding of racial hierarchies in elite social worlds, as these students identify with the experiences of other students of color on campus. Black students may also view their experiences in elite social worlds as continually marked by particular microaggressions (discussed further below and in the next chapter) such as the comparison of not being white, and possibly not "black enough," as stereotypes are often used to mark the experiences and bodies of these students (see the recent #iTooAmHarvard organizing efforts on social media platforms).

How students identified with multiple racial and ethnic groups at the end of college influenced their racial ideologies. These findings provide some support for social identity theory about the importance of ingroup bias, but also provide more contrasting perspectives for how singular ingroup-outgroup approaches can gloss over the everyday consideration of multiple groups shaping people's view of race and inequality. For example, white students who felt closer toward Latinos at the end of college had less prejudice toward that particular ethnic group, while more ingroup closeness increased such prejudice. This is consistent with social identity theory's (Stets and Burke 2000) findings in previous studies, but the multidimensionality of social identity was also found in this model, as higher levels of closeness toward blacks also increased white students' prejudice toward Latinos. This supports the need to broaden social identity theory's often-used singular ingroup-outgroup comparisons to a more multidimensional approach (see Ashmore, Deaux, and McLaughlin-Volpe 2004; Thoits and Virshup 1997). Although the closeness levels that served as proxy measures for multidimensional social identity among elite college students were not often significant in these models, these measures did have more influence on students' racial prejudice than on their views of inequality. Interestingly, students of color who had higher levels of closeness to Asians and Pacific Islanders at the end of college generally had higher levels of racial prejudice, particularly among black and Asian and Pacific Islander students. How these higher levels of closeness to Asian and Pacific Islander students increase prejudice among students of color may relate to aspects of group threat to social positions on campus and in society, often buttressed by the model minority myth and its running theme of zero-sum games for resources. That is to say, the competitiveness of elite social worlds amplifies non–Asian and Pacific Islander students' beliefs in the model minority myth and the need to differentiate between ingroup members and outgroups competing for the same resources and opportunities. It cannot be overemphasized how detrimental it is for students, Asian and Pacific Islander or not, to embrace the model minority myth if they are to understand the discrimination and inequalities facing members of these ethnic groups.[3]

Higher levels of closeness toward whites at the end of college almost unanimously increased elite college students' individualistic views of racial inequality.

These are quite powerful findings given that students were not specifically asked about the successes and failures of whites during their participation in the NLSF project. However, arguably, students respond to these questions using the "bar of whiteness," which connects how closeness to whites increases racial individualism among elite college students. The elite social worlds of these students accentuate this bar of whiteness and provide a comparative measure of assimilative progress for students of color in these elite social worlds. That is, whites' higher social positions in society and within these institutions is the unspoken bar used to compare people of color, and is increasingly used as the assumption of individualism and a colorblind meritocracy emphasized by elite social worlds is simultaneously intertwined with whiteness despite the growing racial and ethnic diversity of members in the elite segment of society.[4]

The influences of whiteness in elite social worlds and the lives of the students embedded within them is further shown by the continuing significance of how close students were to whites at the beginning of college. Higher levels of closeness at college entrance increased white and Asian and Pacific Islander students' racial prejudice, while this entering level of closeness to whites was particularly impactful on students of color's views of inequality, increasing their individualistic explanations. Elite college students' closeness to whites when they enter college has a lasting effect on their views after college, which speaks volumes for how students are socialized to view whiteness and inequality (see also Hagerman 2014; Johnson 2015; Lewis 2003; Lewis-McCoy 2014). These socialization experiences around whiteness at an early age increase the belief in individual efforts as a determinant of a person's social position in society, which is buttressed by the elite social worlds of their campuses, including how students understand their admittance to such institutions in relation to their own merit (see Warikoo 2016).

Students' racialized social identities may have another influence on their views of race and inequality; they may act as mediators for race-related social interactions in college. As discussed in the previous chapter, the connections drawn between people of different groups can influence their social interactions with those individuals, and is noted in other intergroup relations work (see Sidanius et al. 2008; Tajfel 1982; Tajfel and Turner 1997; also Warikoo 2016, 113–136). What is important to note at this point is the complexity of not only how students identify with different racial and ethnic groups, but how these identifications are linked to experiences within elite social worlds shaped by whiteness, and structured by a racial hierarchy of social interactions influencing students' racial ideology.

The Influence of Campus Context

Similar to students' social interactions, the campus context was an important influence on their racial ideology. However, the campus context was more influential on elite college students' racial prejudice than it was on their views of inequality. A few specific findings stand out as crafting elite college students' racial ideology while on campus. The first, a college experience closely related to the social interactions during college, was the experiences students had in courses that often discuss race and inequality, such as those in ethnic and gender studies. Elite college students were rarely influenced by these courses, and their experiences in such courses actually increased the prejudice of two student groups. For black and Latino students, completing more ethnic and gender studies courses increased their prejudice toward whites and Asians and Pacific Islanders. Although these courses may be viewed as divisive (as argued most recently in Arizona around Chicano studies in public schools), this would miss the point that learning about race and inequality is not a linear path for most people. That is, the histories and wide range of other information these courses contain can be difficult for students to grapple with in relation to not only how they understand the information presented in the classroom, but also how students are reconciling such histories and information with their own lived experiences and group positioning in contemporary society. Perhaps the most concerning finding from the models is that these courses do not influence elite college students' views of racial inequality. As argued at the outset and throughout this volume, these findings may relate more to the belief in a colorblind meritocracy structuring the cumulative individual efforts underlying social positions in society, not simply how hard they work. Additionally, the pedagogical approaches taken in these courses, particularly those utilizing a "power analysis" frame challenging popular narratives of history and racial progress (see Warikoo 2016, 63–85; also Warikoo and Deckman 2014), could influence whether and how students are influenced by these courses, similar to the differential effects of diversity programs for students.

Perceptions of the campus climate had limited influence on elite college students' racial ideology, but these effects present some interesting findings. Students of color who perceived a more racially hostile campus climate at their institutions were more prejudiced toward whites at the end of college. Given the continuing racial hostility on campuses across the United States perpetrated by white students prior to and after the 2016 presidential election, such as the recent incidents at Duke University, Yale University, the Universities of Mississippi and Oklahoma, and other institutions (see Wise 2008a, 2008b for more examples), the campus climate measures seem to congeal around white students' discrimination against students of color. Among Asian and Pacific Islander and Latino students, a more racially hostile campus climate increased their prejudice towards blacks as well. These findings may relate to student groups navigating these campuses from "the racial middle" whereby the limited social experiences students have with diverse peers prior to college may manifest themselves in awkward and possibly negative interactions on campus, not necessarily with black students in particular. Perhaps these measures may tap a perspective of campus hostility among these students centering on more visible targeting of and resistance by black students of discriminatory acts on campus. These findings raise an important point of how racism on college campuses stratifies student groups. Racially hostile campus environments create and perpetuate dividing lines among students of color. Such environments reduce students' sense of belonging (see Locks and colleagues 2008), and limit how students confronting racism on campus can connect and work together to push for equitable and inclusive spaces. Lastly, that white students were unaffected by racially hostility on campus is unsurprising, as they constitute the majority of students on campus, were the original group of students these institutions were established for (see Wilder 2013), and continue to reap the most benefits of their attendance (Binder, Davis, and Bloom 2016; Rivera 2015).

Students' perceptions of racial groups' visibility and the representation of students of color on campus presented a series of findings hinting at the development of group positions among elite college students. A person's sense of group position, similar to the arguments of social identity theory, develops through their consideration of their relationships to their own group as well as the members of other groups, which distill into a general perspective of where they fall in terms of their position in society (for further discussion of the group position perspective developed by Blumer 1958, see Bobo 1999; Bobo and Tuan 2006). Group positions emerge from patterns of social interactions over time, and often relate to perceptions of threat and competition for resources. Group positions are also closely tied to perceptions of threat as group visibility and representation of people of color increases in communities (examples of the racial threat literature include Blalock 1967; Fossett and Kiecolt 1989; Taylor and Schroeder 2010). As noted further below, the institutions included in this study are not only highly selective but are highly competitive, which can influence students to form traditional notions of group positions over resources and opportunities to achieve higher status positions. However, this group positioning among elite college students was almost wholly restricted to shaping their views of race rather than influencing their views of racial inequality. Students who noted other groups on campus were more visible than their own group were often less prejudiced toward those specific groups as well as others on campus, which somewhat counters group position research. The group position perspective comes into view when specifically considering students of color. More Latino student visibility on campus increased black students' prejudice toward whites while increasing Asian and Pacific Islander students' prejudice overall. Also, greater white student visibility on campus increased Latino students' prejudice toward whites. In relation to students' views of racial inequality, more Latino student visibility on campus increased Asian and Pacific Islander students' racial individualism in all models except for the model specifically examining individual efforts among blacks. Similarly, greater black student visibility on campus increased Latino students' racial individualism in all models except for the specific model examining their views about blacks.

Closely related to perceptions of visibility is the representation of students of color. As found with the visibility measures, the student representation measures mainly influenced elite college students' views of race. In general, higher levels of racial and ethnic diversity on elite college campuses had prejudice-reducing effects for students, which counters the noted perspective that more visibility and representation may increase students' perceptions of threat to resources and opportunities in highly competitive environments. However, for students of color at these institutions, more Asian and Pacific Islander student representation on campus increased their prejudice toward whites. This particular finding may relate to perceived threats of scarce resources and opportunities on campus for students of color linked with a belief in the model minority myth pitting Asians and Pacific Islanders as the most competitive to whites. These opportunities and resources are often hoarded by whites, who are the dominant group on campus. Interestingly, more Asian and Pacific Islander representation on campus increased Latino students' individualistic views of racial inequality. Again, this may link to the competitive cultures of these campuses and the pitting of students of color against each other for scarce resources, which increases Latino students' narrow belief that how to get these scarce resources and opportunities is through their individual efforts, somewhat similar to the findings described by Rivera (2015). In a study of how elite college students pursue highly coveted jobs and internships, Rivera notes how students of color were often at a disadvantage to their white peers at elite colleges because of the "insider" perspective of what a well-rounded, not necessarily highest-achieving, applicant for elite firm positions looks like to recruiters, which often reflected the characteristics of white students also interviewing for these positions.

The type of institution elite college students attended also had a variety of influences on their racial ideology development during college. Consistent with other patterns, where elite college students studied was more influential on their views of race than on their views of inequality. When examining racial prejudice levels, students attending a private research university or liberal arts college were less prejudiced than their peers at public research universities. However, different institutional environments did increase students' racial prejudice toward particular groups. For example, black and Latino students at private research universities had higher levels of prejudice toward whites and Asians and Pacific Islanders at the end of college. Why these two groups were found to have more prejudice based on the type of institution they attended may relate to specific climate issues on those campuses, and may also relate to the competitive culture among these students, whereby a series of microaggressions or negative experiences with white and Asian and Pacific Islander peers on projects or other competitive activities heighten black and Latino students' prejudice toward these groups.[5]

Precollege Experiences and Other Key Findings

Many of the remaining factors influencing elite college students' racial ideology at the end of college related to their precollege social experiences. Although not all of these findings are discussed further in this section, what must be said is that the college-going experience did not eliminate the residual effects of these experiences from childhood. These findings indicate a misplaced view of education, and colleges and universities in particular, as society's "great equalizers" in many ways. What is seen throughout this chapter are the experiences and attitudes elite college students bring with them to college, which continue to shape their views even after college.[6] This is most clearly found for all student groups analyzed in this study, as their entering prejudice levels as well as their racial individualism levels continued to predict their views of race and inequality after four years on campus. Although it may be naïve to assume four years of college experiences could completely erase the foundational views of race and inequality for students, the fact that every entering college measure for students' racial ideology was still a strong predictor, even with the many measures included in the models relating to students' college-going experience, indicates how difficult it is to reduce prejudicial and individualistic views of race and inequality during college. These "carry-over" effects from the beginning of college varied by group, as Asian and Pacific Islander students exhibited the strongest influences of these first-year measures, followed by white students, and then Latino students as well as black students.

In relation to the changes in elite college students' views of racial inequality, the analyses in this chapter identified that students were less supportive of highly individualistic views of racial inequality by the end of college. Despite this presumably positive finding, it is important to recall that although someone is not as supportive of such views of racial inequality does not mean they support the view that structural factors impact a person's life chances or position in society (see Hunt 2007). Particularly concerning is the possibility for the development of racial apathy among students, whereby they view the deeply entrenched racial inequality in society as permanent and unfixable (Forman 2004). Further, the particular population of students examined in this study suggests that their elite social world may craft their views of the importance of individual efforts in a different but vital way. Extending the work of Khan (2011) on students' experiences at an elite boarding school, Rivera's examination of how elite college students are piped into top-ranked businesses, firms, and law schools, and Royster's study of white and black vocational high school students, elite college students may still be highly supportive of the importance of individual efforts in the mobility (or not) of different groups in society. However, it is not how hard a person works, but *how* a person's efforts matter in regards to their social position. Elite college students are highly favored in the recruitment and hiring at elite businesses, firms, and law schools, but which students are advantaged within this exclusive group depends on where elite college students invest their efforts during college

(Rivera 2015, 92–101). In relation to Royster's (2003) finding that black vocational high school students were kept out of apprentice opportunities for blue-collar jobs regardless of their grades or performance on various job-related tasks, students of color at elite colleges are similarly disadvantaged, as they are not landing as many top positions after college despite their grades and test scores (Rivera 2015). These studies shed light on the importance of students' shaping a certain image and knowledge of elite social worlds through the investment in prestigious organization memberships during school and college in addition to participation in high-status activities (i.e., debate versus the outdoors club) and athletics (i.e., squash versus baseball). That is, elite students, particularly white students, understand the signals these activities communicate to possible employers (Khan 2011; Rivera 2015). Thus, given the advantages white students have in elite social worlds, they can focus more on crafting such images and knowledge, while through the limited cross-race interactions during college, students of color receive little information on how to extend their efforts beyond their studies to particular social activities. In the end, the lack of support by elite college students of the idea of how important a person's efforts are to their social position, may indicate that elite college students highly value individual efforts through a "work smarter, not harder" mantra. Put differently, it is how you invest your efforts across multiple activities and interests, not how hard you work on a few, that importantly shapes a person's social position. Again, it is the ease of privilege that links how the culture and social structure of elite colleges influence the mental structures of students (i.e., their racial ideology).[7] Although elite college students are not completely blind to structural inequalities, they may navigate interactions and opportunities using a more nuanced approach to individualism than often accounted for in discussions of people's beliefs about race and inequality.

Turning to precollege experiences and friendships of elite college students, these measures exerted many influences on students' racial ideology at the end of college. Childhood friendships continued to shape elite college students' racial prejudice at the end of college more than their views of racial inequality. Among students, more white and black precollege friendships had prejudice-increasing effects, while Latino friendships exhibited prejudice-reducing effects across groups. However, students' level of racial individualism was mostly shaped by Latino and Asian and Pacific Islander friendships established prior to college. White students' views of racial inequality were not influenced by these friendships.

Similar to the influences of precollege friendships, the social environments that elite college students experienced prior to entering college impacted their prejudice levels more than their racial individualism levels at the end of college. Interestingly, students who attended private schools prior to college were generally less prejudiced, particularly toward Asians and Pacific Islanders. However,

this was not found for racial individualism, as private school attendance amplified Asian and Pacific Islander students' individualistic views for their own ethnic group members. School and neighborhood segregation exerted contrasting
effects on students' prejudice levels, as coming from a more segregated school
prior to college often reduced prejudice among elite college students, while
coming from a more segregated neighborhood often increased students' prejudice at the end of college, particularly toward blacks and Latinos. These findings
may relate to exclusionary views taken to residential choices of ideal neighborhood composition, which are closely tied to perceptions of racial threat similar
to those found in national studies (see Blalock 1967; Blumer 1958; Charles 2003,
2007; Fossett and Kiecolt 1989; Schuman et al. 1997; Taylor and Schroder 2010).
Again, these social environments rarely influenced students' views of racial
inequality, but Asian and Pacific Islander students were the most influenced, as
coming from a more segregated school resulted in more critical perspectives on
other group members' efforts.

CONCLUSION

The social interactions of elite college students impacted their racial ideology,
and in many cases reduced their prejudiced views and reliance on individualistic
explanations for racial inequality. However, interacting across racial and ethnic
lines did not dramatically shape students' views of race and inequality, as roughly
half of all possible influences of social interactions on their views significantly
influenced them. More often than not, students' views of race and inequality are
unaffected by whom they interact with during college or whether it is through
friendships, dating, rooming together, or participating in the same student organization. These findings do not necessarily counter the long-standing research
in intergroup relations as much as they uncover more of the complexity surrounding how social interactions may or may not influence students' racial ideology over time. All of these findings point to a disturbing reality on elite college
campuses and the framing of "race relations," as elite college students may not
fully view their peers as relatable or even equal when race or ethnicity is considered. More discussion is needed to untangle how elite college students' social
interactions are guided by their identities and the culture and structure of their
institutions. In the next chapter, I provide an in-depth examination of how the
race-related histories, cultures, and patterns of interactions embedded within
elite colleges and universities intersect with the experiences of their students to
provide clarification of how an increasingly racially and ethnically diverse student population may not interact or learn more from one another in regard to
race and inequality.

5 · WHEN THINGS FALL APART
Identities and Interactions within an Intersected Habitus

The previous chapters paint a concerning picture: the segment of college students with the most resources and opportunities, those who disproportionately take leadership roles throughout society, have limited social interactions across racial and ethnic lines that shape their views of race, with even less influence on their views of racial inequality. When we step back to examine the main findings from these earlier chapters, the importance of considering the impact these elite colleges have on crystallizing students' views of race and inequality, and even their day-to-day interactions (or not) across racial and ethnic lines informing these views, comes into focus.

As found in Chapter Two, elite college students hold moderately strong individualistic views of racial inequality and varying levels of racial prejudice when they enter college. That is, elite college students do not view one another as equals with regards to their traits or characteristics, and generally support the view that the lower social positions of racial and ethnic minorities are a result of individual efforts and capabilities, eschewing external structural and cultural factors influencing a person's social position. Even at their college entrance, these students were powerfully shaped by their racialized social identities, while their friendships prior to college had few effects on their racial ideology. These findings indicated how ingroup and outgroup bias shapes elite college students' connections to groups as well as their beliefs about racial inequality in society. Further, students had distinct friendship networks with limited interaction across racial and ethnic lines that rarely influenced their views of race and inequality. Despite the constrained social networks and narrow views of race and inequality among students, there still existed an opportunity for them to broaden their views as well as whom they interacted with once they arrived at elite institutions.

Unfortunately, the limited friendship diversity and distinct networks among elite college students prior to college were not confined to their precollege lives, as found in Chapter Three. Throughout college these students were positioned within a larger racial hierarchy of social interaction. The examination of elite college students' social interactions identified that white students were the most homophilous in their social interactions during college, as nearly 70% of all people they interacted with during this time were white. This is not surprising, as these campuses continue to host a predominantly white student body. Asian and Pacific Islander students split their interactions mostly between whites and other Asians and Pacific Islanders while on campus. Latino students were the most integrated into elite college campuses regarding their social interactions, in which they experienced more diversity, but still mostly interacted with whites while on campus. Black students, on the other hand, were the most segregated group of students on campus, as they often interacted with other black students, but were also the last group other students interacted with on campus. These findings highlight an important social structure on campus: students draw experiences and knowledge from social interactions shaping their education and solidifying their views of race and inequality prior to entering the workforce after college. Students' identities continued to shape elite college students' lives—in this case, whom they interacted with during college in various forms—but so too did other race-related campus experiences. Perceptions of the campus climate and student group visibility and representation also informed elite college students' social interactions. Thus, the college environment can play an important role in continuing to craft students' social interactions and how friendships and even dating are not simply laissez-faire exercises in social interaction.

When elite college students exit their institutions and enter the workforce, their racial ideologies are mostly intact from their precollege views of race and inequality, but are also significantly modified by their racialized social identity, their college environments, and to a lesser extent their social interactions during college, particularly those that are more intimate such as romantic relationships, friendships, and roommates. As explored in Chapter Four, elite college students were generally less prejudiced toward each other's groups, while they still held strong positive bias toward Asians and Pacific Islanders at the end of college. These students also held lower levels of individualistic views of racial inequality, meaning they did not completely adhere to views of individual capabilities and efforts as sole determinants of people of color's social positions. Though these results may appear encouraging at first glance, a subtle and subversive reality may surround these findings and is discussed further in this chapter. Diverse social interactions had limited effects on elite college students' racial ideology, particularly their racial individualism. Approximately one-half of all possible intergroup contact effects existed in the analyses with only one-third reducing students' racial prejudice or support for individualistic views of racial inequality. The remaining effects increased students' racial prejudice or racial individualism. That is, interacting across racial and ethnic lines, be it friendships, romantic relationships, among roommates, or in student organizations of different compositions, were not the driving force for the change in elite college students' racial ideology. However, students' racialized social identities more readily shaped their views of race and inequality, but were also malleable themselves compared to their entering levels discussed in Chapter Two. All of these findings present a complicated puzzle of how college students navigate their elite social worlds, craft their identities, and position themselves in relation to race and inequality. Further, although one could view these findings as the result of individual beliefs and resistance to change by these students, a larger influence on how elite college students interact on campus and shift their views of race and inequality is at play: the structure and culture of the institution itself.

The current chapter delves into the above-mentioned findings with particular attention to examining the importance of how higher education institutions themselves can dictate the degree of interaction across racial and ethnic lines and solidify particular views of race and inequality. First, I explore how the framework of organizational racial habitus can assist us with understanding the elite social worlds these students live and study in. This discussion brings together literature on how the culture and structure in these elite social worlds shape students' race-related experiences and correspondingly reproduce racial inequality in both student interactions and racial ideologies. Next, I discuss the importance of linking the racialized social identities of students to this organizational habitus of elite colleges and universities. How students identify with multiple groups and literally relate to one another through social interaction takes on new meaning and importance with this framing in mind. Finally, I discuss what these findings and theoretical perspectives mean for social interactions and their impact on students' racial ideology when we consider the spatial aspects of college campuses surrounding students.

THE COLLEGE EXPERIENCE: ORGANIZATIONAL RACIAL HABITUS AND ELITE COLLEGE STUDENTS

The elite social worlds in which these students live and study contain important cultural and structural components that shape their identities, ideologies, and interactions. The college experience around issues and interactions of race hinges on two forms of habitus intertwining to reproduce racial inequality within and outside these elite social worlds. It is because of this dynamic that these campuses produce graduates who may appear more diverse in racial and ethnic representation, but are also in close alignment with previous graduates' views of race and inequality. In this section I discuss the importance of framing this study's findings with the conceptions of "organizational racial habitus" (Carter 2012; McDonough 1997) and "individual racial habitus."[1] Through such conceptualization and framing of elite college students' experiences, identities, and ideologies, we can see how elite social worlds can (re)produce racial inequalities while pushing for "diversity" frameworks and policies on multiple levels (Berrey 2015, 55–123; also noted in Warikoo 2016).

The concept of "habitus" was put forth by sociologist Pierre Bourdieu to codify how a person's environment and material conditions, related to their class position, produce and organize everyday life. More fully, Bourdieu defines habitus as

> systems of durable, transposable dispositions, structured structures predisposed to function as structuring structures, that is, as principles of the generation and structuring of practices and representations which can be objectively "regulated" and "regular" without in any way being the product of obedience to rules, objectively adapted to their goals without presupposing a conscious aiming at ends or an express mastery of the operations necessary to attain them and, being all this, collectively orchestrated without being the product of the orchestrating action of a conductor. (Bourdieu 1977, 72)

That is, the habitus is a result of the social conditions and related practices and interactions of everyday life that shape a person's perception of their location and relationship to others around them, and ultimately provides "reason" for their actions while navigating the social world. These "reasons" for action are justified by underlying, and often unconscious, interests serving people from similar class locations, which assist them with navigating social interactions and situations throughout their lives (also referred to as "schemes" by Bourdieu 1977). People with similar class locations share a habitus that produces similar situations for them to navigate more readily than people of another class location. As Bourdieu specifically notes, "'interpersonal relations' are never, except in appearance, individual-to-individual relationships and . . . the truth of the interaction is never entirely contained in the interaction" (Bourdieu 1977, 81). Thus, we must understand social interactions as embedded within the habitus informing both interaction and situation, which is a sociohistorical product leading to individual and collective practices. People (re)produce and also are products of the habitus by giving meaning to interactions. Although a college student has their own habitus informed by the conditions of their environment, they are also embedded within an organization that carries with it a set of collective interests, practices, and situations forming an organizational habitus, meaning that habitus can have multiple levels, and a person's experiences reflect the intersection of these multiple levels.

Young elites attending the highly selective institutions examined in the current study inhabit the most socioeconomically advantaged and privileged position compared to most college students.[2] Their childhood and young adulthood is often spent in elite social worlds assisting with the construction of their class habitus. This class position and experiences, their habitus, shapes their views of opportunities, resources, and inequality. As noted above, the habitus also shapes young elites' social interactions with their peers on campus, such that the success and failure of someone is viewed as the result of individual efforts and capabilities given that everyone around them is part of the proclaimed "best and brightest" and justified by their meritocratic beliefs.[3] Importantly, students' habitus is not limited to class but extends to and is intertwined with race. The habitus of elite college students, as is argued throughout this volume, suggests that racial inequality is, again, the result of individual efforts and capabilities, an ideology building on the rights movements' arguments to shift to more individualistic discussions of people acknowledging diversity rather than to rely on group-based and essentialist views (see also Khan 2011, 2015; Khan and Jerolmack 2013). This individualistic view of inequality buoys colorblindness to shun discussions of racial discrimination and structural inequalities as having significant influences on people's experiences and positions. Such views of racial inequality were found in the current study as well as other examinations of young elites and students at similar institutions (see Espenshade and Radford 2009; Khan 2011; Massey et al. 2003; Sidanius et al. 2008; Warikoo 2016; Warikoo and Novais 2015). Although the elite college students examined in this study decreased their reliance on such individualistic perspectives of racial inequality, they still held such views as part of their disposition to inequality within and outside of their elite social worlds, and critically, this does not indicate they readily acknowledge the far-reaching effects of structural inequality (see also Hunt 2007). An even more concerning possibility is that not only are elite college students not readily acknowledging structural inequalities, they may become more racially apathetic as they see racial inequality as an unchanging societal norm (Forman 2004).

Returning to the argument put forth at the outset of this volume, young elites enact privilege in their everyday lives resulting from their social position and habitus. The "ease of privilege" allows young elites to navigate their social worlds without fully recognizing inequality's impact on their experiences or those of others around them (Khan 2011, 77–113). This allows students to rationalize inequality and who their peers are at elite colleges by using the ultimate attribution error to explain racial inequality and buffer their prejudicial views. That is, when a student has an experience or comes across particular information countering their prejudiced views of a group, they rationalize this experience or information to make it an exception to their stereotypical beliefs such that the person they interact with is "lucky," was extremely motivated, countered their views because of a special advantage in life, or were part of a whole experience that resulted from a manipulated situation (Pettigrew 1979). However, what privilege can do for young elites in supporting particular views of race and inequality and shaping their social interactions takes on new meaning when considering that students' habitus is influenced by the habitus of the colleges and universities they attend, which increases the availability bias of elite college students.

Recognizing how a student's habitus is shaped by the larger organizational habitus is critical to understanding their social interactions and racial ideologies. Elite colleges and universities operate from a unique social location in society, a reflection of their organizational habitus within the elite social world.[4] The institutions included in this study continue to rely on young elites and their families for admissions and financial support, if not more, as they have for well over a century (the reliance on these elite families for students is well documented in Bowen and Bok 1998; Bowen, Kurzweil, and Tobin 2005; Espenshade and Radford 2009; Karabel 2005; Massey et al. 2003; Soares 2007; and Wilder 2013). Importantly, the framing of college choice discussions centers on students having the agency to apply to and attend a college or university. When coupled with the strong belief in meritocracy among young elites as found in Warikoo's (2016) research, this further disconnects the popular narrative from the reality of college admissions decisions. However, when we revisit how selective admissions function (i.e., exclusivity and prestige hinge on rejection and exceptionalism), this general framework misses how elite institutions reproduce generations of students who may not differ dramatically from graduates of the past: it is not the student who selects the college, but the college which selects the student. This reality allows elite colleges to utilize their organizational habitus to select students who "fit" their ideal or archetypical students—those with social locations and experiences similar to those of current and past students. In the end it is a self-fulfilling prophecy of who attends and what social interactions they may experience regarding race.

These interactions within the racial hierarchy on campus become "natural" and justifiable as "how things are" for students and arguably administrators as well, blinding them to how the intersection of individual and organizational racial habitus structures their interactions, similar to the dynamics found in other studies of social interaction and residential perceptions (see Bonilla-Silva and Embrick 2007; Mayorga-Gallo 2014). This reliance on students from similar social locations buttresses particular views of race and inequality and patterns of social interaction. These characteristics of their campuses shelter elite college students from larger realities outside their elite social worlds such as limited social mobility, resources, and opportunities, and increasing racial inequality, ultimately increasing their availability bias (Khan 2015, 2011). The organizational habitus of these institutions structures particular experiences and situations around elite college students that build on their earlier lives in elite social worlds. Young white elites' continual experience with highly successful people of color establishes the "exception as the rule" for framing racial inequality in broader society from their particular social position in an elite social world. Thus, the disproportionately low numbers of students of color on their campuses are viewed as the result of a functional meritocratic system, not evidence of racial discrimination and inequality in the broader society.[5] This can also serve as an insidious belief to discount students of color who protest racial discrimination, for example, as no longer fitting the mold as the "right" student or possibly as "hypersensitive." Such beliefs can ultimately undercut discussions and possible changes using social justice efforts on and around campus toward equity and inclusion. Considering this perspective with the sheer lack of interracial contact effects in the analyses, the availability bias and ultimate attribution error buoyed by elite colleges' racial habitus is arguably a reflection of students' ability to ease through these interactions, as their privileged locations rarely put them in situations that do not frequently justify their views of race and inequality.[6]

The habitus of these institutions supports the meritocratic notion that their students are the "best and brightest," and since the rights movements of the mid-twentieth century, increasingly argues that this notion includes diversity in various forms as part and parcel of elite status in higher education (Berrey 2015, 55–123). This establishes all students, including the increasing numbers of students of color, as intelligent, hardworking, and talented people who found their way to campus via meritocracy, which supports young elites' views of success and inequality. This limits the realization among these students of the racial discrimination that occurs in broader society as well as on their own campuses, lending credence to colorblind and individualistic views. As Khan (2011, 52–64) and Warikoo (2016; Warikoo and Novais 2015) note, when their elite social world intersects with the larger social world, young elites can rationalize racial inequality by using colorblindness built on individual and cultural explanations for why some people are their peers on campus, while others work in dining facilities serving them food.

The perspective of colleges having an organizational habitus builds on the development of campus climate research originating from the expansive college impact literature. This area of research identifies how colleges differentially influence students' academic and social lives. The field of campus climate research developed as scholars examined how students and their colleges changed with the increasing racial diversity of the student body following the post–World War II expansion of higher education, integration, the civil rights movement, and student movements during the mid-twentieth century. Sylvia Hurtado and her colleagues (1999, 3–7) developed a contextualized and sociohistorical approach to identify several dimensions of the campus climate, specifically (1) a sociohistorical legacy of inclusion or exclusion; (2) a psychological dimension of race-related attitudes and perceptions of discrimination; (3) a behavioral dimension relating to students' social interactions and involvement in diverse campus spaces; and (4) a compositional component relating to the racial and ethnic diversity of the students, faculty, and staff. These four dimensions interact to form the overall campus climate, which is influenced by external societal forces. Previous research (Bowen and Bok 1998; Charles et al. 2009; Espenshade and Radford 2009; Gurin et al. 2002; Hurtado et al. 1999) identified the negative effects of limited racial diversity and social interactions on campus, racially contentious environments, lax institutional policies supporting diversity and the academic success of students of color, and a failure to address the historical legacies of racism. Campus climates influence many situations in students' lives, yet these situations are arguably linked by the structured realities of culture embedded within the organizational racial habitus of an institution, further informing students' own racial habitus that they operate from prior to entering college.

The broadened application of habitus to an organizational level extends notions of the campus climate from attitudes and perceptions of campus life to the entrenched racialized patterns of cultural dispositions and interactions on an organizational level, and those formed in larger society. These racialized patterns within the organizational racial habitus can influence students' social adjustment and academic performance throughout college, not only their social interactions (see also Carter 2012; McDonough 1997). That is, an organization can emit a particular set of cultural dispositions and accepted patterns of interactions in relation to race and achievement, influencing campus policies and practices beyond faculty, staff, and students. The policies and practices reify or modify these dispositions and interactions, establishing the experience of college for many students of color as a prolonged stereotype threat situation (see the in-depth discussions provided by Claude Steele and Joshua Aronson: Steele 1997, 2010; Steele and Aronson 1995, 2004). At the K–12 level, scholars have also identified the context around racialized tracking and disciplinary policies in a similar vein; for examples of how the structures of schools such as academic tracks are racialized and influence both academic and social pursuits among students, see Lewis and Diamond (2015) and Tyson (2011). This perspective arguably provides a crucial approach to understanding college racial dynamics in the proclaimed era of colorblindness, when racism and racial inequality exist without a plethora of "racists" (Bonilla-Silva 2014).

Although research on college students and their institutions has not necessarily used a similar framing of race, interaction, and ideology as described above around the conception of habitus, a few studies provide examples of how both levels of habitus intertwine to produce particular forms of interactions and views of race and inequality. Recently, Julie Park's (2014b) ethnography of an evangelical Christian student group at a California university indicates how an organization that deliberately structures activities around a perspective of racial reconciliation can have positive results in line with intergroup contact theory's arguments for the five key conditions that can reduce prejudice and build a sense of community across group lines. However, Park's study further indicates that this is not an easy or linear process, as combatting student underrepresentation and a university's larger position toward race, diversity, and inequality can have substantial impacts on how student-led organizations on campus facilitate cross-group interactions and increase discussion of racism and inequality in broader society. Similarly, the work of Natasha Warikoo pinpoints how colorblindness intertwines with narrow perspectives of diversity to rebut in-depth considerations of power relations in society around race by white students, who also view limited social interactions with students of color as "self-segregation" by non-white students, further isolating their consideration of how racial inequality manifests on their own campuses and influences their lives, while students of color are more engaged with considerations of power and inequality. Further, Warikoo found white students to hold a degree of social interaction entitlement, feeling students of color must interact with them given their framing of diversity as collective merit, which suggests that such cross-race interactions are needed by white students if they are to gain diversity-related knowledge supposedly held automatically by students of color to aid their academic and career pursuits (Warikoo 2016, 103–104; also Warikoo and Deckman 2014; Warikoo and Novais 2015; Moore and Bell 2011). In other words, white students argued for a racial capital approach of diversity on campus: as whiteness is constructed as emptiness and without diversity (white debt), the knowledge of diversity supposedly held by particular students of color will give them the necessary knowledge of race and inequality to be a better student, professional, and person (color capital).[7] Ellen Berrey (2015) also notes how universities justify diversity from narrow perspectives, limiting their efforts to combat racial discrimination on campus and educational disparities afflicting students of color.[8] Such narrow perspectives constrain even the most well-supported and structured approaches among students, faculty, and staff on and off campus. Additionally, the research by Joe Feagin, Hernan Vera, and Nikitah Imani (1996) on students of color's experiences on a Florida campus; Wendy Leo Moore's (2008) pivotal examination of how law schools structure student interactions with each other, with curricular offerings that discuss race and inequality and link to broader legal battles for racial justice; and the study by Leslie H. Picca and Joe R. Feagin (2007) on white college students' navigation of social interactions and views of race on campus, uncover how the perspectives and experiences students bring to college intertwine with the organizational racial habitus of their campuses to shape their social interactions and racial ideology. These studies indicate how passive and superficial attention to the structure and culture of an institution can reproduce racial discrimination and inequality among students, while continually racializing spaces for student interactions.

Through the integrated perspective of how structure and culture intertwine around student experiences and performance, we can better understand how changes of institutional structures and policies can assist or hinder efforts toward racial equality. That is, the above approach to examining how the individual-level and organizational-level racial habitus intertwine in the elite social world answers the call by Mitchell Stevens, Elizabeth Armstrong, and Richard Arum (2008) for a more ambitious examination of the sociology of higher education by situating colleges within the societal contexts that influence students, their interactions, and how these institutions can influence racial inequality among their own students and across society. Although most diversity and inclusion policies are enacted with the goal of reducing disparity in various capacities, they may have the opposite effect if larger cultural and structural changes do not precede or accompany them, or are simply not taken into full account.[9] As important as it is to understand how multiple levels of the habitus intertwine to influence student experiences and ideologies, it is also critical to examine how elite college students' identities factor into our understanding of whom they interact with and what they take away from their interactions while on campus.

BOUND IN IDENTITIES AND HIERARCHY ON CAMPUSES

Throughout the analyses of elite college students' interactions and views of race and inequality, one group of measures most consistently influenced students' interactions as well as their racial prejudice and individualism levels: their racialized social identities. Unlike previous studies of social identities, the current study examined racialized social identity with a multidimensional approach (see also Ashmore, Deaux, and McLaughlin-Volpe 2004; Thoits and Virshup 1997). This approach emphasized that ingroup-outgroup dynamics informing social identities are not necessarily a binary, but more of a relational understanding of group membership among multiple groups. A person making ingroup and outgroup comparisons takes into consideration more than one outgroup to build a positive social identity, while at the same time making sense of these multiple racial and ethnic categories with their associated meanings and histories. As mentioned previously, these findings suggest it is not a matter of "which group are you a part of," but more of "how much of a connection with each group do you have?"

The current study sheds light on important contexts and situations activating elite college students' social identity. The analyses indicate how students' racialized social identities and their maintenance of these identities comparing multiple groups at once can make identity a salient part of both interaction and racial ideology. Further, this study notes how aspects of the habitus and racial ideology intertwine around elite college students' racialized social identity, complicating our understanding of how "ingroups" are conceived in society. Specifically, elite college students hold particular perspectives of what individuality and diversity mean regarding race, and subsequently racial inequality, into their understanding of their racialized social identities. The hegemonic aspect of racialized social identity makes group memberships and associated beliefs of group capabilities more rigid despite how loosely elite college students hold to them. As seen in the previous chapter, white and black students generally reported they were less close to their own racial group, but also less close to other groups as well after they completed college. The obvious difference was for Latino and Asian and Pacific Islander students, who grew closer to each other as well as blacks by the end of college, while not necessarily feeling significantly less close to their own groups. These findings indicate racialized social identity is not only multidimensional, but also malleable. Additionally, no student group identified exclusively with one or another racial or ethnic group, as elite college students had quite low closeness ratings across the board.

The patterns of social interaction on elite college campuses reaffirm these loose group memberships for students, further hardening their beliefs in racial group boundaries. This arguably solidifies a more individualistic racialized social identity whereby elite college students disassociate themselves from traditional racial group membership, while still holding loosely to that membership. Thus, as Matthew Hughey (2012, 12–14 and 186–190) and Amanda Lewis (2004) suggest, racial identities form as hegemonic identities with continuums built off of relationships with ingroup and outgroup members. This hegemonic identity is loose but inflexible at the same time, which can make racialized social identities more rigid, as elite college students can dismiss varying approaches to race, identity, and their relationship to inequality that do not fit their socialized views from earlier in their lives. At the same time, young elites can decouple how they, themselves, fit within these racial group memberships and relationships, preserving views of themselves as individuals who do not follow general patterns or stereotypes of their affiliated racial or ethnic group. This makes ingroup and outgroup bias more heuristic as young elites use it to reflect on group boundaries, making membership a default reality in their lives, not necessarily viewing it as a malleable, socially constructed aspect of life. The ability to rely on this racially individualistic approach to identity even when considering multiple groups is buoyed by the habitus of the elite social world, which is explicitly intertwined by whiteness and white privilege. Elite social worlds were and continue to be constructed by whites, which allows them the luxury of not seeing themselves as members of the specific racial category "white" generally. Although whites were less likely to identify with their racial ingroup compared to other groups, this is arguably because the elite conception of the "individual" is based on the construction of whiteness as an integral part of these social worlds. This possibility is amplified by the racial hierarchy of social interactions on campus, which reifies the information and perspectives that elite college students gain from such interactions, further solidifying beliefs in group boundaries. This perspective of social identity's multidimensionality embedded within the social structural characteristics of a multilevel habitus expands our understanding of social identity theory and how people "[act] in the context of, referring to, and reaffirming social structure" as it relates to race and everyday life (Stets and Burke 2000, 232; see also Thoits and Virshup 1997).

When we consider the above expansion of social identity theory, we notice that elite college students' multidimensional identities play off their perceptions of group memberships and relationships in varying ways. The analyses provide support for social identity theory in some ways, but also for conflicting findings somewhat countering the theory. However, what is important is not whether ingroup and outgroup bias increases racial prejudice or individualism, but how these biases are informed by elite college students' associations with multiple group memberships. This consideration also assists with examining how identities embedded within the elite social world can influence patterns of interaction of these elites and vice versa, as discussed by William Domhoff (1978) and Shamus Khan (2012). Among white and Asian and Pacific Islander students, their racialized social identities had limited influences on their social interactions during college. These findings appear to be a function of their homophilous social networks spanning all four forms of social interaction, in which they interacted mainly with each other and less so with blacks and Latinos. Some support for the ingroup-outgroup bias hypotheses of social identity theory existed for these two student groups, but interestingly in relation to how white and Asian and Pacific Islander students interacted with each other rather than other groups.

Among black students, ingroup bias played an important role particularly for interactions with other whites and blacks, but more closeness with other groups generally increased their interactions with them as well. Latino students displayed the most complicated findings in relation to their closeness levels and social interactions. For these students, more ingroup or outgroup closeness to a certain racial or ethnic group did not necessarily correspond to particular increases or decreases in friendships, romantic relationships, or roommates with that group, or memberships in student organizations composed of that group. For both black and Latino students, again, these findings are closely tied to the patterns of social interactions found on elite college campuses. However, it should be reiterated that these elite social worlds are interlaced with whiteness and white privilege, heightening students of color's understandings of their positions as non-whites on these campuses similar to those found by Gaztambide-Fernandez and DiAquoi (2010). Moreover, the lower levels of closeness toward whites, but generally higher levels of closeness of Latino and Asian and Pacific Islander students toward each minority group, may indicate that these students identify with other groups' experiences within these exclusive, elite, and white social worlds. Black students were slightly less close to each group at the end of college, but this may reflect the habitus and racial hierarchy of these elite campuses as the students also identify with the experiences of other students of color on campus.

A related point, equally important to the discussion of the hegemonic character and multidimensionality of racialized social identity among elite college students, corresponds to how these identities influenced students' views of race and inequality. The generally low and loose group connections that elite college students had toward each racial and ethnic group could, at first glance, suggest students were more colorblind and individual as they identified with the perception of a more open and diverse elite social world often shunning explicit racial or ethnic group memberships (see Khan 2011; Khan and Jerolmack 2013), but this possibility is eliminated when we consider that these closeness levels had significant influences on their views of race and inequality. Racialized social identity had more influence on elite college students' views of race than inequality, further buttressing their view of racial individualism and the importance of individual efforts to social mobility; or more disturbingly, they were apathetic to both individual and structural influences on inequality as they viewed racial inequality as a fixed aspect of society (Forman 2004). Again, mixed results support social identity theory, but the multidimensionality indicates how the associations elite college students have to other racial and ethnic groups also influence their views of race and inequality, not limited to a simplified ingroup-outgroup binary.

Considering the impact of racialized social identity on elite college students' racial individualism, the analyses indicated that higher levels of closeness to whites at the end of college increased all student groups' views that racial inequality was almost solely determined by individual efforts. Further, this influence of whiteness in elite social worlds is quite powerful given that the survey questions never asked students about whites explicitly, meaning students arguably used a "bar of whiteness" to compare racial and ethnic minority success in society. That is, whites' generally higher social positions in society are the unspoken bar used to compare other groups, and elite social worlds accentuate this comparison. The influence of whiteness in elite social worlds was also found when considering the impact of how close students felt to whites at the beginning of college. Higher levels of closeness toward whites at college entrance continued to increase white and Asian and Pacific Islander students' racial prejudice at the end of college, while also increasing students of color's end-of-college views of racial inequality as highly determined by individual efforts. These findings support previous research on early socialization around whiteness and inequality, whereby these experiences can increase beliefs in individual efforts as a determinant of a person's social position in society (see Hagerman 2014; Johnson 2015; Lewis 2003; Lewis-McCoy 2014), further buoying the rationalization of their experiences and interactions on their elite campuses. These findings of how identity and interaction are embedded in unique ways within the habitus of elite social worlds can have critical implications for understanding research on college students using intergroup contact theory in the future.

CIRCUMVENTED RELATIONS AND
SPACES ON COLLEGE CAMPUSES

The current study builds on the century-long research of intergroup relations (seminal discussions and reviews of the long history of research in this area include Allport 1954; Pettigrew 1998; Pettigrew and Tropp 2011; and Williams 1947). This area of research extends our knowledge of what conditions and processes lead to prejudice reduction, with many studies finding that increased interactions across racial and ethnic lines can reduce a person's racial prejudice. However, the current study did not find such overarching positive results. As mentioned earlier, only one-half of all possible contact effects were significant in the analyses, and only one-third of those that were significant reduced elite college students' racial individualism or prejudice. As argued, it is the ease of privilege of elite college students on their campuses, coupled with the structure and culture of their institutions—that is, the intersection of individual and organizational racial habitus—that allows students to experience cross-race interactions while maintaining their views of race and inequality. This reality of campus life can shape the views of students, faculty, and staff on these campuses, and also perspectives of progress by these institutions.

As noted at the outset of this volume, the general agreement among scholars is that the current dominant form of racial prejudice is subtler than the traditional Jim Crow prejudice, which exhibited beliefs in racial inferiority, both biologically and culturally (see Bobo et al. 1997, 2012; Hughes 1997; Kinder and Sanders 1996; Schuman et al. 1997). Specifically, research shows adherence to colorblindness increases traditional or explicit forms of racial prejudice among most study participants, particularly whites (see also Apfelbaum, Sommers, and Norton 2008; Mazzoco, Cooper, and Flint 2012; Neville et al. 2000, 2005; Oh et al. 2010; Richeson and Nussbaum 2004; Ryan et al. 2007). Previous research supports Eduardo Bonilla-Silva's (2014) notion that people of color hold less colorblind racial attitudes, particularly blacks and Latinos (see Neville et al. 2005; Ryan et al. 2007; Warikoo 2016, 43–61). Studies of colorblind attitudes (Mazzoco, Cooper, and Flint 2012; Oh et al. 2010) found people with higher levels of colorblind racial attitudes were more likely to oppose affirmative action policies, a contentious issue within higher education discussions. These studies are in line with the minimization and abstract liberalism frames of Bonilla-Silva's (2014) colorblind racial ideology, whereby the downplaying of racism is combined with opposition to governmental efforts to increase racial equality, and this arguably extends to college campuses as well. Importantly, the use of colorblind attitudes and behaviors is situational, and can influence engaging in cross-race interactions (Apfelbaum, Sommers, and Norton 2008; also Warikoo 2016, 113–136). Taken together, these studies support the argument that universities pushing limited understandings of "diversity" can buttress racial inequality among students (see the discussion of the evolution of diversity framing used by the University of Michigan in Berrey 2015, 55–123; also Warikoo 2016; Warikoo and Deckman 2014), but also can limit the possible benefits of cross-race interactions given the framing of each other race as diverse and the best and brightest, all of which is a reflection of the habitus of both students and institutions in the elite social world. Through diluting diversity by orienting it around individuality, this framing is related to a general tendency to remove discussions of power and history from conversations around race in academia (see Steinberg 2007; also Warikoo 2016, 43–61).

A further consideration of the space and campus context literally setting the stage for social interactions is needed to fully understand how people navigate these interactions. Importantly, considering spatial aspects of race on college campuses expands discussions of diversity and inclusion away from the aptly used demographic framing whereby the increase in students of color is a key indicator of whether an institution is considered "diverse" or "inclusive" (this is elaborated on below). Research by Leslie Houts Picca and Joe Feagin (2007), building on Erving Goffman's (1959) dramaturgical work, examines the racialized stages of interaction and challenges the popular notion that the form and levels of racial prejudice among whites has changed in recent decades. Specifically, Picca and Feagin emphasize that social space is racialized and the meanings and use of social spaces are generally controlled by whites. With this in mind, two racialized stages exist: backstages and frontstages.

Racialized backstages refer to spaces where whites conduct racial performances with people they perceive to also be white. Within these spaces, whites have relatively high levels of comfort, learn about racial matters from a white perspective, increase their cultural capital with other trusted whites, and develop their everyday information and skills to gain advantages in different sectors of society (Picca and Feagin 2007, 91–142). Furthermore, whites use their social networks of friends, family, and intimate partners in these racialized backstages to construct their understandings of racial boundaries in society and reproduce racist ideas, sustaining the overarching white racial frame (Picca and Feagin 2007, 91–142; see also Myers 2005). Hughey (2011) also emphasizes the power of backstage settings for white men to reproduce and reinforce understandings of white supremacy and white masculinity in other organizations and informal gatherings. Racialized frontstages are the public, more diverse, and multicultural spaces that have varying histories and character. Examples of these settings are city streets, shopping areas, public parks, and other public-use spaces. They sometimes are referred to as "cosmopolitan canopies" (Anderson 2011).

A "two-faced" quality of interactions among college students was present in Picca and Feagin's research (2007, 19 and 255–256). Specifically, the researchers found whites to participate in racist performances, many times in the form of racist joking, or to communicate their views of racial and ethnic groups through their attitudes, beliefs, and emotions among a group of white friends. Picca and Feagin note that light, "white" skin is the "passport" into racialized backstages, but this does not prevent people of other racial and ethnic groups from some-times entering these backstages if they have lighter skin color (Picca and Feagin 2007, 23–24 and 183–194). The researchers also note the differences in transition to and possible "slippage" from a backstage to a frontstage when people of color are present. In such situations where the racialized backstage and frontstage intersect, whites "switch face" to accommodate the new actors into the space and try to appear colorblind or "nonracist." Picca and Feagin's research among college students found that when a person of color approached the group, white students would shift their discussion to a "colorblind" approach so they would not "appear racist," and would seem to have an innocent conversation (Picca and Feagin 2007, 183–194). This approach to avoid sanctioning or accusations of "being a racist" was also found in Natasha Warikoo's (2016, 113–136) examination of elite college students at Brown and Harvard. When we meld this research with the previous discussion of how the different aspects of race and social interactions have changed over the last century, we see how the context of society, and colleges and universities, can profoundly influence not only social interactions, but also the theoretical perspectives developed to understand these interactions.

As noted throughout this volume, the history of American higher education is one of exclusion and elitism rather than equity and inclusion, privileging white students from higher socioeconomic backgrounds and social networks, and it was founded for such groups of students (Bowen, Kurzweil, and Tobin 2005; Espenshade and Radford 2009; Karabel 2005; Soares 2007; Thelin 2004; Wilder 2013). This history is amplified by aspects such as the use of standardized tests for college admissions, originally developed to prevent Jewish and black students from entering the elite echelons of American higher education (Soares 2007). Ironically, using these tests can influence students to believe in a "color-blind meritocracy" and the framing of abstract liberalism (Bonilla-Silva 2014, 78–84; also Warikoo 2016, 87–112), whereby they believe everyone who works hard, regardless of race, has an equal chance of doing well enough on college entrance exams to attend any college they wish. Students who enter highly selective colleges such as those included in the current study receive a reaffirming label of the "best and brightest" given their social location within an elite social world reflecting this highly competitive admissions system, which strengthens beliefs that structural inequalities do not have important influences on a person's life chances. Even though the civil rights movement led to many legal and social gains for people of color, once on campus these groups still face racial discrimination and underrepresentation. Therefore, rather than considering the majority of our colleges and universities as "just colleges" that are not "racially tagged" like historically black colleges and universities (HBCUs), these institutions should be considered historically white colleges and universities (HWCUs) (for additional discussions on how colleges and universities are racialized organizations, see Allen, Epps, and Haniff 1991; Bonilla-Silva 2012; Brunsma, Brown, and Placier 2013). This framing explicitly includes those institutions considered "elite" given that their selective admissions are based on exclusivity.

The reframing of the majority of colleges and universities as HWCUs places the appropriate context around social interaction on campus. Often, these institutions are referred to as predominantly white institutions (PWIs) and treated as "benign" settings for people to interact across racial and ethnic lines. It is even now common for colleges and universities to be ranked by their racial and ethnic diversity as a proximate measure for how inclusive these campuses are for students (see Priceonomics 2016). However, such designation only indicates the demographic characteristics of a college, whereas there exists much more on campus that influences social interactions and racial ideologies. As recent student protests across the nation pinpoint, increased racial and ethnic diversity on a campus does not mean it is a "racism-free" campus. HWCUs have particular histories, curricula, symbols, culture, and traditions that privilege white students over students of color (Bonilla-Silva 2012, 184–186). These features create a situation where whiteness is normalized (Lewis 2004), often hiding the negative racial climates containing racial discrimination, restricting students' interactions with each other, and establishing "walls of whiteness" difficult to bring down.[10] The reproduction of whiteness on college campuses is carried into the towns where HWCUs are located, whereby local businesses and people cater to the mostly white student interests (Bonilla-Silva 2012, 184–186). This norm of whiteness creates an "epistemology of ignorance" among white students, who struggle when confronted with the gravity of race and racism in society, particularly in relation to racial disparities.[11] As discussed above, this interlacing of racial and class privilege of elite social worlds embedded within the habitus are critical to the framing of students' social interactions and their racial ideology development during college.

Considering college campuses and the racialized spaces surrounding students, racialized backstages can include dorm rooms, discussions at dining hall tables, and other areas in which people can somewhat seclude themselves from others. Racialized frontstages on campus include athletic locker rooms, bars, classrooms, dining halls, and lawns. This suggests laboratories and other campus facilities used for more experimental intergroup contact research could be considered racialized frontstages, meaning that participants likely modify their interactions with people of other races and ethnicities during studies to align with perceived socially desirable responses. Several aspects of intergroup contact studies in these settings should be considered in relation to how people interact across racial and ethnic lines. First, Kristen Myers found similar racialized stages among college students, and emphasizes that whites still structure the boundaries of social interactions and the understandings of whiteness, blackness, and brownness for students to navigate on campus (Myers 2005, 61–90). That is, the dispositions and patterns of interactions proliferating across an institution can have meaningful impacts on whether students of different groups interact, how they understand such interactions, and what possible changes in views of race and inequality may result from these interactions.

Second, previous research points out the different responses on similar racial attitude items given by college students on surveys compared to face-to-face interviews, whereby they give more "racially progressive" responses on surveys (Bonilla-Silva and Forman 2000). Thus, how college students may respond on campus climate surveys may not necessarily be selecting a true response as much as one that they view as the most socially desirable response on the surveys in order to not appear racist or bigoted. As such, Warikoo (2016, 113–136) and Apfelbaum and colleagues (2008) found white college students' use of colorblind attitudes and behaviors in interracial interactions is situational, which hints at the importance of how students of different races and ethnicities view the spaces available for social interaction on campus. Additionally, as Wendy Leo Moore (2008) notes in her study of law schools, racialized spaces continue into professional schools and even influence whether students of color attend off-campus social events. Moore's research identifies how the hostility toward particular courses such as those focusing on civil rights law can make racialized spaces out of the curriculum, stigmatizing faculty and students and echoing the racial hostility of campuses. The hostility or devaluing of particular recent additions to the college curriculum such as black studies, ethnic studies, and women's and gender studies can then take the form of microaggressions, or subtle slights, toward students in those majors in social interactions, with questions such as "why did you major in *that*?" or "what can you do with *that* major?" (see Solorzano, Ceja, and Yosso 2000; Sue, Capodliupo, and Holder 2008).

Lastly, the "two-faced" aspect of social interaction on college campuses may not function as Picca and Feagin describe, particularly on elite college campuses (Picca and Feagin 2007, 19 and 255–256). Given the intersection of individual and organizational racial habitus surrounding and often scripting student interactions, when we consider white students' limited changes to their racial ideology as a result of social interactions, the frontstage and backstage differentiation may not readily exist for these students at elite colleges. That is, the colleges' habitus reinforces whiteness in conjunction with diversity as individuality for white students to perform regardless of space, providing a colorblind lens to understanding their social interactions, and ultimately, racial inequality. This reinforcement of narrow views of racial inequality further solidifies a racial optic for students to continuously rely on when examining inequalities as the result of what those who are not in their privileged positions must have done wrong, absolving the intertwined influence of elitism and whiteness in these social worlds and beyond (Steinberg 2007, 66–67; also Warikoo 2016; Warikoo and Novais 2015).

When we consider how these spaces are framed by the campus racial climate, we must also note how racial hostility and discrimination is framed within the organizational racial habitus of institutions with both whiteness and the persistence of colorblind beliefs. Researchers have found whites to readily dismiss racist attitudes, statements, and acts by other whites as the isolated actions of bigots, and possibly to point out that the person under scrutiny "has a few black friends" to dismiss their actions (Brunsma, Brown, and Placier 2013; Myers 2005; Picca and Feagin 2007). Such dismissal of racist acts limits the ability of whites to develop cross-race empathy, keeping them detached from the experiences of others, and lines up with the minimization frame of colorblindness (Bonilla-Silva 2014, 91–95). Additionally, the dismissal of racist acts allows the events and discrimination to persist on HWCU campuses and keeps these incidents detached from the larger problem, associating such racist incidents with "individual" issues. The use of colorblind attitudes and behaviors by whites on campus also decreases their negative perceptions of the campus racial climate (see Worthington et al. 2008). Therefore, racist parties and costumes (Mueller, Dirks, and Picca 2007; Wise 2008a, 2008b), the use of racial epithets and slurs on campus as "free speech" (Wise 2008b), and the targeting of racial and ethnic studies programs first during times of financial difficulties (Eaton and White 2010) are dislocated from systemic racism and less likely to register on the "racial radar" of white students. Even more concerning is the framing of these incidents by administrators because they can frame critiques and incidents of racial discrimination as "teachable moments," circumventing the ability to create more equitable and supportive campuses of the increasingly diverse student bodies, even with diversity workshops (Berrey 2015, 55–123; see also Warikoo and Deckman 2014). Utilizing the abstract liberalism frame of colorblind racial ideology allows whites to argue campus administrators should not "force" diversity issues, but should allow interactions to develop more freely, further disconnecting specific acts of racism on campus from historical trends. This reflects similar writings on laissez-faire racism by Lawrence Bobo, whereby whites argue for a more free-flowing market dynamic, a "hands-off" approach, to racial issues and interactions (Bobo 1999). Thus, diversity efforts are met with increased levels of racial resentment (Tuch and Hughes 2011) among whites, which exists among white students as seen in the current study as well as others (Berrey 2015, 55–123; see also Warikoo and Novais 2015; Whitt et al. 2001). Furthermore, this hands-off desire leads white students to rationalize their almost exclusively white networks as part of a naturally occurring phenomenon in society and on campus (such as "birds of a feather flock together"; McPherson, Smith-Lovin, and Cook 2001), rather than specific segregating choices. As found in the current study, a racial hierarchy exists on campus that is not simply the product of student choices, but an embedded pattern of social interaction. Returning to the intersection of individual- and organizational-level habitus with one another framing elite college students' interactions, these racialized spaces and the current era of colorblindness hinder the ability to create an inclusive campus environment, to reduce prejudice among students, and ultimately to bring down the spatial, curricular, and ideological walls of whiteness on campus (Brunsma, Brown, and Placier 2013).

The limited influence of social interactions across race and ethnicity is arguably attributable not only to the racial hierarchy that exists on campus, but also to how students befriend others while in college. As Stark's (2015) recent analyses indicate, children with higher levels of prejudice will not only avoid befriending peers of different races or ethnicities, they will also avoid befriending same group peers who are friends with peers of different races or ethnicities. Thus, elite college students could create buffer zones in their social networks from not only outgroup members, but also those ingroup members who are considered "fringe" in their beliefs or social interactions (i.e., group members with more outgroup friendships). When we add in recent research indicating that students enter college with low desires for and expectations of interacting with students of color during college (Espenshade and Radford 2009, 389; see also Pryor et al. 2007), and that campuses allow students plenty of opportunities to avoid each other so they do not have to interact with someone of a different race or ethnicity (Picca and Feagin 2007, 91–142) or from a different social class position, then the interactions likely taking place across racial lines may often be superficial and limited in duration at best. Moreover, HWCUs such as nearly all of the institutions examined in the current study allow racialized backstages to persist in many forms, giving white students the opportunity to continue using racist framings and conceptions of people of color, and separating those friends they do have of different racial and ethnic groups by using the ultimate attribution error (Pettigrew 1979). Also, given the racial privilege of whites who buttress the racial hierarchy of social interactions on campus, when students enter more public frontstages on campus, another aspect of social interactions must be considered in relation to the campus climate. This is most obvious when we consider the influence of metastereotypes and microaggressions (Shelton and Richeson 2006; Shelton, Richeson, and Salvator 2005; Solorzano, Ceja, and Yosso 2000; Sue, Capodliupo, and Holder 2008; Torres and Charles 2004; Tropp 2007) related to the campus racial climate (Hurtado et al. 1999) and indicative of the particular organizational racial habitus of elite institutions. Microaggressions are misinterpreted and often thought of as "small" given the wording, but it actually means they occur on an individual level. Here, everyday racial slights towards students of color reinforce racism through verbal and nonverbal forms. In metastereotype situations, students of color are familiar with racial stereotyping about their groups, and skeptical about their interactions with whites with this in mind, which influences their participation in cross-race interactions and how much any person in these situations learns from peers. In relation to metastereotypes, it is important to note that students are skeptical of a person not because of their racial appearance, but because of continued experiences with racism on and around campus, which influences their views and social interaction decisions.[12]

With this in mind, if a racist incident occurs on campus, students of color may wonder if they would be supported by the administration with quick and appropriate action. Doubts can undermine the formation of sustained cross-race interactions and modify their views of race and inequality. Pettigrew and Tropp suggest support by authorities or institutional support for intergroup contact situations is perhaps the most important condition for reducing prejudice (Pettigrew and Tropp 2011, 69–72). In light of this, the extent of support for cross-race interaction and equality among all racial and ethnic groups within the context of a racialized environment such as an HWCU campus is important to consider. The misinterpretation of intergroup contact discussions—that interaction in and of itself will reduce prejudice—still exists (see also Pettigrew 1998), and this reality at HWCUs suggests that simply bringing students of color to campus will not address systemic racism and structures of inequality. The authority figures at these institutions need to disassemble these long-held structures and cultures on campus; doing so could increase the positive effects of interracial interaction and also increase the sense of belonging of students of color.

All of this points to the power of the intersected individual and organizational racial habitus of elite college students in the emerging era of colorblindness. The beliefs in a colorblind meritocracy, which limit people's understanding of structural inequality and how much people actually achieve "on their own," strengthen the cognitive aspects of racial prejudice. These beliefs are further solidified by young elites' view of themselves as diverse individuals who are the "best and brightest" (Khan 2011; Khan and Jerolmack 2013; Warikoo 2016), which is buoyed by elite colleges' views and privileged interactions with them as well (Berrey 2015; Bowen and Bok 1998; Bowen, Kurzweil, and Tobin 2005; Espenshade and Radford 2009; Karabel 2005). The meta-analysis conducted by Pettigrew and Tropp (2011) points to a disturbing trend in intergroup contact studies, which is possibly a direct result of our changing eras of racial dynamics surrounding elite college students. The influence of cross-group interactions on the beliefs and stereotypes representing cognitive measures of prejudice has fallen over the last several decades, while such interactions have increasingly influenced measures of affective prejudice (i.e., favorability and emotions) (Pettigrew and Tropp 2011, 97–114). One interpretation of such findings relating to race is that the limited integration in social spaces following the civil rights movement has increased people's closeness to people of other races and ethnicities, but has not fully changed their beliefs and stereotypes about those groups. Additionally, fewer people may be willing to identify themselves with the Jim Crow style of bigotry, which could lead to a minimization of the importance of cognitive racial prejudice. If we consider the current era of colorblindness and the deemphasizing of race by focusing on diversity as individualism, then these findings make disturbing sense. The current study suggests the habitus surrounding life in elite social worlds is a possible driver of how elite college students racially identify, what they understand these group memberships to mean, how frequently and in what ways they interact with peers during college, and what impact these identities and interactions can have on their racial ideology following college graduation.

Taken together, what do the current study's findings mean for the use of intergroup contact theory today, particularly as it relates to the study of elite college students? That is, do the many non-findings indicate the need to disregard this theory of cross-group interactions and how they influence a person's beliefs about race? Put simply, no, they do not, but we need to look further into the contexts influencing social interactions where power and inequality exist in relation to race. Throughout this volume's analyses, social interactions had many influences on elite college students' racial prejudice, which is central to intergroup relations research. However, the complex set of cultural and structural realities surrounding social interactions, beliefs about race and identity, and how colleges and universities operate from a particular racial habitus establish a difficult situation to transform for students' education, both academically and socially. In order to establish equitable and inclusive campuses, not simply ones that are diverse in relation to the demographics, we must recontextualize social interactions to focus on the institutional structures supporting racial hierarchies of interaction. That is, to understand ideologies and interactions, we must understand the conditions, and avoid obscuring the sociohistorical aspects of relationships, which includes power and privilege (Steinberg 2007, 81–84). This reality was noted over 50 years ago by esteemed social psychologist Thomas Pettigrew: "I think one of the great fallacies we have had in the field of race relations for many, many decades has been to worry about attitudes rather than about conditions. It is a crude but, I think, generally correct statement to say that attitudes are more often a result than a cause of most of our race-relations situations" (Pettigrew 1966, 312). Given that this research area is built on the study of reducing prejudicial views, what is in need of further research is how cross-group interactions could be structured differently to break down detrimental views of how racial inequality manifests in society, and what should be done to create a more equitable and socially just society. Young elites often do not experience situations challenging their views about racial inequality; thus, identifying how interactions could do just that is important. Such a process would most likely not be linear in progression, and similar to some of the findings for taking ethnic and gender studies courses and diversity programs for students to engage in conversations about race and inequality (Warikoo 2016, 63–85; also Warikoo and Deckman 2014), may create situations making students uncomfortable with modifying how they understand racial inequality within and outside of their elite social worlds. However, both cultural and structural changes are simultaneously needed on campuses to modify the racial ideologies of students that reinforce racial inequality in the broader society (see Pettigrew and Martin 1987).

CONCLUSION

This volume concerns itself with what is often referred to as the study of "race relations." However, this is a misnomer that construes power dynamics and important contexts in society and college campuses relating to race and racism (Steinberg 2007). The reality on elite college campuses is not of an institution bringing together a broad range of racially and ethnically diverse students interacting with each other in racial harmony, as is often portrayed by elite colleges themselves (Berrey 2015, 79–123; also Warikoo 2016). Rather, a racial hierarchy of social interaction marking the intersection of the individual and organizational racial habitus structures students' interactions, reinforcing narrow perspectives of race, identity, and inequality. The racialized spaces on campus buttress this reality, and the ethos of "the best and brightest" familiar in educational institutions of the elite social world (Bourdieu 1996; Khan 2011, 2015; Khan and Jerolmack 2013) interlaces students' experiences, limiting not only their interactions, but what they take from these interactions and relate to discussions of racial inequality in the broader social world. As the concluding chapter discusses, this reality among elite college students may support the continued growth of racial inequality on these college campuses, but also in broader society heavily shaped by graduates of these institutions.

6 · INTERACTING FUTURES AND THE REPRODUCTION OF RACIAL INEQUALITY

The discussion of how elite college students interact and how these interactions do or do not influence their views of race and inequality provides a cautionary note for the oft-told narrative around the college-going experience. Many times, family and friends relay the belief and value of attending college based on the opportunity to meet peers from differing backgrounds and perspectives on the world, enhancing the student's education (Byrd 2015). This perspective of the diverse interactions as part of the college experience is used in what is described as the "educational benefits of diversity" position taken by colleges and universities to sell how diversity is an important part of the academic and social opportunities of their campus for students and the broader society (Berrey 2015, 55–123; see also Smith 2016). Further, research has noted many benefits, including increasing knowledge about cultural, racial, and social issues; increasing student retention and graduation rates as well as academic performance; and many other student outcomes (see antonio and Muniz 2007; Chang 2002; Chang et al. 2003, 2004, 2006; Gurin et al. 2002; Orfield 2001, among others). However, this strongly held perspective can overshadow important cultural and structural issues existing on college campuses that lead to racial discrimination and inequality. Thus, the view that diverse interactions will occur and change the perspectives of a student during college arguably establishes a "sincere fiction," an enduring folktale distorting the history of interactions and institutions shaped by whiteness, overselling the perspective of students having an abundance of opportunities to interact with people who are different from them, while also buffering important considerations of how racial inequality influences who these peers are on campus, and how these interactions may influence their views of race and inequality when they graduate from college.[1] These sincere fictions orient students toward particular views of their elite colleges, their classmates, and their positioning in both the elite and the broader social world, providing a thinly veiled view of, and some would say blindness to, how whiteness intertwines with elitism to shape their campus experiences.

The examination of elite college campuses also provides a cautionary tale for understanding racial inequality in the broader social world and the role these young elites who attend such highly selective and prestigious institutions have in perpetuating such inequality after they graduate. The overwhelming advantages that graduates of these colleges and universities have in graduate school admissions and the workforce (Khan 2012; Rivera 2015) indicate how these students' interactions may hold the key to why a seemingly more racially progressive generation of students (Apollon 2011; Bonilla-Silva 2014; Pew Research Center 2010, 2014) could perpetuate racial inequality despite their educations at institutions that pride themselves on their diversity and academic excellence (Berrey 2015, 73–77). In what follows, I suture the many findings of this volume together to provide a general narrative of the college-going experience of elite college students and how this experience shapes their views of race and inequality when they complete their degrees. Then, I discuss why further consideration of colleges' racial habitus sheds light on how these findings of students' interactions and views are somewhat unsurprising when we consider the mindset of young elites concerning diversity, individuality, and race on these campuses. With this in mind, I discuss the recent protests against racism and inequality on college campuses with a critical eye toward the rhetoric of the "educational benefits of diversity" framing many of these protests, which blinds people from understanding central issues at the heart of these protests. Finally, I consider the importance of pursuing organizational change within elite colleges and universities, and higher education as a whole, to create a more holistic education incorporating social interaction with their coursework to combat the reproduction of racial inequality, specifically by those who graduate from elite institutions.

SOCIAL INTERACTION AND SHIFTING RACIAL IDEOLOGIES DURING COLLEGE

It is important to discuss the major trends found in this study in the college-going experience of elite college students. However, the sheer number of variables and findings across the four student groups included in this study could make this narrative confusing and less informative. Therefore, I provide four general narratives for each elite college student group centering on the four research questions guiding this study in relation to the frequency of social interactions, the form of interactions (i.e., friendship, romantic relationship, roommate, student organization), how students' social interactions related to their racial prejudice and individualism, and how their racialized social identities shaped both their interactions and their views of race and inequality during college.

In order to assist with creating these narratives, I will note what students bring with them to college in relation to their precollege views, race-related social interactions, and general backgrounds shaping these early views. Then I will describe the overall patterns of social interactions for each student group during college. Finally, I will describe what changes occur in elite college students' racial prejudice and individualism, and how social interactions and their racialized social identities influence students' racial ideology as they graduate from college and enter the workforce. Before we proceed, it should be emphasized that these are general narratives for each student group hinging on the central findings relating to their social interactions and identities. As seen throughout this volume, there are many differences not only across elite college student groups, but also within each group regarding their views, identities, and experiences during college. Thus, these narratives should not be taken as rigid and all-encompassing; rather, they provide an orientation to the common experiences connecting members of these groups during their time on elite college campuses.

White Students

Among elite college students, whites entered these institutions as the best-off socioeconomically, having spent their childhoods living in predominantly white neighborhoods and attended high school with mostly white peers. These almost exclusively white social environments corresponded to limited racial and ethnic diversity among white students' friendship networks, as nearly 80% of their friends were also white. Generally, they felt closest to other whites, but moderately so, as students also had somewhat similar levels of closeness to other racial and ethnic groups. These students carried with them low levels of racial prejudice toward blacks and Latinos, viewing them as less capable and hardworking compared to whites. However, white students did not hold the same views of Asians and Pacific Islanders. Instead, whites viewed Asian and Pacific Islander students more favorably than their own group. When it came to their views of racial inequality when they entered college, whites held moderately strongly to the perspective of people of color that they do not achieve more in life through hard work and education and have only themselves to blame.

As students pursued their degrees, they sustained fairly homophilous social networks across different forms of interaction. White students typically befriended other whites with only a few friends from other races and ethnicities. Although they mainly dated white partners throughout college, students also had interracial relationships, particularly with Asian and Pacific Islander partners. White students roomed with nearly all white roommates during college, and most of the student organizations they joined were predominantly white as well. Thus, their social interactions reflected their social environments from childhood throughout college: predominantly white. Whom students were friends with prior to college had a variety of influences on how they interacted with people of color, and with whom, during college. Across these influences a subtle pattern emerges, with more white friendships prior to college shaping white students' interactions into a reified pattern of predominantly white friendships, romantic relationships, roommates, and peers in their student organizations, which often reduces their interactions with others. Although having more friends of different races and ethnicities prior to college can lead to corresponding interactions with those groups, these interactions did not take place with the general exception of a slight increase in white students' interactions with Asians and Pacific Islanders during college. Although white students' racialized social identities had important influences on their racial ideology, the same cannot be said for their racialized social identities' relationship to whom they interacted with during college. Many times, how close they felt to different races and ethnicities when they entered college did not have a bearing on whom they befriended, dated, roomed with, or sat next to in student organizations, although feeling closer to Asians and Pacific Islanders increased white students' interactions with members of that particular group.

When students graduated from college, their views of race and inequality changed in small but important ways. White students did not hold substantial racial prejudice toward blacks and Latinos, as they did when they entered college, having almost nonexistent levels of prejudice toward those groups at the end of college. Their positive racial bias toward Asians and Pacific Islanders increased over college as well. White students' support for individualistic views of racial inequality also decreased throughout college, but they might not fully consider structural inequalities in society. Considering the important influence of racialized social identities shaping white students' views and interactions throughout college, students felt less close toward each racial and ethnic group, with the largest decrease in closeness to their own group. These changes were associated with a variety of experiences during college, with social interactions playing a more prominent role in shaping white students' views of race during college than their views of inequality.

Friendships with different groups during college did not always shape white students' views of race and inequality, but a few trends were evident. Friendships with whites and Latinos during college most consistently influenced white students, as more of such friendships reduced students' prejudice toward blacks and Latinos, while also often reducing their support for individualistic views of racial inequality. Friendships did not always have positive influences on white students' views of race, however, as more white and Asian and Pacific Islander friendships increased their prejudice toward Asians and Pacific Islanders during college. Whom whites dated during college had contrasting influences on their racial ideology when they left college, as students who dated black partners often held less prejudice and less support for racial individualism, while the opposite effect existed for dating

Latino partners during college. More roommate diversity during college generally lowered white students' prejudice toward blacks and Latinos, and often rooming with other whites or Asians and Pacific Islanders decreased their support for racial individualism. For those students who joined mostly white student organizations during college, they had lower levels of prejudice toward all racial and ethnic minorities as well as having less support for individualistic views of inequality toward blacks. However, more memberships in organizations mostly composed of Asian and Pacific Islander students increased white students' support for racial individualism, particularly toward blacks.

The racialized social identities among white students had limited influence on their views of race and inequality when they left college, but two important trends existed that are important for understanding how these students navigated their elite social worlds and related to other groups. First, white students who felt closer to blacks when they entered college also had less racial prejudice toward people of color at the end of college. Feeling closer to blacks at the end of college only influenced white students' support for individualistic explanations of racial inequality toward blacks, reducing their support when they left college. Second, white students who felt closer to other whites before or during college were more prejudiced toward blacks and Latinos when they left college. Additionally, feeling closer to whites at the end of college overwhelmingly increased their support for individualistic views of racial inequality, and feeling closer to whites also increased their support for such views specifically toward blacks. All of these findings indicate the tenuous influence that social interactions have on white students' racial ideology, but also show how these elite colleges are limited in shaping such views while influencing their social interactions more frequently.

Black Students

Black students were often the least well-off socioeconomically when they entered elite colleges and universities. Oftentimes, black students lived in segregated or integrated neighborhoods and attended high schools with similar student compositions, the least likely to live or study in predominantly white communities. Half of black students' friends when they entered college were also black and nearly one-third of their friends were white, owing to the more racially diverse communities they lived in prior to college. Black students felt closest, though moderately so, to other blacks at college entrance, and were much less close to other groups. Black students held low levels of racial prejudice toward Latinos when they entered college, but had slight positive racial bias toward whites and particularly Asians and Pacific Islanders. When students stepped onto campus, they were not completely sold on the perspective that if people of color do not do well in life, it is the result of their individual efforts. They held moderate support for these views, though they were slightly more supportive of this view for Asians and Pacific Islanders' success.

Throughout college, black students were more likely to interact with other blacks than any other racial or ethnic group. A majority of their friends were black, though they did have several white friends on average during college. Black students did not exclusively date black partners, as they often dated white partners as well. Regarding roommates and the organizations they joined during college, black students often roomed with either black or white roommates and frequently joined organizations that were predominantly composed of either group as well. Generally, feeling closer to each race or ethnicity increased black students' interactions with members of those groups during college, while feeling closer to other groups sometimes influenced whether black students formed friendships or dated members of other races and ethnicities. Black students' experiences with more diverse friendship networks prior to college had sporadic impacts on whom they interacted with in college and in what ways they interacted with members of different groups. Although having more friends of each group prior to college often increased diverse interactions, these precollege experiences had the opposite effect for black students' romantic relationships, which suggests that such college interactions may hinge on other contextual information in relation to the campus community that influences whether these students dated partners of different races or ethnicities.

When black students graduated from college, they left with slight prejudice toward whites, but positive racial bias toward Latinos and Asians and Pacific Islanders. These changes were the result of increased prejudice toward both whites and Asians and Pacific Islanders despite the latter group still being viewed more positively than the students' own group. Black students were also less supportive than they had been at college entrance for individualistic views of racial inequality. Regarding their racialized social identities, black students were somewhat less close to all groups at the end of college, but continued to feel moderately close to other blacks. Although racialized social identity was an influential factor for how black students developed their early views of race and inequality prior to college, this was not the case when they left college, as their racialized social identities rarely influenced these views. However, black students' social interactions throughout college did substantially influence their racial prejudice, but it was not nearly as influential on their views of racial inequality.

Most social interactions during college influenced black students' prejudice toward whites and Asians and Pacific Islanders, with fewer effects on their prejudice toward Latinos. Although social interactions during college less frequently influenced black students' views of racial inequality, most interactions impacting their views reduced their support for racial individualism. In relation to their friendships during college, more friendship diversity corresponded to higher levels of prejudice toward whites and Asians and Pacific Islanders. Whom black students dated during college had contrasting influences on their racial prejudice and views of inequality. Students who dated Latino partners often had higher racial prejudice and more support for individualistic views of inequality overall, while black students who dated Asian and Pacific Islander partners often had less prejudice and were less supportive of individualistic views of racial inequality. Dating white partners decreased black students' prejudice toward whites, but increased their prejudice toward Latinos and Asians and Pacific Islanders. In relation to dating other blacks, students often had less prejudice toward Latinos and more prejudice toward whites and Asians and Pacific Islanders, and were generally less supportive of racial individualism. Black students who had more roommate diversity during college were less prejudiced toward Latinos when they graduated, while rooming with other black students reduced their prejudice overall. The composition of black students' organizational memberships was also important for shaping their prejudice toward different groups, as more memberships in predominantly white student organizations reduced their prejudice toward whites, while more memberships in predominantly black and Latino student organizations decreased their prejudice toward whites and Asians and Pacific Islanders.

The racialized social identities among black students sporadically influenced their racial ideology, and were not limited to their end-of-college evaluations of how close they felt to each group, as their early levels of closeness to groups also factored in to their end-of-college views. When black students reflected on how close they felt toward multiple groups at the end of college, feeling closer toward whites lowered their prejudice toward both whites and Asians and Pacific Islanders. Moreover, feeling closer toward whites lessened black students' support for individualistic views of racial inequality when considering people of color as a whole. Students who felt closer toward Asians and Pacific Islanders at the end of college were less prejudiced towards Latinos and Asians and Pacific Islanders. Generally, black students who felt closer toward other blacks when they entered college were less prejudiced toward both whites and Asians and Pacific Islanders as well. These same students were also less supportive of racial individualism. However, black students who felt closer toward whites when they entered college were more supportive of individualistic views of racial inequality when they left college. When taken as a whole, the social interactions during college are an important influence on black students' racial ideology when they graduate, and their racialized social identities play a subtle role in shaping their interactions and racial ideology.

Latino Students

Latino students were from similarly less well-off socioeconomic backgrounds compared to black students who entered elite colleges and universities. A majority of Latino students lived in predominantly white communities prior to attending college, but these residential situations only corresponded to a slight majority of them attending high schools that were predominantly white. Additionally, these students were more likely than other student groups to study in racially integrated schools. These fairly diverse communities shaped Latino students' precollege friendships, as only one-quarter of their friends identified as also Latino, while slightly more than half were white, with the remaining friends almost evenly split between blacks and Asians and Pacific Islanders. Although Latino students entered college feeling closest to their own group, they were only moderately so, and were similarly close to other racial and ethnic groups. Latino students generally held low levels of racial prejudice toward blacks at college entrance, but they held positive racial bias toward whites and Asians and Pacific Islanders. When students entered college they were moderately supportive of the view that racial inequality was mostly the result of individual efforts, with the strongest support for this view for explaining Asian and Pacific Islander success.

Latino students had the most diverse social interactions throughout college compared to other students. A majority of their friends were white, and they had friendships across race and ethnicity with others as well, not only among other Latinos. They frequently dated across racial and ethnic lines, not showing a preference for partners of a certain group. Reflecting the campus environment, most of their roommates were white, as were most of the students in the organizations they joined during college. Oftentimes, Latino students' social interactions drew on experiences with their precollege friends and their racialized social identities. Students' racialized social identities influenced their social interactions with the exception of their student organization memberships. Generally, feeling closer to a group corresponded with more frequent social interactions during college among Latino students. Although feeling closer to different groups did not necessarily mean Latino students would not interact with another group, a persistent finding was Latino students' closeness to blacks, and Asians and Pacific Islanders often had the inverse effect on those interactions. That is, the closer Latino students felt to blacks when they entered college, oftentimes the fewer interactions they had with Asians and Pacific Islanders, and vice versa. Regarding their friendships prior to college, Latino students often had fewer interactions with people of color and more interactions with whites even though they had racially diverse friendship networks when entering college.

Latino students left college with lower levels of prejudice and less support for individualistic views of racial inequality compared to when they entered college. Latino students held less prejudice toward blacks, but had positive racial bias toward whites and Asians and Pacific Islanders. Students did not necessarily feel any closer to Asians and Pacific Islanders or other Latinos at the end of college, but were slightly closer toward blacks and less so toward whites. Latino students' racial ideology at the end of college was shaped frequently by their social interactions. These social interactions during college were more influential on their racial prejudice than on their racial individualism. More diversity in college friendships often increased Latino students' prejudice toward whites and Asians and Pacific Islanders, with little influence on their views of racial inequality. Whom students dated while in college differed in how these interactions impacted their racial prejudice and views of inequality. Latino students who often dated other Latino partners were more prejudiced by the end of college and more supportive of racial individualism, but those students who often dated Asian and Pacific Islander partners were less prejudiced when they left college. Although frequently dating black partners during college increased Latino students' prejudice toward whites and Asians and Pacific Islanders, it decreased such prejudice toward blacks while also decreasing their support for individualistic views of racial inequality. More roommate diversity reduced Latino students' prejudice toward blacks, with some contrasting effects relating to their prejudice toward whites. However, having more black roommates during college increased students' support for racial individualism, while frequently rooming with other Latinos and Asians and Pacific Islanders during college decreased support for individualistic views of racial inequality. Latino students who joined more student organizations composed predominantly of one group or another, particularly white and other Latino students, were less prejudiced when they left college. Similarly, students who were members of mostly white or black student organizations were less supportive of individualistic views of racial inequality.

Latino students' racialized social identities were not as influential as their social interactions on their racial ideology. However, their identities still shaped their views in important ways, particularly how they related to whites and the continual influence of their precollege identity development. Latino students' levels of closeness at the end of college often influenced their prejudice in contrasting ways toward whites and Asians and Pacific Islanders, while their connections to whites prior to and during college greatly influenced their support for racial individualism. Students' closeness toward blacks when they entered college often reduced their prejudice toward whites and Asians and Pacific Islanders, while feeling closer toward Asians and Pacific Islanders increased their prejudice toward these two groups. In relation to their support for individualistic views of racial inequality, Latino students who felt closer toward whites prior to and during college were much more supportive of racial individualism when they graduated. Their connections to other Latinos at the end of college and blacks prior to stepping foot onto campus played a lesser role in shaping their views of inequality, as feeling closer to these two groups somewhat reduced their support for racial individualism when they left college. In summary, Latino students were integrated into campus life in many ways, with numerous influences on their racial ideology at the end of college. For these students, social interactions, when compared to their racialized social identities, were more integral to shaping their racial prejudice and support for racial individualism compared to other students.

Asian and Pacific Islander Students

Asian and Pacific Islander students entered elite colleges in a socioeconomically well-off position. Most students lived in predominantly white neighborhoods and also attended predominantly white high schools. In line with other students of color, half of Asian and Pacific Islander students' precollege friends were white, while slightly more than one-third of their friends were other Asians and Pacific Islanders. Students felt closest to other Asians and Pacific Islanders, but moderately so, and were similarly close toward whites and slightly less close toward other groups when they entered college. Asian and Pacific Islander students held low levels of racial prejudice toward all three outgroups when they entered college, the only student group to do so. In relation to their early views of inequality, these students were moderately supportive of the view that people of color only have themselves to blame for not achieving more in life, and were more supportive of this view for their own group.

Asian and Pacific Islander students typically interacted with whites or other Asians and Pacific Islanders during their college experience. A majority of their friends were either whites or Asians and Pacific Islanders; most of their romantic relationships, and their roommates and peers in their student organizations, were also members of these two groups. Many of the characteristics and experiences that shape Asian and Pacific Islander students' social interactions during college often hinged on interacting with whites and Asians and Pacific Islanders, while a common link seemed to exist between blacks and Latinos among their interactions. Students' racialized social identities, while shaping Asian and Pacific Islander students' social interactions in varying ways, reflected an important relationship and their connections with whites. For these students, feeling closer to whites not only increased their interactions with whites in varying capacities during college, it also reduced their interactions with other Asians and Pacific Islanders. The reverse effect existed for closeness to other Asians and Pacific Islanders. Precollege friendship diversity often corresponded to increased diversity in social interactions among Asian and Pacific Islander students, as more friendships with members of each group increased interactions with such groups, with the overarching exception of romantic relationships. In this case, precollege friendship diversity limited Asian and Pacific Islander students' romantic relationships with people of color in college, but generally increased their relationships with white partners.

When Asian and Pacific Islander students graduated from college, they held lower levels of prejudice and racial individualism than when they first stepped onto campus. However, these students still held racial prejudice toward whites, blacks, and Latinos. Asian and Pacific Islander students were generally closer to other students of color when they left college and less so toward whites. For these students, social interactions during college prominently influenced Asian and Pacific Islander students' views of race by the time they graduated. Although these aspects of campus life were also important for shaping students' views of racial inequality, they were much less influential compared to the impact they had on students' racial prejudice. Additionally, Asian and Pacific Islander students' racialized social identities influenced their racial prejudice at the end of college, and to a lesser degree, their support for racial individualism.

Asian and Pacific Islander students' friendships presented a complex set of social interactions shaping their racial ideology during college. More friendship diversity often corresponded with increased prejudice toward whites, while more friendships with whites and Latinos during college reduced students' prejudice toward Latinos. Although Asian and Pacific Islander students' friendships were not as influential on their support for racial individualism, consistently having more white friends during college reduced their support for individualistic views of inequality. Whom Asian and Pacific Islander students dated during college had contrasting influences on their racial prejudice and support for racial individualism, as students who frequently dated black or Asian and Pacific Islander partners were generally less prejudiced and supportive of individualistic views of racial inequality, while students who frequently dated Latino partners were more prejudiced and supportive of racial individualism at the end of college. Students who dated whites during college were less prejudiced toward whites, but more so toward Latinos, and were less supportive of individualistic views of racial inequality. The diversity of Asian and Pacific Islander students' roommates during college was highly influential on their views of race at the end of college, as more racial diversity among their roommates consistently reduced their prejudice toward other groups. Students' roommates were less influential on their views of racial inequality, as Asian and Pacific Islander students who more frequently roomed with black roommates were more supportive of racial individualism. Also, Asian and Pacific Islander students who joined organizations that were predominantly white or Latino often held less prejudice overall when they left college.

Similar to white students, Asian and Pacific Islander students' racialized social identities were an important part of their lives shaping their racial ideology. Moreover, these influences were not restricted to their connections with one group or another, nor were their identities at the beginning of college trumped by their closeness to groups at the end of college. Students who felt closer toward other Asians and Pacific Islanders at the end of college increased their racial prejudice toward other groups, while feeling closer toward blacks somewhat reduced their prejudice toward whites and blacks. However, their racialized social identities at the beginning of college were much more influential on their views of race than their identities at the end of college. Generally, students who felt closer to other people of color when they entered college were less prejudiced when they left, but those students who felt closer toward whites were more prejudiced toward other groups. Asian and Pacific Islander students' connection with whites was the prominent influence among their identities on their end-of-college views of racial inequality. Students who felt closer toward whites at the beginning of or during college were more supportive of individualistic views of racial inequality when they graduated. Asian and Pacific Islander students who felt closer toward blacks and Latinos at the beginning of college were somewhat less supportive of such views of racial inequality at the end of college. Taken together, Asian and Pacific Islander students are impacted by their social interactions while at elite colleges. These experiences shape their racial ideology in important ways, and their racialized social identities are important to these views as well.

These four general narratives describe the paths students take while they navigate the social world of elite colleges, and indicate how their social interactions during college influence their views of race and inequality. These narratives also indicate how limited social interactions can be on students' racial ideologies, particularly for white students, which suggests that a focus solely on social interactions and their associated effects does not present the broader picture of social interaction and inequality in these worlds. The campus environments are not restricted to whom students interact with or how they interacted with them during college, nor are these campuses constrained to influencing students' views of race and inequality. The simultaneous set of cultural and structural influences represented by institutions' racial habitus can directly and indirectly shape students' social interactions, and limit the influences of social interactions on students' racial ideology, particularly regarding racial inequality. Given this context, students consider group relationships, their connections with such groups, how these patterns play out on their college campuses, and what this means for broader understandings of race and inequality. As I summarize below, a fuller consideration of the culture and structure of these college campuses brings to light why students' social interactions in college may not influence their views by the time they leave college and enter the workforce.

"RACE RELATIONS" AND THE REPRODUCTION OF INEQUALITY

The four narratives of race, identity, and social interaction among elite colleges given above may appear fairly positive, as social interactions did have important influences on students' views of race and inequality, reducing prejudice and individualistic views of inequality on occasion. However, these interactions were only partially successful, as most social interactions among students had no influence on their racial ideologies, and increased their prejudice and support for individualistic views of racial inequality at times. The elite colleges and universities examined in this study influence their students' outcomes from their initial contact around applications to when students enter their halls of academic and social pursuits. Through their organizational habitus, the ideal or prototypical student "fitting" on campus reflects the institution's alums in many ways, buffering young elites from fully relating their experiences and educations in the elite social world with broader society before they even enroll in courses. Once on campus, the intersection of individual and organizational racial habitus structures the interactions that students have with one another and their perceptions of the campus at large, which ultimately limits their knowledge of how race and inequality function in society. The "ease of privilege" surrounding these social interactions, even those across racial and ethnic lines, allows students to rationalize inequality using narrowly tailored views of individuality, diversity, and meritocracy. The characteristics of their campuses heighten the availability bias (Khan 2011; also Khan 2015; Khan and Jerolmack 2013) of elite college students and arguably increase the likelihood of committing an ultimate attribution error (Pettigrew 1979) when confronting information or experiences that counter their beliefs of why and how racial inequality exists in society. That is, the organizational habitus of elite institutions structures particular experiences and situations around students, extending similar experiences from their childhoods in elite social worlds and further hindering their education about the social world outside of the classroom.

Though the racial and ethnic diversity of elites has increased in recent decades (see an overview by Khan 2012), the early experiences young elites have with highly successful people of color in these elite social worlds can establish the perception of these individuals as an exception to a rule of racial inequality in broader society, because only highly intelligent and hardworking people are able to achieve such high status positions in their minds: a highly individualistic view shaping their perception of themselves as part of the "best and brightest" (similar findings are noted in Warikoo 2016). The dramatically lower number of students of color on elite college campuses can then be viewed as a result of a meritocracy, negating any evidence that racial discrimination or inequality on campus or in broader society exists and influences who sits next to them in the classroom. The limited interracial contact effects, particularly on students' views of racial inequality, in this study are arguably a result of this availability bias and ultimate attribution supported by elite colleges' racial habitus, which allows students to navigate these social interactions with ease from their privileged positions. They rarely find themselves in situations not justifying their views of race and inequality, and they possibly avoid uncomfortable situations altogether so as to not appear "racist" (the active avoidance of uncomfortable situations around race and inequality is noted by Warikoo 2016, 113–136; see also Apfelbaum, Sommers, and Norton 2008).

Elite colleges and universities educate students who are engaged in an intricate dance between conceptions of identity and inequality framing their interactions and what they take away from them during college. As evidenced in this study, elite college students held low and somewhat loose identification with their racial or ethnic group, and oftentimes this extended to their connections with other groups. These racialized social identities are multidimensional, as young elites consider their group membership and relationship to multiple racial and ethnic outgroups. Through early socialization around group memberships, elite college students have particular orientations to race and ethnicity that are also framed by the conception of "diversity" as individuality assisting them with further loosening, or decoupling, their connection with racial or ethnic groups. This allows elite college students to avoid general group stereotypes of affiliated racial or ethnic group memberships, but importantly, to preserve the positive view of themselves as individuals. This view of diversity as a group of unique individuals is strongly supported in elite social worlds, and is extended through the legal defense and rhetoric around diversity in higher education, which often announces that anyone can be "diverse" when you consider unlimited characteristics, making the concept amorphous and nearly without measure (Berrey 2015, 55–123; also Khan 2011; Khan and Jerolmack 2013; Warikoo 2016, 87–112). As argued throughout this volume, the ability to rely on racially individualistic views of not only inequality but identity as well is supported by the habitus of the elite social world inexplicitly intertwined by whiteness, in which such views of individuality and diversity are built.

With this in mind, we have to ask: What sort of "relations" occurs on elite college campuses across racial and ethnic lines? The limited effects of social interactions suggest that elite college students are not necessarily interacting with peers much different from themselves, particularly in relation to social location. As described in Chapter Two, the students attending the institutions examined in this study come from better socioeconomic positions than most students in higher education. When we combine these similar class locations with the belief in diversity as individuality among elite, high-achieving students, then the answer to the question may hinge on the belief of individuals who are wholly accountable for their actions and outcomes in a colorblind meritocratic world. Such reliance on racial individualism can be used by these students to deny discrimination and inequality in the elite and broader social world. For example, if a black student describes to a white student an experience where they were discriminated against by a teaching assistant in a biology class by not receiving any feedback on a test unlike their mostly white classmates, even though they all performed poorly on the test, the white student could rationalize this situation as one in which the student did not deserve such feedback because they performed poorly. That is, the reliance on highly individualistic conceptions of identity and inequality form around social interactions to justify racial discrimination, in this case as simple poor performance or lack of effort on the part of the black student. Race is argued not to be an excuse for the student performing poorly on the test as that *individual* student performed poorly and should do better in the class on their own. The rationalization dismisses the fact that only the black student who performed poorly did not receive feedback from the teaching assistant in the class, but the white students who also performed poorly did receive such feedback, which can influence their progress in the class, ultimately perpetuate racial disparities inside the particular class, and contribute to the underrepresentation of scientists of color in the field produced by that institution as a whole. The black student's experience is not viewed as an example of discrimination in the colorblind era, simply an individual failure. The white student, on the other hand, could go about their day thinking about the interaction as simply one student who "couldn't hack it among the best and brightest"; that an individual was without the capability to succeed, not that the opportunity structure was restricted for them on a campus where the institution and students construct the organizational racial habitus as one of equal opportunity for only the most deserving and highest-achieving students.[2] Thus, the racial hierarchy of social interaction on college campuses not only limits the amount of interaction between different student groups, but also limits the opportunity to fully consider their peers' experiences as part of their own college experience, given the framing of race and inequality within and outside these elite social worlds. This example of two college students interacting and dismissing racial discrimination and broader patterns of inequality on campus is missed by the common framing of social interactions, in college and society at large, without the important consideration of power and history shaping such interactions (see Steinberg 2007).

Graduates of these highly selective institutions disproportionately have access to influential positions in a variety of sectors of society, from business and law to politics (Binder, Davis, and Bloom 2016; Domhoff 1978; Khan 2012; Rivera 2015; Zweigenhaft and Domhoff 1991). However, the circumscribed interactions on campus limiting their understanding of race and inequality also create blind spots for many young elites, as the organizational habitus of elite colleges is not assisting with increasing students' "cultural toolkits." These toolkits provide students with culture as a resource to draw upon varying habits, skills, and styles to make sense of their world and support their decisions or "strategies of action" (Swidler 1986). When we contextualize these toolkits to the findings of the current study, it is apparent that elite colleges are often constrained by their organizational habitus to reinforcing the habitus that students bring with them to college and helping them conform to particular approaches of race, diversity, and individualism rewarded by the institution, which does not allow students to fully expand their toolkits for understanding racial inequality (how elite institutions can shape students' racial ideology and perceptions of social interaction is also noted by Warikoo 2016, 63–86). Although these institutions often provide many curricular opportunities to learn about global inequalities, students are not frequently linking how the content of these discussions is manifest in their everyday lives through their social interactions, or how they themselves may perpetuate these inequalities given their privileged social positions. It is at the intersection of culture and structure that the importance of the habitus for shaping the daily lives and perceptions of inequality among elite college students comes into view. As these students often interact with peers from similar social locations, they can build off of the individuality as diversity perspective to eschew the realities of racism today both on and off campus in favor of the mythical colorblind meritocracy. However, although elite college students may not always view racial inequality as important to their everyday lives, this does not mean all students on these college campuses are not thrust into the reality that racial discrimination and inequality influences their paths through life. As noted above and detailed in the previous chapter, elite colleges are intertwined with whiteness, making these institutions difficult places for students of color to navigate.[3] Although previous research identifies the different approaches that students of color as well as lower socioeconomic students use to refine their cultural toolkits to navigate these elite social worlds, which were designed to perpetuate white privilege and racial inequality (Armstrong and Hamilton 2013; Gaztambide-Fernandez and DiAquoi 2010; Jack 2016), recent events on college and university campuses across the nation remind both students and institutions that one tool for combatting racism and racial inequality on campus and in broader society is protest for social justice.

PROTESTING THE EVERYDAY LIFE OF CAMPUS RACISM

With what seemed like a slow creep and then a sudden pounce on the nation's consciousness, the fall of 2015 witnessed a level of student activism and protest not witnessed since the 1960s and 1970s. Although these protests were not necessarily new, the sheer force that students of color, particularly black students, wielded to call attention to the structural inequalities and everyday racism interlacing their campuses and daily lives put campus administrators on notice that speaking to "diversity" and "inclusion" was not enough; things needed to change (Pauley and Andrews 2015). The use of social media to support these efforts made these protests visible in ways not seen before, which added further momentum to protestors' efforts by gaining support beyond their campus communities and linking to students protesting racism and inequalities at other institutions. If administrators were not willing to create a more equitable campus for students, as seen at the University of Missouri, the university that was arguably the catalyst for larger nationwide protests by students, then they might be packing their bags and vacating their offices as students exerted round-the-clock pressure on their institutions' administrators to be more accountable for addressing systemic inequalities on campus (Kingkade, Workneh, and Grenoble 2015). Although a glance at the protests could be washed over by cynicism and dismissal, a closer examination of the demands of these student protests indicates how important both structural and cultural changes on campus are in order to create a more equitable environment for both academic and social life for students.

An analysis of the fall 2015 student activists' demands done by researchers at the American Council on Education (ACE) found student demands were centered on campus-wide changes in the areas of policy, leadership, resources, composition of student and faculty bodies, training, curricular offerings, and support services (Chessman and Wyat 2016). The demands examined by these researchers spanned multiple types of institutions and included eight NLSF institutions included in the current study in addition to other Ivy League and highly selective colleges and universities. Considering the demand for increased diversity on campus, over 50% of the demands by student activists focused on increasing student diversity, and fully 80% called for more faculty diversity at their institutions. Students often demanded more institutional support services beyond cultural centers, as they called for more academic and mental health services, indicating that the current services do not meet the needs of all students on campus. Diversity training, particularly for faculty and staff, was a central demand of student activists, as nearly 60% of all demands issued across the nation noted such needs on their campuses. The campus leadership was called upon to increase diversity advocacy on campus and in the larger community, clarify the role of campus police agencies, and revise policies on a number of issues including affordability and hate speech, and it was emphasized that the campus leadership needed to acknowledge the history and current existence of racism on campus. Student activists clearly articulated, again, the need for campus leadership to engage in institutional transformation beyond buzzwords and packaged statements, to create a truly equitable campus.

These calls by student activists for substantive structural and cultural change on college campuses indicate how the "educational benefits of diversity" rhetoric of these institutions can gloss over or dismiss racial discrimination and inequality on their own campuses (Berrey 2015, 55–123; also Byrd 2015). Further, by focusing on college admissions in many legal cases, such as the recent *Fisher I* and *Fisher II* cases, rather than linking college admissions to larger aspects of students' lives after they arrive on campus and once they leave college to enter the larger social world for work, universities miss an important opportunity to strive toward many of their public commitments to be global leaders and improve society. Such responsibility begins on their own campuses and through their efforts within their institutions. University leaders make diversity "marketable" and sell why it is important to education, limiting the examination of other aspects of campus life that could undercut these educational benefits for students (Berrey 2015, 77–123). Importantly, by pushing the "educational benefits of diversity" approach, university administrators focus their efforts for justifying why racial and ethnic diversity is important to the education of white students, and leave untouched the dangerous assumption that students of color automatically benefit from their attendance at these historically white colleges and universities. Moreover, the selling of diversity aids in shifting conversations of meritocracy and inequality away from examining flaws in the college admissions process and reliance on test scores and narrow measures of student achievement, which can leave unexamined the myths about racial inequality and student performance in college (Alon and Tienda 2007; Warikoo 2016). As the recent protests against racism on college campuses show, students of color are battling for not only the opportunity to study at these institutions, but to be considered "worthy," to be fully supported and to matter, by the predominantly white students and faculty. It is also important to note that racism afflicts faculty's lives as well; specific acts of vandalism, symbolic violence, and microaggressions indicate how racism manifests at multiple levels for community members on campus (for a more sociohistorical analysis of racism on one campus linking multiple aspects of the institution, see Combs et al. 2016). Although these campuses vary in their capacity to quickly and effectively address issues of racism and inequality identified by students, it is critical to note that the recent rise in protests signals the resistance and solidarity of students who are finding ways to aspire and achieve despite the constrained realities of their campuses. The findings from the current study support the positioning that multiple avenues must be taken to improve the campus environment for students and faculty of color rather than settling on an either-or approach to tackle race-related campus issues (see Pettigrew and Martin 1987; also expanding conversations of equality and inclusion beyond student demographics to faculty and administrative leadership efforts in Smith 2016). Without significant efforts to tear down the "walls of whiteness" on elite college campuses in addition to all college campuses identified as "historically white colleges or universities" (i.e., institutions with an organizational racial habitus that buoys elitism and white privilege), the future leadership of the business and political world, who disproportionately attend these institutions, will receive educations and experiences that justify their views of individuality and meritocracy, blinding them to understanding how structural aspects of society perpetuate racial inequality without any racists to blame (Bonilla-Silva 2014).

FUTURE EDUCATIONS, INTERACTIONS, AND INEQUALITIES

The examination of how elite college students' social interactions tenuously shape their views of race and inequality sheds light on how difficult it is to undermine a social world built on exclusion and the social interests of a small segment of the population. This difficulty is nowhere seen more clearly than in the limited influence social interactions had on students' support for individualistic views of racial inequality: that the success of people of color is a direct result of their individual efforts to achieve socioeconomic success. Although students were generally less supportive of such views of racial inequality when they graduated college, these findings do not necessarily indicate students are fully aware of the structural realities continually undergirding racial inequality around the globe. Additionally, among elite college students, whites were least impacted by their social interactions during college, while students of color were more readily influenced by such interactions. In light of these findings, pursuing a path toward reconfiguring the racial habitus of elite colleges and universities to provide a broader education on inequality is needed to counteract the perpetuation of racial inequalities on campus and in the future as students enter prominent positions in society. As it currently stands, if institutions with the most resources and opportunities are failing to educate their students on the mechanisms of racial inequality, power, and the importance of history to understanding current circumstances in society, then a fundamental change in how we view race, merit, and inequality must occur not only on these campuses, but also across all of higher education and the broader society.[4]

Elite colleges and universities direct their students toward certain perspectives enhancing elites' interests and positions as a whole, which reinforces racial inequality (Bartels 2008; Bourdieu 1996; Domhoff 1978; Khan 2012). This academic and social education builds on the hierarchy of social interactions on campus, while assisting young elites with crystallizing their views of racial inequality. Despite the demographic changes of elites globally, institutions aligned with the elite social world such as colleges and universities make it advantageous to align oneself with the existing elite establishment's positions and perspectives. As Shamus Khan poignantly notes, even though people of color are increasing in representation among the global elite, they are doing so within the context and structure policed by institutions such as highly selective and prestigious higher education institutions that often require them to commit to such institutional arrangements and positions (Khan 2012). However, although students of color attend many gatekeeping institutions such as highly selective colleges and universities, this does not mean these students successfully join the ranks of the elite, nor does it mean their experiences within these institutions are discrimination-free or healthy for their pursuit of identifying their place within this elite social world (see Charles et al. 2009, 150–204; also Gaztambide-Fernandez and DiAquoi 2010; Jack 2016; Khan 2011; Torres and Charles 2004). The racial inequality manifesting on campus through the social networks is aligned with a racial hierarchy continually privileging white students' education, and ultimately, their advantages in pursuing high-status positions throughout society. As Rivera's (2015) examination of the hiring processes among elite firms in business, consulting, and law shows, students of color continue to be at a disadvantage even when they attend elite colleges and universities, as they are shut out from many status-signaling cultural activities and opportunities that would complement their degrees. The cultural opportunities are signals for recruiters and firms looking to hire those "fitting" their firm's culture, which operates in a vein similar to the organizational racial habitus of elite colleges and universities, selecting employees in this case that fit their mold and leaving little room for organizational change. Thus, the reproduction of inequality is continually buttressed by the colleges and universities held as the vanguard of higher education opportunities and their alumni, ensuring continued elite positioning despite global changes, which include the diversification of the elite themselves (Bourdieu 1996; Bourdieu and Passeron 1990).

Perhaps the most pernicious aspect of the racial habitus of elite colleges and universities is the framing of diversity as individuality noted above. The legal focus around affirmative action lawsuits has buoyed such framing of diversity away from race to one in which almost everyone is considered "diverse"; it can now include "intellectually diverse" people (Berrey 2015, 55–123). The tailoring of diversity as individuality further supports the active work of elites to define and isolate themselves by using framing that supports the belief in a colorblind meritocracy rewarding hard work and intellect (Khan 2011; Khan and Jerolmack 2013; Warikoo 2016, 87–112). As described throughout this volume, this aspect of young elites' racial ideology situates themselves and others as individuals beyond racial discrimination, which further solidifies their belief in their privileged positions and increasing advantages gained in elite social worlds as a result of such a meritocratic and discrimination-free society. When we couple this reality to this study's findings that social interactions, and many times other race-related experiences on campus, had limited influence on students' views of racial inequality, we see why tackling the culture and structure embodied by many policies on colleges campuses is important to educate students on inequality in a variety of ways.

The risk of not attempting to change the racial habitus of colleges and universities and the policies reinforcing this campus reality is the possibility that students may become racially apathetic. That is, given the immense difficulty of reducing racial inequality and the seemingly inevitable reality that such inequality will continue throughout their lives, students may not view this social issue as "fixable" (Forman 2004). As seen in this volume, elite college students reduced their support for individualistic views of racial inequality, but this does not necessarily indicate they fully understand how structural aspects of inequality continue to influence people's lives beyond their individual efforts. Moreover, these findings may hint at the acclimation of young elites to a dangerous view of racial inequality within their elite social world building on the rhetoric of their institutions selling the benefits of diversity for their educations and their economic advantages (Berrey 2015, 78–123; see also Warikoo 2016). That is, if diversity is equated to individuality, and this diversity is important for both education and markets, then racial inequality is ultimately the cost of business, as not everyone can be the CEO of a Fortune 500 corporation. This rationalization blinds students from considering how their own positions, both socially and later in the workforce, may perpetuate racial inequality through colorblind and apathetic complicity. Although these data were collected prior to Barack Obama's taking the oath of office to be president, the findings of this study may only be reinforced in light of recent calls for postracism and the increasing support for individualistic views of racial inequality (Bonilla-Silva 2014, 255–300). The symbolic progress of the first black president provides ample cover for such arguments of individualism, but also allows for other pernicious stereotypes to be used to justify racial inequalities in society. Further, the recent protests on college campuses can be framed as misguided or even as "racist" as people increasingly discuss achievement as an individually attained aspect of life. Making calls for "all lives matter" serves both as a reinforcement for racial individualism, but also white privilege in higher education and society in general. That is, "all lives matter" is arguably the epitome of the diversity as individuality perspective taken in higher education, which readily dismisses broader issues of racial discrimination and oppression facing communities of color on and off campuses, and the policies put forth to tackle such realities.

Elite institutions' approach to diversity and inclusion provides an amorphous set of concepts framing their plans to accomplish their goals (Berrey 2015, 55–77; also Iverson 2012). Through these constructions of diversity, institutions continually frame groups as outside of their institutional norms, while homogenizing group differences and relying on the shared values of groups to build their campus communities (Iverson 2012). That is, institutions rarely examine themselves for why underrepresentation of racial and ethnic groups continues to mark the reality of their students and faculty. Institutions spend many efforts on reformulating policies for access and opportunity such as affirmative action, and perhaps set aside large amounts of money to increase faculty diversity through cluster-hiring initiatives such as in the recent cases at Brown and Yale Universities and the University of Missouri, among others. However, these policy approaches miss the important caveat of intergroup contact theory concerning how contact in and of itself does not reduce prejudicial views (Pettigrew 1998) when applying their approaches to increasing diversity on campus; that is, increased racial and ethnic diversity on campus does not make such campuses "inclusive" nor discrimination-free. When institutions do incorporate particular courses and workshops discussing race and inequality for students to engage in, the approaches taken in these programs can have varying effects on what students learn, including reinforcing their beliefs in meritocracy and framing diversity as individuality (Warikoo 2016, 63–85; also Warikoo and Deckman 2014). Further, the enforcement of nondiscrimination and equal opportunity policies is critical to reinforcing administrative support for not only interracial interactions, which is the crux of intergroup relations research, but also to the reduction and one day the elimination of incidents and perspectives undercutting the values many institutions state in relation to equality and social justice. It is the difficulties in changing access policies targeted by lawsuits, such as affirmative action policies in college admissions, that indicate the importance of uncovering how integral the racial habitus of colleges and universities is to perpetuating racial inequality (see also Alon and Tienda 2007). These attacks are often by people educated at higher education institutions such as elite colleges and universities, who lead efforts to dismantle race-conscious policies in favor of more colorblind approaches hinging on the elite social world's conception of meritocracy and individuality.

Institutional efforts to shift the cultural and structural aspects of everyday life are complicated by the nuances of individual campuses. As this study found, students at liberal arts colleges and private and public research universities often exhibited more or fewer interactions of various kinds, and differed in their views of racial inequality on occasion. Although these individual campus differences were not explored in depth, these differences by institutional type inform how institutional leaders must adjust their approaches to similar efforts to address histories and contemporary realities of racism and inequality on their campuses. Broad brushstroke efforts to address racism and inequality in higher education can go awry unless the specific institutional context anchors such conversations and efforts. For example, recent efforts to document the roles of colleges and universities in the American slave trade are under way on many campuses, including Harvard and Georgetown Universities.[5] In the particular case of Georgetown, university officials acknowledge the sale of 272 slaves in 1838 to sustain the fledgling institution at the time, and have begun steps to situate conversations of racism and inequality throughout the university curriculum in the newly founded Department of African American Studies, and also to offer the same admissions advantages to descendants of the slaves sold by the university as are offered to legacy students (i.e., students whose parents or other family members attended the same institution). However, these efforts are not without criticism of not thoroughly addressing the sociohistorical legacy of the decisions, handling racism on the campus today, or moving closer toward closure of the harm caused to the families descended from the slaves owned and sold by the university (Cottom 2016; New York Times Editorial Board 2016; Swarns 2016). Yale University has also grappled with its history of slavery and pro-slavery connections, specifically in relation to a residential college bearing the name of John C. Calhoun, a pro-slavery leader in US history. A protracted discussion of whether or not to remove the name of Calhoun from the college has sparked protests building off of student activists' demands for administrators to combat racism on campus and to remove a stained-glass picture in a building depicting black slaves working in the fields (Associated Press 2016; Greenberg 2016; Remnick 2016). Yale has pledged $50 million toward faculty diversity efforts to recruit and retain top faculty (Yale University 2015). Yet these efforts are overshadowed by the continuing struggle for equity and inclusion of students of color, which have direct impacts on the university's ability to educate future faculty of color whom they one day may seek to hire through faculty diversity initiatives such as the one they recently began. These two examples indicate the importance of examining the nuances of one's own campus to design policies and other approaches to tackle cultural and structural changes to address racism and inequality on campus, which begins, as this study notes, with understanding how these aspects of institutions intersect and influence students' experiences and views of race and inequality.

Ultimately, the findings from this study shed light on the ongoing reality that race is an integral part of young elites' everyday life during college, informing how they will view racial inequality when they enter high-status positions in the workforce. By relying on loosely coupled understandings of groups and identities, elite college students navigate a social world structuring their interactions, educating them with particular notions of culture and individuality, and shielding them from full awareness of how their own educations make them complicit in perpetuating racial inequality despite perhaps thinking positively of their peers of different races and ethnicities. Arguably, most historically white colleges and universities, elite or otherwise, produce a self-fulfilling prophecy undercutting their own efforts to break down the "walls of whiteness" (Brunsma, Brown, and Placier 2013) and continuing to privilege white students over students of color. The racial habitus of these institutions selects similar students of generations past who are navigating social environments still struggling to fully accept them as equals. The recent protests across the nation indicate racism and inequality continue to be markers of higher education, including at highly selective and prestigious institutions such as those in the current study. Without deliberately remaking aspects of colleges' and universities' racial habitus, little may change the institutions held up as the vanguard of higher education, and we will continue to witness students graduate from institutions learning little from their race-related experiences and interactions, and possibly avoiding particular situations altogether, by relying on their early socialized beliefs about race and inequality to assist them with navigating their social worlds. This reality will perpetuate not only racial inequality in the broader social world, but higher education's role in contributing to such inequality for generations to come.

APPENDIX: METHODOLOGY

The National Longitudinal Survey of Freshmen (NLSF) was originally collected from a sample of first-year students entering 28 of the most selective colleges and universities in the United States during the fall semester 1999 by Douglas Massey and colleagues (Massey et al. 2003). These highly selective colleges were selected based on students' average SAT scores and class ranks, and the institutions' *U.S. News & World Report College Rankings*. Over the five waves that followed this cohort of students until their anticipated spring 2003 graduation, a wealth of data in relation to their social backgrounds, academic and social experiences prior to college, and experiences and perceptions throughout college, both academic and social, were collected. This study employed a variety of quantitative analyses to examine how students interacted with one another across racial and ethnic lines, and how these interactions influenced their racial attitudes and views of racial inequality. The groups of variables included in this study are detailed below, followed by tables presenting the descriptive statistics and reliability measures of scales constructed for use in this study.

MEASURES

The models in the study have eight overarching groups of variables: traditional racial prejudice, racial individualism, social closeness, forms of interracial contact, social characteristics, family characteristics, characteristics of precollege environments, and college-level characteristics.

Traditional Racial Prejudice

Traditional racial prejudice served as one of the dependent variables. Traditional racial prejudice consists of overt beliefs and stereotypes about a racial or ethnic group with a general premise that one group is biologically, and increasingly in recent years culturally, inferior compared to the individual's group. Traditional racial prejudice is often referred to as "biological racism," "Jim Crow racism," and "old-fashioned racism" (Bonilla-Silva 2014; Hughes 1997; Kinder and Sanders 1996). Common among all of these conceptions of traditional racial prejudice are negative beliefs about a group's intelligence and work ethic, and the disdain for interracial dating, marriage, and overall integration of a racial or ethnic group into the same spaces as the dominant racial or ethnic group. Items measuring racial prejudice were collected during Waves 1 and 5, and were included in factor analyses to identify the structure of traditional racial prejudice among college students.

Among each student group, a small set of measures tapped into students' traditional racial prejudice toward outgroups. As an example of these measures, for white students, the items used to create the traditional racial prejudice measures included their ratings of blacks, Asian Americans, Latinos, and whites on four racial prejudice items in Waves 1 and 5. All items were coded to have the negative perceptions of each racial group equal higher scores and included: the perception of group intelligence on a scale of intelligent (1) to unintelligent (7); group work ethic on a scale of hardworking (1) to lazy (7); group preference for welfare on a scale of preference for self-support (1) to preference for welfare (7); and group initiative of sticking to tasks on a scale of stick to task (1) to give up easily (7). A difference score was created for each of these three items in both Waves 1 and 5 by taking the racial outgroup item score and subtracting the white racial group score, giving a difference score of how white college students perceived the three racial outgroups on each item in relation to how they viewed their own racial group (range = −6 to 6). For example, if a white college student rated blacks as a "6" on the intelligence scale and whites as a "5," then the difference score would equal "1," reflecting the lower rating a student gave blacks in relation to whites. Three separate scales were then created by averaging the group-specific difference score items, representing traditional anti-black prejudice, traditional anti-Latino prejudice, and traditional anti-Asian prejudice. A similar process was used to create traditional racial prejudice scales for each racial and ethnic outgroup for black, Asian and Pacific Islander, and Latino students.

Racial Individualism

In the first wave, students were asked their level of agreement (0 = strongly disagree, 10 = strongly agree) on two items each regarding blacks, Latinos, and Asian and Pacific Islanders, stating that (1) a person of each group only has himself to blame for not doing better and needs to try harder to do better; and (2) a person of each group who is educated and does what is considered "proper" will get ahead in society. These two items are similar to other measures of racial individualism and resentment. Moreover, these measures tap into the highly individualistic beliefs that have dominated perspectives of racial inequality since the 1960s across multiple racial and ethnic groups. A scale measuring racial individualism for each racial and ethnic group was created in addition to an overall scale combining the items for all three groups.

Several items were analyzed to identify whether a racial individualism scale could also be constructed from Wave 5. As with the items in Wave 1, students were asked their level of agreement (0 = strongly disagree, 10 = strongly agree) on one item that corresponds to the first wave items used to create the racial individualism scales. Students were asked their level of agreement on items regarding blacks, Latinos, and Asians and Pacific Islanders, stating that a person of each group only has himself to blame for not doing better and needs to try harder to do better. Each of these items served as group-specific racial individualism scales, and similar to the approach used for the Wave 1, an overall scale was created that combines the items for all three groups.

Social Closeness

Generally, "having a particular social identity means being at one with a certain group, being like others in the group, and seeing things from the group's perspective" (Stets and Burke 2000, 226). Several measures in the first and fifth waves of the NLSF were used as proxy measures for students' racialized social identity. In Wave 1, students were asked to indicate how close they felt to ideas of different groups, including poor, middle-class, and rich members of white, black, Asian American, and Latino groups, and how close they felt to young white, black, Asian American, and Latino men and women ("tell me how close you feel to the people in terms of your ideas and feelings about things"; 0 = very distant, 10 = very close). Similarly, in Wave 5 students were asked how close they felt to the ideas of particular racial and ethnic groups, to poor, middle-class, and rich members and college students of the four racial-ethnic groups ("how close do you feel to [racial-ethnic group] in terms of your ideas and feelings about things"; 0 = very distant, 10 = very close). An index was calculated for students' closeness to each group in Wave 1 using the following five items for each group: poor members of each group, middle-class members of each group, rich members of each group, and young men and women members of each group. A similar index was calculated for social closeness to each racial and ethnic group in Wave 5, using the same items for each racial and ethnic group: poor members, middle-class members, and rich members. However, the items asking students about their level of closeness to young men and women of each racial and ethnic group were not included in Wave 5; items asking students how close they felt to students of each group at their college were included in the survey. The closeness items in Wave 1 that measured how close students felt to young men and women of different racial and ethnic groups were included in the Wave 1 closeness scales, with the assumption that students thought of their peers when responding to the questions in Wave 5 concerning separate racial and ethnic student groups at their college. For each group of closeness items in Wave 1 that corresponded to a particular group, the average was taken to create ingroup and outgroup closeness scales. A similar process was conducted for the Wave 5 closeness items.

Interracial and Intraracial Contact

Four forms of interracial contact with each specific racial and ethnic group were measured: interracial friendships, interracial dating, living arrangements, and student organizations. Interracial friendships were measured in Waves 1, 2, 3, and 5. In the first two waves, students were asked how many of ten friends were white, black, Asian and Pacific Islander, or Latino. In these two waves, the proportion of friends for students of each group was calculated by counting the number of friends in each racial or ethnic group and dividing each number by the total number of friends reported, to create proportions of white friends, black friends, Latino friends, and Asian and Pacific Islander friends. In the third and fifth waves students were asked the race of their four closest friends. The proportions of outgroup friendships were calculated in a similar way for the third and fifth waves. These outgroup friendship proportions were used to create composite indexes of friendship with each racial and ethnic outgroup during college. Each specific racial or ethnic group proportion in Wave 2 was added to the corresponding proportion from Waves 3 and 5 and divided by three to create these indexes.

Data on students' dating patterns across racial and ethnic lines were collected in Waves 2, 3, 4, and 5. In each wave, students were asked if they had dated someone in the past year and what their race or ethnicity was. The students could report dating members of the following groups: whites, blacks, Latinos, Asians and Pacific Islanders, and other racial or ethnic groups. Dichotomous variables were created for each group where "1" indicates that the student reported dating someone of that race and "0" indicates that the student did not report dating anyone of that race during that year. A composite index of interracial dating for each racial and ethnic group was created using a process similar to the one used to create the interracial friendship indexes. The index consisted of adding the group-specific dating items in each wave together and then dividing by four (the number of waves the items were asked in).

Data on students' living arrangements were collected during Waves 3 and 4 of the study. In both waves students were asked the number of whites, blacks, Asians and Pacific Islanders, and Latinos who resided in the same residence (0 to 50 individuals). The proportions of roommates of each racial or ethnic group were calculated by dividing the number of roommates from each group by the total number of roommates of the student. Indexes of interracial living arrangements were calculated by adding each specific racial and ethnic group proportion to the corresponding proportion from the other wave and dividing by two.

Data on students' participation in on-campus organizations were collected during Waves 3 and 4. Students indicated the perceived racial or ethnic majority of the group. In Wave 3, students could indicate their membership in eleven student organizations, but in Wave 4 students were only allowed to indicate their membership in two student organizations. In each wave students were asked to identify which student organizations were majority white, black, Latino, Asian and Pacific Islander, and equally integrated. A proportion of student groups that were a majority of each specific racial or ethnic group was created by counting the number of student groups that had a majority of a particular group and then dividing this number by the total number of student organization memberships. An index of interracial student organizations that are a majority of each specific racial and ethnic group was created by adding each proportion from the two waves for each group, and dividing by two. In addition to each form of interracial contact, intraracial (within group) contact was calculated for each racial and ethnic student group in this study using processes similar to those described above.

Ethnic and Gender Studies Courses

As students' views toward racial and ethnic groups different from their own can be influenced by the coursework they take during college, this study considers how many ethnic and gender studies courses they took during college. The total number of courses under African or Afro-American Studies, American Studies, Asian-Mideast Studies, Latin American or Latino Studies, Other Ethnic or Area Studies, and Women's Studies were considered across all waves of NLSF data (range = 0 to 14 total courses).

Racial Diversity Visibility and Commitment

Students were asked their level of agreement about the visibility of the four racial and ethnic groups on their college campus. These items were coded: students who strongly disagreed that a racial or ethnic group was visible on their college campus were coded "0" and students who strongly agreed that a racial or ethnic group was visible were coded "10." Student visibility scores were created by subtracting the visibility of their own racial or ethnic group's visibility on campus from each outgroup. Students were also asked their perception of the commitment by their college to diversity (1 = way too little, 5 = way too much).

Campus Racial Climate

In Waves 2 through 4 the NLSF contained identical measures of the perceived campus racial climate. Ten items from Waves 2 and 3 were selected to measure the campus racial climate. Students were asked how frequently they felt self-conscious when they were with students or faculty because of their race or ethnicity; felt self-conscious on campus because of their race or ethnicity; heard derogatory remarks about a racial or ethnic group from faculty, staff, or students; experienced racial discrimination or harassment on campus; felt they received an unfair grade from a professor because of their race or ethnicity; felt discouraged to speak up (participate) in class by a professor because of their (the student's) race or ethnicity; and felt discouraged by a professor to pursue a particular course of study or major because of their (the student's) race or ethnicity. In Wave 4, several of the questions used in Waves 2 and 3 to measure perceptions of the campus racial climate were collapsed into five questions. The five frequency items were: felt self-conscious since the beginning of the academic year because of their race or ethnicity; were made to feel self-conscious on campus because of their race or ethnicity; heard racial or ethnic derogatory remarks on campus; felt they received an unfair grade from a professor because of their (the student's) race or ethnicity; and felt discouraged to speak up in class by a professor because of their (the student's) race or ethnicity (1 = never, 5 = very often). A scale for each wave for the campus climate was created by averaging the climate items in each wave. These three scales were then added together and divided by three to establish a campus climate scale.

Social Characteristics

Gender was a dichotomous variable (0 = male, 1 = female). Race was a set of four dichotomous variables (1 = member of race, 0 = not member of race) that identify white students, black students, Asian and Pacific Islander students, and Latino students. Interviewers identified a student's skin color on a continuum of very light (0) to very dark (10). Dichotomous variables identified whether students were born in the United States (0 = no, 1 = yes), and whether they identified as Protestant, Catholic, or another religion (0 = no, 1 = yes). Students' religiosity was measured on a scale ranging from "extremely not religious" (0) to "extremely religious" (10). Dichotomous variables also identified whether the student attended high school in the Northeast, Midwest, West, or South.

Family Characteristics

Mothers' and fathers' education ranged from grade school (1) to graduate/professional degree completion (7). Family income ranged from under $20,000 a year (1) to over $200,000 a year (11). Additionally, whether a students' parent(s) owned a home at college entrance (0 = no, 1 = yes) was included in the study's models.

Characteristics of Precollege Environments

Measures of precollege environments and experiences with inter- and intraracial interactions were included in the models. Given the highly segregated school system in the United States, schools and neighborhoods were considered "integrated" if they had less than 30% black and Latino students in the school or residents in the neighborhood. "Mixed" schools and neighborhoods contained more than 30% but less than 70% black and Latino students in schools or residents in neighborhoods. Lastly, schools and neighborhoods were considered "segregated" if they had 70% or more black and Latino students in schools or residents in neighborhoods. A singular scale was constructed for school and neighborhood segregation (1 = integrated; 2 = mixed; 3= segregated).

College-level Characteristics

The proportions of black students, Asian and Pacific Islander students, and Latino students on campus in Wave 4 were entered into each model.

ADDRESSING MISSING DATA

Like most datasets, the NLSF contains missing data. Once the measures were created, a dataset for each racial-ethnic student group was created. Each dataset contained only those data and measures for that racial or ethnic group. The EM algorithm used the group-specific measures to produce more accurate estimates using the characteristics and experiences of each racial or ethnic group and created an imputed dataset to analyze for the purposes of this project.

The EM algorithm is a two-step iterative process to impute or fill in missing observations in a dataset. The first step (the E step) consists of replacing the missing value with a predicted score, which results from a series of regressions where all other variables serve as predictors of the missing value for the variable that contains missing data in each case. The sums, sums of squares, and cross products are then calculated. In the second step (the M step) maximum likelihood estimation produces a covariance matrix and regression coefficients using the raw and imputed data that are used to calculate new estimates for the missing data points for the next E step, when the process begins again. The EM algorithm cycles through these steps until the changes in the covariance matrices resulting from the M step fall below a preset criterion, indicating that the changes are small and trivial (see Duncan, Duncan, and Lu 1998; Enders 2001).

ANALYTIC STRATEGIES

Beyond the descriptive statistics to examine the different characteristics of students, and the factor analyses that aided in the creation of the scales included in the current study's models, hierarchical regressions were tested to assess (1) how the social backgrounds of students informed their racial prejudice levels entering college; (2) how students' social backgrounds, entering racial prejudice levels, and experiences on campus influenced their inter- and intraracial interactions during college; and (3) how inter- and intraracial interactions affected racial prejudice among each racial and ethnic college student group. Analyses of elite college students utilized an imputed dataset using the process noted above, and included 867 whites, 796 blacks, 835 Asians and Pacific Islanders, and 753 Latinos. As noted in Chapter One, only those students who successfully completed their college degrees at the same NLSF institution they entered in the fall of 1999 were included in the current study. Two forms of analyses dominated this study's examination of these three areas of interracial interactions. First, hierarchical regressions were conducted in the study. In hierarchical regression analysis, blocks of independent variables are entered in different models to build to a full model. With each additional block of variables, the amount of variance explained by the additional variables was calculated along with the total amount of variance explained by all of the variables in the model. Furthermore, the changing influence of the independent variables on the dependent variable that occurs with each additional block of variables can be identified through checking the output of results.

Cross-sectional studies, though helpful for examining intergroup contact effects at one point in time, cannot accurately measure sustained intergroup contact effects, which are more influential in reducing racial prejudice. A longitudinal approach to studying intergroup contact effects has advantages over cross-sectional studies because the effects of intergroup contact on racial prejudice tend to accumulate over time. The use of a hierarchical regression allows this study to examine how the effects of interacting across racial-ethnic lines develop using composite indexes of the different forms of interracial contact during college.

The current study analyzed the four racial and ethnic groups separately. This approach was chosen in light of critiques of status attainment research, in which researchers used racial or ethnic groups as "controls" in models, and assumed that the designated paths of influence are the same for individuals despite their race. This approach would not present an accurate account of students' intergroup contact in the college environment. Preliminary analyses explored the possibility of also subdividing by class, but the colleges in the NLSF dataset have limited class variability.

Hierarchical regression models were constructed similar to those in Sidanius and colleagues' study of UCLA students (Sidanius et al. 2008). Two groups of models were estimated: group-specific racial prejudice, and racial resentment. For traditional prejudice toward each racial and ethnic outgroup, the first model contained only the focal racial or ethnic outgroup contact variables: inter- and intraracial friendships in college, inter- and intraracial dating in college, rooming with the specific racial or ethnic outgroup, and participation in student organizations composed of members mostly of the primary racial or ethnic outgroup. The second model contained the focal racial or ethnic outgroup contact variables and the variables in Wave 5 (senior year): scales measuring students' racial or ethnic group visibility on campus compared to other groups, perceived college commitment to diversity, the campus racial climate scale, a scale of racialized social identity measured by social closeness to the racial or ethnic ingroup, and a scale of social closeness toward the specific racial or ethnic outgroup. Other variables included in Model 2 were the measures taken at college entrance such as group-specific racial prejudice, closeness to the racial or ethnic ingroup, closeness to the specific racial or ethnic outgroup, interracial friendships, school and neighborhood segregation, student's skin color, and whether the student was a woman. Also included as control variables were father's and mother's education, family income, the region of the United States where they attended high school, whether the student was an international student, and whether the student identified as a Christian. Model 3 added the four forms of interracial contact for the two remaining outgroups and the friendship proportions from Wave 1 for each group. A similar process was used to estimate a model of racial resentment for each racial or ethnic student group. This model contained all indexes of inter- and intraracial interaction during college, a scale of social closeness to the racial or ethnic ingroup, a scale of social closeness toward each racial or ethnic group in waves 1 and 5, the proportion of friendships during high school with each outgroup, and the same control variables used in the traditional racial prejudice models.

SCALES UTILIZED IN STUDY

As noted above, the current study used several scales to examine the influence of inter- and intraracial interactions on elite college students' views of race and inequality. Below, the construction of the two dependent variable scales for traditional racial prejudice and racial individualism is presented for each of the four racial and ethnic student groups (see Tables A.1 and A.2). Also presented is the construction of the campus racial climate scale, which incorporated several survey measures within and across each wave of the NLSF (see Table A.3). In each table, the means, standard deviations, and Cronbach alphas for each of the reliability analyses are reported.

TABLE A.1   Means, standard deviations of traditional racial prejudice scales

Variable	White	Black	Latino	Asian & Pacific Islander
Anti-white racial prejudice (first-year)[a]	——	.597	.491	.545
Laziness difference score	——	.34 (1.58)	.24 (1.39)	1.00 (1.39)
Unintelligence difference score	——	.02 (.94)	−.20 (.86)	.45 (.82)
Preference for welfare difference score	——	−.52 (1.39)	−.69 (1.45)	.44 (1.07)
Lack of sticking with tasks difference score	——	−.10 (1.60)	−.02 (1.26)	.85 (1.18)
Anti-black racial prejudice (first-year)[a]	.638	——	.421	.659
Laziness difference score	.15 (.90)	——	.19 (.95)	1.07 (1.63)
Unintelligence difference score	.29 (.73)	——	.04 (.53)	.86 (1.19)
Preference for welfare difference score	.61 (1.10)	——	.15 (.82)	1.38 (1.56)
Lack of sticking with tasks difference score	.07 (.92)	——	.09 (.84)	.91 (1.29)
Anti-Latino racial prejudice (first-year)[a]	.659	.346	——	.670
Laziness difference score	.14 (1.08)	−.01 (.98)	——	1.08 (1.70)
Unintelligence difference score	.38 (.88)	.30 (.67)	——	.97 (1.32)
Preference for welfare difference score	.61 (1.17)	.05 (.75)	——	1.40 (1.59)
Lack of sticking with tasks difference score	.16 (.90)	.07 (.93)	——	1.02 (1.31)

(continued)

TABLE A.1   (CONTINUED)

Variable	White	Black	Latino	Asian & Pacific Islander
Anti-Asian racial prejudice (first-year)[a]	.645	.644	.594	——
Laziness difference score	−.81 (1.21)	−.81 (1.63)	−.73 (1.48)	——
Unintelligence difference score	−.45 (.82)	−.61 (1.11)	−.79 (1.24)	——
Preference for welfare difference score	−.31 (.82)	−1.09 (1.52)	−1.07 (1.58)	——
Lack of sticking with tasks difference score	−.70 (1.02)	−.95 (1.58)	−.82 (1.32)	——
Anti-white racial prejudice (fourth-year)[a]	——	.508	.464	.537
Laziness difference score	——	.41 (1.23)	.23 (1.15)	.85 (1.16)
Unintelligence difference score	——	.06 (.65)	−.14 (.70)	.31 (.75)
Preference for welfare difference score	——	−.28 (1.22)	−.35 (1.01)	.37 (1.01)
Lack of sticking with tasks difference score	——	.06 (1.08)	.07 (.94)	.53 (.91)
Anti-black racial prejudice (fourth-year)[a]	.467	——	.474	.696
Laziness difference score	−.04 (.73)	——	.18 (.80)	.80 (1.20)
Unintelligence difference score	.10 (.45)	——	-.01 (.32)	.48 (.92)
Preference for welfare difference score	.22 (.85)	——	.09 (.55)	.78 (1.36)
Lack of sticking with tasks difference score	−.03 (.65)	——	.06 (.57)	.56 (.95)
Anti-Latino racial prejudice (fourth-year)[a]	.478	.453	——	.655
Laziness difference score	−.13 (.93)	−.17 (.85)	——	.70 (1.16)
Unintelligence difference score	.16 (.56)	.08 (.37)	——	.51 (.97)
Preference for welfare difference score	.22 (.86)	−.03 (.47)	——	.73 (1.36)
Lack of sticking with tasks difference score	−.00 (.70)	−.04 (.66)	——	.54 (.91)
Anti-Asian racial prejudice (fourth-year)[a]	.687	.656	.700	——
Laziness difference score	−.78 (1.08)	−.59 (1.26)	−.63 (1.23)	——
Unintelligence difference score	−.38 (.72)	−.46 (.84)	−.59 (.93)	——
Preference for welfare difference score	−.28 (.78)	−.79 (1.37)	−.63 (1.19)	——
Lack of sticking with tasks difference score	−.45 (.86)	−.55 (1.16)	−.61 (1.02)	——

NOTE: Nonimputed NLSF data used to create scales; difference scores with the ingroup score given by specified group in each column was subtracted from target outgroup for each item. Standard deviations noted in parentheses.

[a] Cronbach alpha listed for each racial and ethnic group scale of traditional racial prejudice.

TABLE A.2   Means, standard deviations of racial individualism scales

Variable	White	Black	Latino	Asian & Pacific Islander
Overall racial individualism (first-year)[a]	.857	.811	.845	.846
Toward blacks[a]	.535	.465	.446	.491
Educated and does what is proper; will get ahead	6.95 (2.21)	5.97 (2.60)	6.52 (2.63)	6.80 (2.32)
Have only themselves to blame for not doing better; should try harder	3.79 (2.65)	4.15 (2.78)	4.05 (2.80)	4.11 (2.75)
Toward Latinos[a]	.493	.489	.507	.454
Educated and does what is proper; will get ahead	6.68 (2.23)	5.70 (2.46)	6.56 (2.40)	6.51 (2.33)
Have only themselves to blame for not doing better; should try harder	3.53 (2.57)	3.99 (2.61)	4.14 (2.79)	4.05 (2.63)
Toward Asians and Pacific Islanders[a]	.405	.353	.390	.438
Educated and does what is proper; will get ahead	7.61 (2.00)	7.18 (2.38)	7.20 (2.27)	7.29 (2.11)
Have only themselves to blame for not doing better; should try harder	3.49 (2.70)	4.16 (2.73)	4.06 (2.80)	4.43 (2.82)
Overall racial individualism (fourth-year)[a]	.930	.928	.939	.930
Toward blacks				
Have only themselves to blame for not doing better; should try harder	2.50 (2.45)	2.81 (2.75)	2.52 (2.68)	2.99 (2.56)
Toward Latinos				
Have only themselves to blame for not doing better; should try harder	2.14 (2.29)	2.46 (2.51)	2.48 (2.65)	2.64 (2.48)
Toward Asians and Pacific Islanders				
Have only themselves to blame for not doing better; should try harder	2.00 (2.32)	2.60 (2.64)	2.29 (2.61)	2.99 (2.64)

NOTE: Nonimputed NLSF data used to create scales. Standard deviations located in parentheses.
[a] Cronbach alpha listed for each racial and ethnic group scale of racial individualism.

TABLE A.3   Means, standard deviations of campus racial climate scales

Variable	White	Black	Latino	Asian & Pacific Islander
Second-year campus racial climate scale[a]	.717	.827	.776	.743
Felt self-conscious by students because of race/ethnicity	1.26 (.56)	2.03 (.96)	1.60 (.84)	1.63 (.79)
Felt self-conscious by faculty because of race/ethnicity	1.09 (.31)	1.50 (.77)	1.22 (.54)	1.25 (.52)
Felt self-conscious on campus because of race/ethnicity	1.26 (.55)	1.88 (1.00)	1.41 (.74)	1.54 (.75)
Heard racially derogatory remarks from students	1.44 (.72)	1.81 (.94)	1.77 (.90)	1.63 (.77)
Heard racially derogatory remarks from faculty	1.07 (.30)	1.17 (.49)	1.14 (.47)	1.10 (.33)
Hear racially derogatory remarks from staff	1.10 (.38)	1.25 (.61)	1.21 (.53)	1.17 (.45)
Experienced racial discrimination/ harassment on campus	1.12 (.40)	1.37 (.66)	1.22 (.56)	1.22 (.47)
Received unfair grade from professor because of race/ ethnicity	1.02 (.19)	1.20 (.55)	1.07 (.31)	1.08 (.35)
Discouraged from speaking up in class because of race/ethnicity	1.03 (.23)	1.18 (.55)	1.06 (.29)	1.06 (.28)
Discouraged from pursuing course by professor because of race/ ethnicity	1.20 (.49)	1.32 (.68)	1.24 (.63)	1.20 (.53)
Third-year campus racial climate scale[a]	.716	.839	.795	.792
Felt self-conscious by students because of race/ethnicity	1.24 (.50)	1.97 (.99)	1.55 (.79)	1.56 (.71)
Felt self-conscious by faculty because of race/ethnicity	1.09 (.33)	1.53 (.78)	1.22 (.52)	1.22 (.50)
Felt self-conscious on campus because of race/ethnicity	1.29 (.56)	1.89 (1.00)	1.42 (.72)	1.50 (.73)
Heard racially derogatory remarks from students	1.40 (.62)	1.86 (.91)	1.76 (.84)	1.65 (.75)
Heard racially derogatory remarks from faculty	1.09 (.30)	1.19 (.49)	1.13 (.40)	1.10 (.35)
Hear racially derogatory remarks from staff	1.08 (.29)	1.25 (.56)	1.17 (.48)	1.13 (.40)
Experienced racial discrimination/ harassment on campus	1.09 (.32)	1.39 (.67)	1.20 (.46)	1.20 (.47)
Received unfair grade from professor because of race/ ethnicity	1.01 (.12)	1.23 (.59)	1.08 (.33)	1.08 (.32)

(continued)

TABLE A.3   (CONTINUED)

Variable	White	Black	Latino	Asian & Pacific Islander
Discouraged from speaking up in class because of race/ethnicity	1.02 (.13)	1.17 (.52)	1.07 (.37)	1.05 (.26)
Discouraged from pursuing course by professor because of race/ethnicity	1.13 (.41)	1.34 (.69)	1.20 (.59)	1.18 (.51)
Fourth-year campus racial climate scale[a]	.621	.743	.699	.673
Felt self-conscious since fall semester because of race/ethnicity	1.45 (.66)	2.22 (1.01)	1.74 (.88)	1.81 (.84)
Made to feel self-conscious on campus because of race/ethnicity	1.22 (.49)	1.77 (.93)	1.37 (.70)	1.45 (.70)
Heard racially derogatory remarks on campus	1.46 (.69)	1.87 (.87)	1.80 (.87)	1.68 (.78)
Received unfair grade from professor because of race/ethnicity	1.04 (.24)	1.29 (.65)	1.10 (.37)	1.10 (.36)
Discouraged from speaking up in class because of race/ethnicity	1.05 (.27)	1.32 (.67)	1.12 (.42)	1.09 (.36)
Campus racial climate scale (all three scales combined)[a]	.837	.903	.883	.854
All 25 scale items	1.18 (.21)	1.54 (.43)	1.33 (.32)	1.32 (.27)

NOTE: Nonimputed NLSF data used to create scales. Standard deviations located in parentheses.
[a] Cronbach alpha listed for each racial and ethnic group campus racial climate scale.

NOTES

CHAPTER 1 EASING INTO VIEWS OF RACE AND INEQUALITY IN EVERYDAY LIFE ON CAMPUS

1. The student worked on an aspect of a larger project which was incorporated into Espenshade and Radford's *No Longer Separate, Not Yet Equal* (2009).

2. The continual influence of historical legacies of race and racism in higher education on contemporary student experiences is explored in many volumes. A few of these key readings in relation to elite higher education include Bowen and Bok's *The Shape of the River* (1998), Charles and colleagues' *Taming the River* (2009), Espenshade and Radford's *No Longer Separate, Not Yet Equal* (2009), Feagin, Vera, and Imani's *The Agony of Education* (1996), Massey and colleagues' *The Source of the River* (2003), and Sidanius and colleagues' *The Diversity Challenge* (2008). For additional discussions of these legacies interwoven in American higher education history, see Thelin's *A History of American Higher Education* (2004) and Wilder's *Ebony & Ivy* (2013).

3. The work of Shamus Khan (2011; and Khan and Jerolmack 2013) and Warikoo (2016) is pivotal in informing how elite students understand achievement, inequality, and race.

4. Bourdieu's examination of elite higher education in France untangles how perceptions of elite identities intertwine with institutional prerogatives and histories within the field of power. That is, the ideologies of elite students (the "mental structures") are directly and subversively informed by the institutional norms of elite higher education (Bourdieu 1996; Bourdieu and Passeron 1990).

5. The importance of exclusion while embracing the prestige and status of such exclusionary admissions practices is noted in Berrey (2015); Bowen and Bok (1998); Bowen, Kurzweil, and Tobin (2005); Espenshade and Radford (2009); Karabel (2005); Massey et al. (2003); and Soares (2007).

6. The solidification of elites in the global economy is noted in the economic research of Atkinson and Piketty's *Top Incomes over the 20th Century: A Contrast between Continental European and English-Speaking Countries* (2007), Bernstein and Swan's *All the Money in the World: How the Forbes 400 Make—and Spend—Their Fortunes* (2007), and Piketty and Saez's "Income Inequality in the United States, 1913–1998" (2003).

7. For an overview of the changes in racial attitudes in America, see Bobo and colleagues' "The Real Record on Racial Attitudes" (2012), Bobo, Kluegel, and Smith's "Laissez-Faire Racism: The Crystallization of a Kinder, Gentler, Anti-Black Ideology" (1997), Hunt's "African American, Hispanic, and White Beliefs about Black/White Inequality, 1977–2004" (2007), and Schuman and colleagues' *Racial Attitudes in America* (1997).

8. How elites justify their position in relation to higher education and establish distinctions between individuals at both "elite institutions" and other higher education institutions is detailed in Bourdieu's *State Nobility* (1996).

9. The perspective of diversity as individuality is put forth in Khan's work on elites' ideology (2011, 2015; Khan and Jerolmack 2013).

10. This rationalization of inequality is specifically noted in Khan (2011) and Khan and Jerolmack (2013).

11. It is important to note that although students of color at elite colleges may be seen as equally intelligent and hard-working as their white peers, this does not mean that

they are shielded from discrimination explicitly or through microaggressions every day; see Sue, Capodliupo, and Holder's "Racial Microaggressions in the Life Experiences of Black Americans" (2008), and Solorzano, Ceja, and Yosso's "Critical Race Theory, Racial Microaggressions, and Campus Racial Climate: The Experiences of African American College Students" (2000). Nor does this indicate they do not expect discrimination despite their intellectual abilities and work ethic on campus (see Torres and Charles 2004) or sense they are perceived as "worthy" to be admitted to these institutions by their white peers (see Byrd, Brunn-Bevel, and Sexton 2014).

12. The work of Natasha Warikoo (2016; Warikoo and Deckman 2014; Warikoo and Novais 2015) is pivotal in uncovering how elite college students understand "diversity" and particular diversity programs' framing can influence students' views of race, interaction, and inequality.

13. This partial unwillingness to interact across racial and ethnic lines among entering college students is covered in Pryor and colleagues' *The American Freshman: Forty-Year Trends, 1966–2006* (2007).

14. These outcomes of intergroup relations are prominently detailed in the meta-analyses contained in Pettigrew and Tropp's *When Groups Meet* (2011).

15. A synopsis of the social structure and personality framework can be found in McLeod and Lively's "Social Structure and Personality" (2006).

16. Whether this condition is needed prior to or during the intergroup contact situation is debatable (see Bobo 1988).

17. Discussions of the promotion of particular segments of higher education designed and promoted for elites are noted in Bourdieu's *State Nobility* (1996), Bowen, Kurzweil, and Tobin's *Equity and Excellence in American Higher Education* (2005), Thelin's *A History of American Higher Education* (2004), and Wilder's *Ebony & Ivy* (2013).

18. An example of the documentation of this extensive history is Winthrop D. Jordan's *White Over Black* (1968).

19. The conceptualization of racial individualism is noted in Michael Hughes's "Symbolic Racism, Old-Fashioned Racism, and Whites' Opposition to Affirmative Action" (1997), Kinder and Sanders's *Divided by Color* (1996), and Tuch and Hughes's "Whites' Racial Policy Attitudes in the 21st Century: The Continuing Significance of Racial Resentment" (2011).

20. For additional discussions about conceptualizations of laissez-faire racism and the integration of prejudice as a sense of group position, see Bobo's "Group Conflict, Prejudice, and the Paradox of Contemporary Racial Attitudes" (1988), and Bobo and Tuan's *Prejudice in Politics* (2006).

21. The general definition of social identities is elaborated in Brown's "Social Identity Theory: Past Achievements, Current Problems, and Future Challenges" (2000), Hogg and Abrams's *Social Identifications* (1988), and Stets and Burke's "Identity Theory and Social Identity Theory" (2000).

22. This socialization occurs in educational institutions as well. For examples taking place in preschool and elementary schools, see Lewis's *Race in the Schoolyard* (2003), and Van Ausdale and Feagin's *The First R* (2001).

23. For discussion of the College and Beyond dataset, see Bowen and Bok's *The Shape of the River* (1998). Consider the in-depth discussion in Massey and colleagues' *The Source of the River* (2003) for the design and collection of the National Longitudinal Study of Freshmen data. The following institutions are included in the NLSF: Barnard College, Bryn Mawr College, Columbia University, Denison University, Emory University, Georgetown University, Howard University, Kenyon College, Miami University (Ohio), Northwestern University, Oberlin College, Pennsylvania State University, Princeton University, Rice University, Smith College, Stanford University, Swarthmore College, Tufts University, Tulane University, University of California (Berkeley), University of Michigan, University of North Carolina (Chapel Hill),

University of Notre Dame, University of Pennsylvania, Washington University (St. Louis), Wesleyan University, Williams College, and Yale University.

24. With the exception of Howard University, the average percentage of Asian and Pacific Islander students enrolled at these institutions in 1998 was 13.3%, while 6.7% were black students, 5.1% were Latino students, and 70.3% were white students. Also, as the data in this study do not delineate what ethnic groups students identify with outside of panethnic groupings, Latino and Asian and Pacific Islander are used throughout this volume as shorthand for those students. Further research into how students within these groups identify and how this relates to their patterns of interactions, and social and academic outcomes, would elucidate possible racial and ethnic hierarchies within panethnic groups.

CHAPTER 2 LIFE BEFORE COLLEGE

1. Prejudice toward each racial and ethnic ingroup was not examined in this study. Although the concept of self-hatred is related to the work on racial prejudice, the current study was focused on how cross-race interactions influenced racial and ethnic outgroup prejudice.

2. The discussion of growing calls for a postracial and postracism society are elaborated in Bonilla-Silva's *Racism without Racists* (2014), Feagin's *Racist America* (2010), and Kaplan's *The Myth of Post-Racial America* (2011).

3. A variation of this argument was put forth by Wilson in *The Declining Significance of Race* (1978).

4. See, for example, the in-depth studies of UCLA students by Sidanius and colleagues (2008), who included several social characteristics of students to examine the outcomes of inter- and intraracial interactions on campus.

5. See Emerson and colleagues' (1999) study of the relationship between religion, specifically Christianity, and racial inequality. Here, it is important to point out that although people may not be against racial equality, they may use "cultural tools" associated with Christianity such as individualistic arguments to "victim blame" and antistructuralism to explain inequality. These same tools have the possibility to influence students' racial prejudice towards people of color.

6. Oliver and Shapiro (2006; also Shapiro 2004) note the importance of considering the "wealth gap" that contributes to discussions of racial inequality. Fischer (2008) in particular found homeownership influenced the social interactions of elite college students; thus, this component of students' socioeconomic positions may also shape their views of race and inequality. Generally, education is considered to have a "liberalizing" effect on views of race and inequality (see Schuman et al. 1997).

7. Supplementary analyses (not shown here) found elite college students who attended private schools prior to college held lower levels of support for individualistic explanations for racial inequality overall and when considering specific racial and ethnic minority groups, but did not significantly differ in their prejudice toward racial and ethnic groups.

8. Sidanius and colleagues' (2008) UCLA student study did examine how students' social identities influenced their views of racial and ethnic outgroups, but did not explore how these identities crafted whom they interacted with during college or their views of race at the end of college.

9. The inconsistent gender differences in racial attitudes are examined further in Hughes and Tuch (2003).

10. How the cultural frame for achievement and success for Asians and Pacific Islanders shapes the perspectives of students in the context of immigration policies and institutions is poignantly discussed by Jennifer Lee and Min Zhou (2015). Critical for the current study is how individualistic beliefs about success are often devoid of the important cultural and structural contexts that frame how students may perceive their options for attaining academic and career success in their lives.

11. The somewhat tenuous influence of friendships across racial lines is also discussed in relation to whether people, whites in particular, identify people of color as friends who could more accurately be described as "acquaintances" (see Bonilla-Silva and Forman 2000).

CHAPTER 3 MIXING IT UP ON CAMPUS

1. The use of "sincere fictions" to frame history, institutions, and whiteness in relation to "the other" is part of a larger discussion of what Joe Feagin puts forth as the white racial frame, which developed over centuries (see Feagin 2010, 89–91).

2. A large collection of research has uncovered the many advantages of families from well-off socioeconomic positions, those with ties to institutions, and other families tied to elite segments of the population, in the histories of elite colleges and universities through their college admissions practices and other institutional efforts (see Bowen and Bok 1998; Bowen, Kurzweil, and Tobin 2005; Espenshade and Radford 2009; Karabel 2005; Soares 2007; Thelin 2004; Wilder 2013). Also, it is important to point out that not all students at elite colleges are from such high socioeconomic positions. As the work by Jack (2016) points out, class marginality exists at elite colleges in varying degrees for both the "privileged poor" and the "doubly disadvantaged" students who are not from these elite backgrounds, regardless of race or ethnicity.

3. It should be further noted that the Greek system on college campuses is highly racialized, and a result of a policy of racial segregation established in the early twentieth century, that continues to influence the organizations that students join today. This history reflects how organizations become racialized (see Hughey 2013).

4. The odds ratios for each student group pairing were calculated using the odds ratios for each social interaction. This resulted in six odds ratios for each form of social interaction, for a total of twenty-four odds ratios. From these calculations, the average odds ratio of one student group interaction with another student group was calculated to find the overall odds ratio of two groups' interaction during college.

5. Each racialized social identity measure taken at college entrance was entered into the models to examine how the multiple considerations of race and identity influence whom elite college students form relationships with on campus. This allows for further consideration of the complexities of the sociohistorical relations applied to social interaction among racial and ethnic groups, which is often constrained by using a specific ingroup-outgroup approach. That is, given that there are multiple racial outgroups, and different yet interrelated histories between a person's ingroup and each outgroup, it is important to consider how each form of racialized social identity can influence whom elite college students interact with and in what ways they interact (i.e., the form of interaction) with different racial and ethnic outgroups.

6. These differences include the examination of a mother's and father's educational attainment (not a single measure), and the inclusion of more measures of the socioeconomic and religious backgrounds of students, among other variable differences. Additionally, it must be noted that these studies often merge students of color together into diversity indexes or heterogeneity indexes of different forms to analyze cross-race interactions. Unlike previous research, the current study examines the many influences on elite college students' cross-race interactions for each specific racial or ethnic group in order to broaden our understanding of how conceptions of "diversity" actually hide the segregation and racial hierarchy of student life on elite college campuses. For example, although a student may have a higher score on a

heterogeneity index in relation to their friendship network, meaning they have more friends of different races or ethnicities from their own, this same student may not have friendships with one or two racial or ethnic groups, forming relationships with members of one group explicitly.

7. Similarly, Moody (2001) notes school diversity can hit a "critical mass" whereby students begin to select same-race friends more often than different-race friends as the school swings from predominantly white to predominantly black and Latino.

8. In particular, results were similar to those found in Bowman and Park (2014), Charles et al. (2009), Espenshade and Radford (2009), Fischer (2008), Massey et al. (2003), Park and Kim (2013), and Stearns, Buchmann, and Bonneau (2009).

9. Examples of racial discrimination of Latinos and Asians and Pacific Islanders is noted in Chou and Feagin's *The Myth of the Model Minority* (2008), Cobas, Duany, and Feagin's *How the United States Racializes Latinos* (2009), Myers's *Racetalk* (2005), O'Brien's *The Racial Middle* (2008), and Teranishi's *Asians in the Ivory Tower* (2010), among other research.

10. An extensive literature exists on the continuous and contentious struggles for institutional support for racial diversity and inclusion, both in higher education and society as a whole, in a purported equal opportunity society (see Bowen and Bok 1998; Chang et al. 2003; Espenshade and Radford 2009; Feagin, Vera, and Imani 1996; Gurin, Lehman, and Lewis 2004; Hurtado et al. 1999; Orfield 2001; Park 2014b; Peterson et al. 1978).

11. The roommate measures in this study were taken during students' second and third years of college, which is typically when college students can begin choosing who their roommates are for on- and off-campus living situations.

12. For more discussion on the ingroup-outgroup framing of social identities, see the informative article by Stets and Burke (2000). For additional information on similar discussions of intergroup relations, see the work of Thomas Pettigrew, particularly Pettigrew (1998); Pettigrew and Tropp (2011).

CHAPTER 4   GRADUATING RACIAL IDEOLOGIES

1. As only one measure that was used in the first wave of the NLSF was also used in the last wave of the study, these comparisons only use the common measure from both waves to identify any changes in students' views of inequality. Specifically, this measure asked students their level of agreement with the statement that each racial or ethnic group had only themselves to blame for not doing better in life, and that they should have tried harder to be more successful.

2. Natasha Warikoo also finds white students at elite colleges to use multiple race frames, particularly colorblindness, to discuss identity, interactions, and inequality (see Warikoo 2016, 43–61; also Warikoo and Novais 2015).

3. Jennifer Lee and Min Zhou's *The Asian American Achievement Paradox* (2015) provides an in-depth examination of Asians and Pacific Islanders and a full account of how members of these groups navigate the conceptions of success and failure in relation to culture, structure, and group comparisons.

4. Khan (2012) provides a discussion of how the demographic changes in the global elite do not necessarily indicate that group norms are changing more than that the new members are modifying their perspectives to fit within the broader group.

5. Solorzano, Ceja, and Yosso (2000) provide a comprehensive discussion of how microaggressions in everyday interactions influence students of color in college; see also Sue, Capodliupo, and Holder (2008).

6. The continual impact of early views of race and inequality, particularly as they relate to merit, is noted in the interviews carried out by Natasha Warikoo (2016) at Brown University and Harvard University.

7. See Bourdieu's (1989) discussion of how elite higher education institutions in France shape the broader social elites' views of society (mental structures) through the culture and social structure of these institutions.

CHAPTER 5 WHEN THINGS FALL APART

1. For discussions of individual-level habitus and its connections to organizations, including educational institutions, see the research of Bonilla-Silva (2014); also Bonilla-Silva and Embrick (2007); Bourdieu (1996).

2. Many studies of higher education access and opportunity, particularly around highly selective institutions such as those included in the current study, note the unique demographic of these institutions (see Bowen, Kurzweil, and Tobin 2005; Espenshade and Radford 2009; Khan 2011; Massey et al. 2003).

3. Natasha Warikoo (2016) provides an elaboration of how elite college students link their positions at highly selective institutions with race, merit, and inequality.

4. The organizational habitus and its connection to the broader elite social world is explored further in Bourdieu (1996).

5. Similar findings among white elite college students concerning the blindness of low representation of students of color on campus and how such representation influences social interactions is noted by Warikoo (2016; Warikoo and Novais 2015).

6. Subsequent investigations with advanced methods such as structural equation modeling to identify how these social interactions and campus characteristics are further intertwined around students' experiences were mired with pitfalls because of the racial hierarchy of student interactions on these campuses, as the extremely low and sometimes nonexistent correlations hinder further analyses. These statistical realities echo the social reality emanating from the intersection of the individual and organizational racial habitus on these campuses that is an important set of issues to address, not simply a statistical one that needs additional attention by researchers.

7. The racial capital argument focusing on white debt and color capital is put forth in the work of Matthew W. Hughey (2012, 148–169).

8. Berrey (2015, 55–123) explains the shift of the University of Michigan away from social justice arguments in favor of pitching "diversity" as part of its institutional mission as well as what can make students "marketable." These shifts not only moved away from social arguments used by activists, but also limited how much racial inequality on campus was the result of institutional policies.

9. This opposite effect is noted in Berrey's (2015, 55–123) examination of the University of Michigan's diversity efforts and Supreme Court cases.

10. This literal framing of how whiteness structures students' experiences on campuses is discussed by Brunsma, Brown, and Placier (2013). See also Warikoo and Deckman's (2014) examination of how different diversity programs can influence students' views of race and inequality.

11. Brunsma, Brown, and Placier (2013) build on the work of Mills (1997) and the racial contract and its associated epistemology of ignorance.

12. Warikoo (2016, 113–136) also notes the importance of considering metastereotypes and the perpetual dance of attempting to be colorblind and not being seen as "racist" among white students at elite universities.

CHAPTER 6 INTERACTING FUTURES AND THE REPRODUCTION OF RACIAL INEQUALITY

1. Feagin (2009) expounds on how this distorted framing of histories, interactions, and institutions is integral to understanding race, and white supremacy in particular, in society.

2. Natasha Warikoo's (2016) research examines the framing of race, merit, and inequality, and notes how the intertwined views of race and merit among elite college students influence their perceptions of inequality and policies such as affirmative action in college admissions. Here, students actively invoke strong beliefs and adherence to the myth of meritocracy as supporting their positions at elite institutions, and their support for affirmative action often hinges on consideration of whether they would be left out of current or future opportunities in a competitive world.

3. These findings echo the interview responses with students of color at Brown and Harvard Universities in Warikoo (2016).

4. The need for such change around conceptions of race and merit in higher education is powerfully discussed in Warikoo's *The Diversity Bargain* (2016), among other works.

5. Many institutions are taking steps toward reconciling their history and complicity in racism, not only elite colleges and universities. For more discussion of how colleges and universities were involved in such policies and acts as the slave trade well into the eighteenth century, see Wilder (2013); Morris (2016).

REFERENCES

Allen, Walter R., Edgar G. Epps, and Nesha Z. Haniff. 1991. *College in Black and White: African American Students in Predominantly White and in Historically Black Public Universities.* Albany: State University of New York Press.

Allport, Gordon. 1954. *The Nature of Prejudice.* Reading, MA: Addison-Wesley.

Alon, Sigal, and Marta Tienda. 2007. "Diversity, Opportunity, and the Shifting Meritocracy in Higher Education." *American Sociological Review* 72(4): 487–511.

Anderson, Elijah. 2011. *Cosmopolitan Canopy: Race and Civility in Everyday Life.* New York: W. W. Norton & Company.

antonio, anthony l., and Marcela M. Muniz. 2007. "The Sociology of Diversity." Pp. 266–294 in *The Sociology of Higher Education: Contributions and their Contexts.* Edited by Patricia J. Gumport. Stanford, CA: Stanford University Press.

Apfelbaum, Evan P., Samuel R. Sommers, and Michael I. Norton. 2008. "Seeing Race and Seeming Racist? Evaluating Strategic Colorblindness in Social Interaction. *Journal of Personality and Social Psychology* 95(4): 918–932.

Apollon, Dominique. 2011. *Don't Call Them "Post-Racial": Millennials' Attitudes on Race, Racism, and Key Systems in Our Society.* Los Angeles: Applied Research Center.

Armstrong, Elizabeth A., and Laura T. Hamilton. 2013. *Paying for the Party: How College Maintains Inequality.* Boston: Harvard University Press.

Ashmore, Richard D., Kay Deaux, and Tracy McLaughlin-Volpe. 2004. "An Organizing Framework for Collective Identity: Articulation and Significance of Multidimensionality." *Psychological Bulletin* 130(1): 80–114.

Associated Press. 2016. "Yale to Revisit Name of College Honoring Slave Reporter." *Diverse: Issues in Higher Education,* August 1. http://diverseeducation.com/article/85800/.

Astin, Alexander W. 1968. *The College Environment.* Washington, D.C.: American Council on Education.

———. 1993. *What Matters in College? Four Critical Years Revisited.* San Francisco: Jossey-Bass.

Atkinson, A. B., and Thomas Piketty. 2007. *Top Incomes over the 20th Century: A Contrast between Continental European and English-Speaking Countries.* New York: Oxford University Press.

Bahns, Angela J., Kate M. Pickett, and Christian S. Crandall. 2012. "Social Ecology of Similarity: Big Schools, Small Schools, and Social Relationships." *Group Processes & Intergroup Relations* 15(1): 119–131.

Bartels, Larry M. 2008. *Unequal Democracy: The Political Economy of the New Gilded Age.* Princeton, NJ: Princeton University Press.

Bernstein, Peter W., and Annalyn Swan. (Eds.). 2007. *All the Money in the World: How the Forbes 400 Make—and Spend—Their Fortunes:* New York: Knopf.

Berrey, Ellen. 2015. *The Enigma of Diversity: The Language and the Limits of Racial Justice.* Chicago: University of Chicago Press.

Bettie, Julie. 2003. *Women without Class: Girls, Race, and Identity.* Berkeley: University of California Press.

Binder, Amy J., Daniel B. Davis, and Nick Bloom. 2016. "Career Funneling: How Elite Students Learn to Define and Desire 'Prestigious' Jobs." *Sociology of Education* 89(1): 20–39.

Blair, Irene V., Charles M. Judd, Melody S. Sadler, and Christopher Jenkins. 2002. "The Role of Afrocentric Features in Person Perception: Judging by Features and Categories." *Journal of Personality and Social Psychology* 83(1): 5–25.

Blalock, Hubert M. 1967. *Toward a Theory of Minority-Group Relations*. New York: Wiley.

Blau, Peter M., and Joseph E. Schwartz. 1984. *Crosscutting Social Circles: Testing a Macrostructural Theory of Intergroup Relations*. Orlando, FL: Academic Press.

Blumer, Herbert. 1958. "Race Prejudice and a Sense of Group Positioning." *Pacific Sociological Review* 1(1): 3–7.

Bobo, Lawrence. 1988. "Group Conflict, Prejudice, and the Paradox of Contemporary Racial Attitudes." Pp. 85–114 in *Eliminating Racism: Profiles in Controversy*. Edited by P. A. Katz and D. A. Taylor. New York: Plenum Press.

———. 1999. "Prejudice as Group Position: Microfoundations of a Sociological Approach to Racism and Race Relations." *Journal of Social Issues* 55(3): 445–472.

Bobo, Lawrence D., Camille Z. Charles, Maria Krysan, and Alicia D. Simmons. 2012. "The Real Record on Racial Attitudes." Pp. 38–83 in *Social Trends in American Life: Findings from the General Social Survey since 1972*. Edited by P. V. Marsden. Princeton, NJ: Princeton University Press.

Bobo, Lawrence D., James R. Kluegel, and Ryan A. Smith. 1997. "Laissez-Faire Racism: The Crystallization of a Kinder, Gentler, Anti-Black Ideology." Pp. 15–42 in *Racial Attitudes in the 1990s: Continuity and Change*. Edited by S. A. Tuch and J. K. Martin. Westport, CT: Praeger.

Bobo, Lawrence D., and Mia Tuan. 2006. *Prejudice in Politics: Group Position, Public Opinion, and the Wisconsin Treaty Rights Dispute*. Cambridge, MA: Harvard University Press.

Bonacich, Edna. 1973. "A Theory of Middlemen Minorities." *American Sociological Review* 38(5): 583–594.

Bonilla-Silva, Eduardo. 1997. "Rethinking Racism: Toward a Structural Interpretation." *American Sociological Review* 62(3): 465–480.

———. 2004. "From Bi-racial to Tri-racial: Towards a New System of Racial Stratification in the USA." *Ethnic and Racial Studies* 27(6): 931–950.

———. 2012. "The Invisible Weight of Whiteness: The Racial Grammar of Everyday Life in Contemporary America." *Ethnic & Racial Studies* 35(2): 173–194.

———. 2014. *Racism without Racists: Color-blind Racism and the Persistence of Racial Inequality in the United States*. Fourth edition. Lanham, MD: Rowman & Littlefield.

Bonilla-Silva, Eduardo, and David R. Dietrich. 2009. "The Latin Americanization of U.S. Race Relations: A New Pigmentocracy." Pp. 40–60 in *Shades of Difference: Why Skin Color Matters*. Edited by E. N. Glenn. Stanford, CA: Stanford University Press.

Bonilla-Silva, Eduardo, and David Embrick. 2007. "'Every Place has a Ghetto': The Significance of Whites' Social and Residential Segregation." *Symbolic Interaction* 30(3): 323–345.

Bonilla-Silva, Eduardo, and Tyrone A. Forman. 2000. "'I am not a racist but . . . ': Mapping White College Students' Racial Ideology in the USA." *Discourse & Society* 11(1): 50–85.

Bourdieu, Pierre. 1977. *Outline of a Theory of Practice*. New York: Cambridge University Press.

———. [1989] 1996. *The State Nobility: Elite Schools in the Field of Power*. Stanford, CA: Stanford University Press.

Bourdieu, Pierre, and Jean-Claude Passeron. [1977] 1990. *Reproduction in Education, Society, and Culture*. Second edition. Thousand Oaks, CA: Sage.

Bowen, William G., and Derek Bok. 1998. *The Shape of the River: Long-Term Consequences of Considering Race in College and University Admissions*. Princeton, NJ: Princeton University Press.

Bowen, William G., Martin A. Kurzweil, and Eugene M. Tobin. 2005. *Equity and Excellence in American Higher Education.* Charlottesville: University of Virginia Press.

Bowman, Nicholas A. 2012. "Promoting Sustained Engagement with Diversity: The Reciprocal Relationships between Informal and Formal College Diversity Experiences." *Review of Higher Education* 36(1): 1–24.

Bowman, Nicholas A., and Nida Denson. 2012. "What's Past is Prologue: How Precollege Exposure to Racial Diversity Shapes the Impact of College Interracial Interactions." *Research in Higher Education* 53(4): 406–425.

Bowman, Nicholas A., and Julie J. Park. 2014. "Interracial Contact on College Campuses: Comparing and Contrasting Predictors of Cross-Racial Interaction and Interracial Friendships." *Journal of Higher Education* 85(5): 660–690.

Brown, Rupert. 2000. "Social Identity Theory: Past Achievements, Current Problems, and Future Challenges." *European Journal of Social Psychology* 30(6): 745–778.

Brunsma, David L., Eric S. Brown, and Peggy Placier. 2013. "Teaching Race at Historically White Colleges and Universities: Identifying and Dismantling the Walls of Whiteness." *Critical Sociology* 39(5): 717–738.

Buchman, Claudia, Thomas DiPrete, and Anne McDaniel. 2008. "Gender Inequalities in Education." *Annual Review of Sociology* 34: 319–337.

Burkholder, Zoe. 2011. *Color in the Classroom: How American Schools Taught Race, 1900–1954.* New York: Oxford University Press.

Byrd, W. Carson. 2015. "College Diversity Is (But Doesn't Have to Be) For Whites." *Contexts* 14(3): 74–75.

Byrd, W. Carson, Rachelle J. Brunn-Bevel, and Parker Sexton. 2014. "'We Don't All Look Alike': The Academic Performance of Black Student Populations at Elite Colleges." *Du Bois Review* 11(2): 353–385.

Carter, Prudence. 2012. *Stubborn Roots: Race, Culture, and Inequality in U.S. and South African Schools.* New York: Oxford University Press.

Chang, Mitchell J. 2002. "Preservation or Transformation: Where's the Real Educational Discourse on Diversity?" *Review of Higher Education* 25(2): 125–140.

Chang, Mitchell J., Alexander W. Astin, and Dongbin Kim. 2004. "Cross-Racial Interaction among Undergraduates: Some Consequences, Causes, and Patterns." *Research in Higher Education* 45(5): 529–553.

Chang, Mitchell J., Nida Denson, Victor Saenz, and Kimberly Misa. 2006. "The Educational Benefits of Sustaining Cross-Race Interaction among Undergraduates." *Journal of Higher Education* 77(3): 430–455.

Chang, Mitchell J., Daria Witt, James Jones, and Kenji Hakuta. (Eds.). 2003. *Compelling Interest: Examining the Racial Dynamics in Colleges and Universities.* Stanford, CA: Stanford University Press.

Charles, Camille Z. 2003. "The Dynamics of Racial Residential Segregation." *Annual Review of Sociology* 29: 167–207.

———. 2007. "Comfort Zones: Immigration, Acculturation, and the Neighborhood Racial-Composition Preferences of Latinos and Asians." *Du Bois Review* 4(1): 41–77.

Charles, Camille Z., Mary J. Fischer, Margarita A. Mooney, and Douglas S. Massey. 2009. *Taming the River: Negotiating the Academic, Financial, and Social Currents in Selective Colleges and Universities.* Princeton, NJ: Princeton University Press.

Chessman, Hollie, and Lindsay Wyat. 2016. "What Are Students Demanding?" *Higher Education Today: A Blog by ACE.* Retrieved January 13, 2016 (http://higheredtoday.org/2016/01/13/what-are-students-demanding/).

Chou, Rosalind S., and Joe R. Feagin. 2008. *The Myth of the Model Minority: Asian Americans Facing Racism.* Boulder, CO: Paradigm Publishers.

Cobas, Jose A., Jorge Duany, and Joe R. Feagin, eds. 2009. *How the United States Racializes Latinos: White Hegemony and its Consequences.* Boulder, CO: Paradigm.

Combs, Barbara H., Kristen Dellinger, Jeffrey T. Jackson, Kirk A. Johnson, Willa M. Johnson, Jodi Skipper, John Sonnett, James M. Thomas, and Critical Race Studies Group. 2016. "The Symbolic Lynching of James Meredith: A Visual Analysis and Collective Counter Narrative to Racial Discrimination." *Sociology of Race and Ethnicity* 2(3): 338–353.

Cottom, Tressie McMillan. 2016. "Georgetown's Slavery Announcement Is Remarkable. But It's Not Reparations." *Vox.com*, September 2 (http://www.vox.com/2016/9/2/12773110/georgetown-slavery-admission-reparations).

Denson, Nida, and Mitchell J. Chang. 2009. "Racial Diversity Matters: The Impact of Diversity-Related Student Engagement and Institutional Context." *American Educational Research Journal* 46(2): 322–353.

DiMaggio, Paul J., and Walter W. Powell. 1983. "The Iron Cage Revisited: Institutional Isomorphism and Collective Rationality in Organizational Fields." *American Sociological Review* 48(2): 147–160.

DiTomaso, Nancy. 2013. *The American Non-Dilemma: Racial Inequality without Racism.* New York: Russell Sage Foundation.

Domhoff, G. W. 1978. *The Powers That Be: Processes of Ruling-Class Domination in America.* New York: Random House.

Doyle, Jamie M., and Grace Kao. 2007. "Friendship Choices of Multicultural Adolescents: Racial Homophily, Blending, or Amalgamation?" *Social Science Research* 36(2): 633–653.

Duncan, Terry E., Susan C. Duncan, and Fuzhong Lu. 1998. "A Comparison of Model- and Multiple Imputation-Based Approaches to Longitudinal Data with Partial Missingness." *Structural Equation Modeling* 5(1): 1–21.

Eaton, Colin, and Audrey White. 2010. "Protestors Stage Walkout to Fight Proposed Slashes to Ethnic Studies." *The Daily Texan*, December 1. Retrieved January 2, 2011 (http://www.dailytexanonline.com/content/protestors-stage-walkout-to-fight-proposed-slashes-to-ethnic-studies).

Ellison, Christopher G., and Daniel A. Powers. 1994. "The Contact Hypothesis and Racial Attitudes among Black Americans." *Social Science Quarterly* 75(2): 385–400.

Emerson, Michael O., Christian Smith, and David Sikkink. 1999. "Equal in Christ, but Not in the World: White Conservative Protestants and Explanations of Black-White Inequality." *Social Problems* 46(3): 398–417.

Enders, Craig K. 2001. "A Primer on Maximum Likelihood Algorithms Available for Use with Missing Data." *Structural Equation Modeling* 8(1): 128–141.

Espenshade, Thomas J., and Alexandria Walton Radford. 2009. *No Longer Separate, Not Yet Equal: Race and Class in Elite College Admissions and Campus Life.* Princeton, NJ: Princeton University Press.

Feagin, Joe R. 2009. *The White Racial Frame: Centuries of Framing and Counter-Framing.* New York: Routledge.

———. 2010. *Racist America: Roots, Current Realities and Future Reparations.* Second edition. New York: Routledge.

Feagin, Joe R., Hernan Vera, and Nikitah Imani. 1996. *The Agony of Education: Black Students at White Universities.* New York: Routledge.

Filipovic, Jill. 2010. "Stephanie Grace: Racist Harvard Emailer." *Feministe Blog.* Retrieved April 29, 2010 (http://www.feministe.us/blog/archives/2010/04/29/stephanie-grace-racist-harvard-emailer).

Fischer, Mary J. 2008. "Does Campus Diversity Promote Friendship Diversity? A Look at Interracial Friendships." *Social Science Quarterly* 89(3): 631–655.

Forman, Tyrone A. 2004. "Color-blind Racism and Racial Indifference: The Role of Racial Apathy in Facilitating Enduring Inequalities." Pp. 43–66 in *The Changing Terrain of Race and Ethnicity*. Edited by M. Krysan and A. E. Lewis. New York: Russell Sage.

Fossett, Mark A., and K. Jill Kiecolt. 1989. "The Relative Size of Minority Populations and White Racial Attitudes." *Social Science Quarterly* 70(4): 820–835.

Frankenberg, Erica, and Gary Orfield. (Eds.) 2013. *The Resegregation of Suburban Schools: A Hidden Crisis in American Education*. Cambridge, MA: Harvard University Press.

Gaertner, Samuel L., and John F. Dovidio. 2000. *Reducing Intergroup Bias: The Common Ingroup Identity Model*. Philadelphia: Psychology Press.

Gaztambide-Fernandez, Ruben A., and Raygine DiAquoi. 2010. "A Part and Apart: Students of Color Negotiating Boundaries at an Elite Boarding School." Pp. 55–78 in *Educating Elites: Class Privilege and Educational Advantages*. Edited by Adam Howard and Ruben A. Gaztambide-Fernandez. Lanham, MD: Rowman & Littlefield.

Gans, Herbert J. 1999. "The Possibility of a New Racial Hierarchy in the Twenty-First Century United States." Pp. 371–390 in *The Cultural Territories of Race*. Edited by M. Lamont. Chicago: University of Chicago Press.

Goffman, Erving. 1959. *The Presentation of Self in Everyday Life*. Garden City, NY: Doubleday.

Gomez, Christina. 2000. "The Continual Significance of Skin Color: An Exploratory Study of Latinos in the Northeast." *Hispanic Journal of Behavioral Science* 22(1): 94–103.

Greenberg, Zoe. 2016. "Yale Drops Case Against Worker Who Smashed Window Depicting Slaves." *New York Times*, July 12 (http://www.nytimes.com/2016/07/13/nyregion/yale-worker-john-c-calhoun-window-slaves.html).

Gurin, Patricia, Eric L. Dey, Sylvia Hurtado, and Gerald Gurin. 2002. "Diversity and Higher Education: Theory and Impact on Educational Outcomes." *Harvard Educational Review* 72(3): 330–366.

Gurin, Patricia, Jeffrey S. Lehman, and Earl Lewis. 2004. *Defending Diversity: Affirmative Action at the University of Michigan*. Ann Arbor: University of Michigan Press.

Hagerman, Margaret A. 2014. "White Families and Race: Colour-blind and Colour-conscious Approaches to White Racial Socialization." *Ethnic and Racial Studies* 37(14): 2598–2614.

Hall, Wendell D., Alberto F. Cabrera, and Jeffrey F. Milem. 2011. "A Tale of Two Groups: Differences between Minority Students and Non-Minority Students in their Predispositions to and Engagement with Diverse Peers at a Predominately White Institution." *Research in Higher Education* 52(4): 420–439.

Hamilton, Laura T. 2016. *Parenting to a Degree: How Family Matters for College Women's Success*. Chicago: University of Chicago Press.

Harper, Shaun R., and Sylvia Hurtado. 2007. "Nine Themes in Campus Racial Climates and Implications for Institutional Transformation." *New Directions for Student Services* 120: 7–24.

Harris, Angel L. 2011. *Kids Don't Want to Fail: Oppositional Culture and the Black-White Achievement Gap*. Cambridge, MA: Harvard University Press.

Harris, David R., and Jeremiah J. Sim. 2002. "Who is Multiracial? Assessing the Complexity of Lived Race." *American Sociological Review* 67(4): 614–627.

Herring, Cedric, Verna M. Keith, and Hawyard D. Horton. 2004. *Skin Deep: How Race and Complexion Matter in the "Color-Blind" Era*. Urbana: University of Illinois Press.

Hewstone, Miles, and Rupert Brown. (Eds.). 1986. *Contact and Conflict in Intergroup Encounters*. Oxford, UK: Blackwell.

Hochschild, Jennifer L. 1995. *Facing Up to the American Dream: Race, Class, and the Soul of the Nation*. Princeton, NJ: Princeton University Press.

Hogg, Michael A., and Dominic Abrams. 1988. *Social Identifications: A Social Psychology of Intergroup Relations and Group Processes*. London: Routledge.

Howard, Adam, and Ruben Gaztambide-Fernandez. (Eds.). 2010. *Educating Elites: Class Privilege and Educational Advantages*. Lanham, MD: Rowman & Littlefield Education.

Hughes, Michael. 1997. "Symbolic Racism, Old-Fashioned Racism, and Whites' Opposition to Affirmative Action." Pp. 45–75 in *Racial Attitudes in the 1990s: Continuity and Change*. Edited by S. A. Tuch and J. K. Martin. Westport, CT: Praeger.

Hughes, Michael, and Bradley R. Hertel. 1990. "The Significance of Color Remains: A Study of Life Chances, Mate Selection, and Ethnic Consciousness among Black Americans." *Social Forces* 68(4): 1105–1120.

Hughes, Michael, and Steven A. Tuch. 2000. "How Beliefs about Poverty Influence Racial Policy Attitudes: A Study of Whites, African Americans, Hispanics, and Asians in the United States." Pp. 165–190 in *Racialized Politics: The Debate about Racism in America*. Edited by D. O. Sears, J. Sidanius, and L. Bobo. Chicago: University of Chicago Press.

———. 2003. "Gender Differences in Whites' Racial Attitudes: Are Women's Attitudes Really More Favorable?" *Social Psychology Quarterly* 66(4): 384–401.

Hughey, Matthew W. 2011. "Backstage Discourse and the Reproduction of White Masculinity." *Sociological Quarterly* 52(2): 132–153.

———. 2012. *White Bound: Nationalists, Antiracists, and the Shared Meanings of Race*. Stanford, CA: Stanford University Press.

———. 2013. *Race and Ethnicity in Secret and Exclusive Social Orders: Blood and Shadow*. New York: Taylor & Francis.

Hunt, Matthew O. 2007. "African American, Hispanic, and White Beliefs about Black/White Inequality, 1977–2004." *American Sociological Review* 72(3): 390–415.

Hurtado, Sylvia. 2005. "The Next Generation of Diversity and Intergroup Contact Research." *Journal of Social Issues* 61(3): 595–610.

———. 2007. "The Study of College Impact." Pp. 94–112 in *Sociology of Higher Education: Contributions and their Contexts*. Edited by P. Gumport. Baltimore: Johns Hopkins University Press.

Hurtado, Sylvia, Jeffrey Milem, Alma Clayton-Pedersen, and Walter Allen. 1999. *Enacting Diverse Learning Environments: Improving the Climate for Racial/Ethnic Diversity in Higher Education*. ASHE-ERIC Higher Education Report, Volume 26, Number 8. Washington, DC: George Washington University.

Iverson, Susan V. 2012. "Constructing Outsider: The Discursive Framing of Access in University Diversity Policies." *Review of Higher Education* 35(2): 149–177.

Jack, Anthony A. 2016. "(No) Harm in Asking: Class, Acquired Capital, and Academic Engagement at an Elite University." *Sociology of Education* 89(1): 1–19.

Johnson, Heather Beth. 2015. *The American Dream and the Power of Wealth: Choosing Schools and Inheriting Inequality in the Land of Opportunity*. Second edition. New York: Routledge.

Jordan, Winthrop D. 1968. *White Over Black: American Attitudes toward the Negro, 1550–1812*. New York: W. W. Norton.

Khan, Shamus. 2011. *Privilege: The Making of an Adolescent Elite at St. Paul's School*. Princeton, NJ: Princeton University Press.

———. 2012. "The Sociology of Elites." *Annual Review of Sociology* 38: 361–377.

———. 2015. "The Counter-Cyclical Character of the Elite." *Research in the Sociology of Organizations* 43: 81–103.

Khan, Shamus, and Colin Jerolmack. 2013. "Saying Meritocracy and Doing Privilege." *Sociological Quarterly* 54(1): 9–19.

Kao, Grace, and Kara Joyner. 2004. "Do Race and Ethnicity Matter among Friends? Activities among Interracial, Interethnic, and Intraethnic Friends." *Sociological Quarterly* 45(3): 557–573.

———. 2007. "Do Hispanic and Asian Adolescents Practice Panethnicity in Friendship Choices?" *Social Science Quarterly* 87(5): 972–992.

Kaplan, H. Roy. 2011. *The Myth of Post-Racial America: Searching for Equality in the Age of Materialism*. Lanham, MD: Rowman and Littlefield.

Karabel, Jerome. 2005. *The Chosen: The Hidden History of Admission and Exclusion at Harvard, Yale, and Princeton*. New York: Houghton Mifflin.

Kim, Claire J. 1999. "The Racial Triangulation of Asian Americans." *Politics & Society* 27(1): 105–127.

Kinder, Donald R., and Lynn M. Sanders. 1996. *Divided by Color: Racial Politics and Democratic Ideals*. Chicago: University of Chicago Press.

Kingkade, Tyler, Lilly Workneh, and Ryan Grenoble. 2015. "Campus Racism Protests Didn't Come Out of Nowhere, And They Aren't Going Away Quickly." *The Huffington Post*. Retrieved January 13, 2016 (http://www.huffingtonpost.com/entry/campus-racism-protests-didnt-come-out-of-nowhere_us_56464a87e4b08cda3488bfb4).

Kozol, Jonathan. 1991. *Savage Inequalities: Children in America's Schools*. New York: Harper Perennial.

———. 2005. *The Shame of the Nation: The Restoration of Apartheid Schooling in America*. New York: Crown Publishers.

Kraatz, Matthew S., and Edward J. Zajac. 1996. "Exploring the Limits of the New Institutionalism: The Causes and Consequences of Illegitimate Organizational Change." *American Sociological Review* 61(5): 812–836.

Lareau, Annette. 2003. *Unequal Childhoods: Class, Race, and Family Life*. Berkeley: University of California Press.

Lareau, Annette, and Kimberly Goyette. (Eds.). 2014. *Choosing Homes, Choosing Schools*. New York: Russell Sage Foundation.

Lat, David. 2010a. "The Harvard Email Controversy: How It All Began." *Above the Law Blog*. Retrieved May 7, 2010 (http://abovethelaw.com/2010/05/the-harvard-email-controversy-how-it-all-began/).

Lat, David. 2010b. "The Harvard Law School 'Racist' Email Controversy: Dean Martha Minow Weighs In." *Above the Law Blog*. Retrieved April 30, 2010 (http://abovethelaw.com/2010/04/the-harvard-law-school-racist-email-controversy-dean-minow-weighs-in/).

Lee, Jennifer, and Frank Bean. 2007. "Reinventing the Color Line: Immigration and America's New Racial/Ethnic Divide." *Social Forces* 86(2): 561–586.

Lee, Jennifer, and Min Zhou. 2015. *The Asian American Achievement Paradox*. New York: Russell Sage Foundation.

Levin, Shana, Pamela Taylor, and Elena Caudle. 2007. "Interethnic and Interracial Dating in College: A Longitudinal Study." *Journal of Social and Personal Relationships* 24(3): 323–341.

Levin, Shana, Colette Van Laar, and Jim Sidanius. 2003. "The Effects of Ingroup and Outgroup Friendships on Ethnic Attitudes in College: A Longitudinal Study." *Group Processes & Intergroup Relations* 6(1): 76–92.

Lewis, Amanda E. 2003. *Race in the Schoolyard: Negotiating the Color Line in Classrooms and Communities*. New Brunswick, NJ: Rutgers University Press.

———. 2004. "'What Group?' Studying Whites and Whiteness in the Era of 'Colorblindness.'" *Sociological Theory* 22(4): 623–646.

Lewis, Amanda E., and John B. Diamond. 2015. *Despite the Best Intentions: How Racial Inequality Thrives in Good Schools*. New York: Oxford University Press.

Lewis-McCoy, R. L'Heureux. 2014. *Inequality in the Promised Land: Race, Resources, and Suburban Schooling*. Stanford, CA: Stanford University Press.

Locks, Angela M., Sylvia Hurtado, Nicholas A. Bowman, and Leticia Oseguera. 2008. "Extending Notions of Campus Climate and Diversity to Students' Transition to College." *Review of Higher Education* 31(3): 257–285.

Logan, John R., Brian J. Stults, and Reynolds Farley. 2004. "Segregation of Minorities in the Metropolis: Two Decades of Change." *Demography* 41(1): 1–22.

Massey, Douglas S., Camille Z. Charles, Garvey F. Lundy, and Mary J. Fischer. 2003. *The Source of the River: The Social Origins of Freshmen at America's Selective Colleges and Universities*. Princeton, NJ: Princeton University Press.

Massey, Douglas S., and Nancy A. Denton. 1994. *American Apartheid: Segregation and the Making of the Underclass*. Cambridge, MA: Harvard University Press.

Massey, Douglas S., and Margarita Mooney. 2007. "The Effects of America's Three Affirmative Action Programs on Academic Performance." *Social Problems* 54(1): 99–117.

Mayorga-Gallo, Sarah. 2014. *Behind the White Picket Fence: Power and Privilege in a Multiethnic Neighborhood*. Chapel Hill: University of North Carolina Press.

Mazzoco, Philip J., Lyndsee W. Cooper, and Mariagrace Flint. 2012. "Different Shades of Racial Colorblindness: The Role of Prejudice." *Group Processes & Intergroup Relations* 15(2): 167–178.

McClelland, Katherine, and Erika Linnander. 2006. "The Role of Contact and Information in Racial Attitude Change among White College Students." *Sociological Inquiry* 76(1): 81–115.

McDonough, Patricia. 1997. *Choosing Colleges: How Social Class and Schools Structure Opportunity*. Albany: State University of New York Press.

McLeod, Jane D., and Kathryn J. Lively. 2006. "Social Structure and Personality." Pp. 77–102 in *Handbook of Social Psychology*. Edited by J. Delamater. New York: Kluwer Academic/Plenum Publishers.

McPherson, Miller, Lynn Smith-Lovin, and James M. Cook. 2001. "Birds of a Feather: Homophily in Social Networks." *Annual Review of Sociology* 27: 415–444.

Meyer, Heinz-Dieter, and Brian Rowan. (Eds.). 2007. *The New Institutionalism in Education*. Albany: State University of New York Press.

Mills, C. Wright. 1956. *The Power Elite*. New York: Oxford University Press.

Mills, Charles W. 1997. *The Racial Contract*. Ithaca, NY: Cornell University Press.

Moody, James. 2001. "Race, School Integration, and Friendship Segregation in America." *American Journal of Sociology* 107(3): 679–719.

Moore, Wendy Leo. 2008. *Reproducing Racism: White Space, Elite Law Schools, and Racial Inequality*. Lanham, MD: Rowman & Littlefield.

Moore, Wendy Leo, and Joyce Bell. 2011. "Maneuvers of Whiteness: 'Diversity' as a Mechanism of Retrenchment in the Affirmative Action Discourse." *Critical Sociology* 37(5): 597–613.

Morris, Catherine. 2016. "Georgetown, Harvard Embrace Role in Slavery Atonement." *Diverse: Issues in Higher Education*. Accessed September 29 (http://diverseeducation.com/article/87506/).

Mueller, Jennifer C., Danielle Dirks, and Leslie Houts Picca. 2007. "Unmasking Racism: Halloween Costuming and Engagement with the Racial Other." *Qualitative Sociology* 30(3): 315–335.

Myers, Kristen A. 2005. *Racetalk: Racism Hiding in Plain Sight*. Lanham, MD: Rowman and Littlefield.

Neville, Helen A., M. Nikki Coleman, Jameca W. Falconer, and Deadre Holmes. 2005. "Color Blind Racial Ideology and Psychological False Consciousness among African Americans." *Journal of Black Psychology* 31(1): 27–45.

Neville, Helen A., Roderick L. Lily, Georgia Duran, Richard M. Lee, and LaVonne Brown. 2000. "Construction and Initial Validity of the Color-Blind Racial Attitudes Scale (CoBRAS). *Journal of Counseling Psychology* 47(1): 59–70.

New York Times Editorial Board. 2016. "Georgetown Confronts Its Ugly Past." *New York Times*, September 1 (http://www.nytimes.com/2016/09/02/opinion/georgetown-confronts-its-ugly-past.html?_r=0).

North, Anna. 2010. "Meet Harvard's Racist Email Antagonist, Stephanie Grace." Retrieved April 30, 2010 (http://jezebel.com/5527272/meet-harvards-racist-email-antagonist-stephanie-grace).

O'Brien, Eileen. 2008. *The Racial Middle: Latinos and Asian Americans Living Beyond the Racial Divide*. New York: New York University Press.

Oh, Euna, Chun-Chung Choi, Helen A. Neville, Carolyn J. Anderson, and Joycelyn Landrum Brown. 2010. "Beliefs about Affirmative Action: A Test of the Group Self-Interest Racism Beliefs Models." *Journal of Diversity in Higher Education* 3(3): 163–176.

Oliver, Melvin, and Thomas Shapiro. 2006. *Black Wealth / White Wealth: A New Perspective of Racial Inequality*. Second edition. New York: Routledge.

Orfield, Gary. (Ed.). 2001. *The Diversity Challenge: Evidence on the Impact of Affirmative Action*. Cambridge, MA: Harvard University Press.

Pahlke, Erin, Rebecca S. Bigler, and Marie-Anne Suizzo. 2012. "Relations between Colorblind Socialization and Children's Racial Bias: Evidence from European American Mothers and their Preschool Children." *Child Development* 83(4): 1164–1179.

Park, Julie J. 2012. "'Man, this is hard': A Case Study of How Race and Religion Affect Cross Racial Interaction for Black Students." *Review of Higher Education* 35(4): 567–593.

———. 2014a. "Clubs and Campus Racial Climates: Student Organizations and Interracial Friendships." *Journal of College Student Development* 55(7): 641–660.

———. 2014b. *When Diversity Drops: Race, Religion and Affirmative Action in Higher Education*. New Brunswick, NJ: Rutgers University Press.

Park, Julie J., and Stephanie H. Chang. 2015. "Understanding Students' Precollege Experiences with Racial Diversity: The High School as Microsystem." *Journal of College Student Development* 56(4): 349–363.

Park, Julie J., and Young K. Kim. 2013. "Interracial Friendship and Structural Diversity: Trends for Greek, Religious, and Ethnic Student Organizations." *Review of Higher Education* 37(1): 1–24.

Pascarella, Ernest T., and Patrick T. Terenizini. 1991. *How College Affects Students*. San Francisco: Jossey-Bass.

———. 2005. *How College Affects Students: A Third Decade of Research*. San Francisco: Jossey-Bass.

Pauley, Madison, and Becca Andrews. 2015. "Campus Protests Are Spreading Like Wildfire." Mother Jones. Retrieved January 13, 2016 (http://www.motherjones.com/politics/2015/11/missouri-student-protests-racism).

Perry, Pamela. 2002. *Shades of White: White Kids and Racial Identities in High School*. Durham, NC: Duke University Press.

Peterson, Marvin W., Robert T. Blackburn, Zelda F. Gamson, Carlos H. Arce, and Roselle W. Davenport. 1978. *Black Students on White Campuses: The Impacts of Increased Black Enrollments*. Ann Arbor: University of Michigan Institute for Social Research.

Pettigrew, Thomas F. 1966. "Transcript of the American Academy Conference on the Negro American—May 14–15, 1965." *Daedalus* 95(1): 287–441.

———. 1979. "The Ultimate Attribution Error: Extending Allport's Cognitive Analysis of Prejudice." *Personality and Social Psychology Bulletin* 5(4): 461–476.

———. 1997. "The Affective Component of Prejudice: Empirical Support for the New View." Pp. 76–90 in *Racial Attitudes in the 1990s: Continuity and Change.* Edited by S. A. Tuch and J. K. Martin. Westport, CT: Praeger.

———. 1998. "Intergroup Contact Theory." *Annual Review of Psychology* 49: 65–85.

———. 2009. "Secondary Transfer Effects of Contact: Do Intergroup Contact Effects Spread to Noncontacted Groups?" *Social Psychology* 40(1): 55–65.

Pettigrew, Thomas F., and Joanne Martin. 1987. "Shaping the Organizational Context for Black American Inclusion." *Journal of Social Issues* 43(1): 41–78.

Pettigrew, Thomas F., and Roel W. Meertens. 1995. "Subtle and Blatant Prejudice in Western Europe." *European Journal of Social Psychology* 25(1): 57–75.

Pettigrew, Thomas F., and Linda R. Tropp. 2011. *When Groups Meet: The Dynamics of Intergroup Contact.* Philadelphia: Psychology Press.

Pew Research Center. 2010. "Almost All Millennials Accept Interracial Dating and Marriage." February 1. Available at http://www.pewresearch.org/2010/02/01/almost-all-millennials-accept-interracial-dating-and-marriage/.

———. 2014. "Millennials in Adulthood: Detached from Institutions, Networked with Friends." March 7. Available at http://www.pewsocialtrends.org/2014/03/07/millennials-in-adulthood/.

Picca, Leslie H., and Joe R. Feagin. 2007. *Two-Faced Racism: Whites in the Backstage and Frontstage.* Lanham, MD: Rowman & Littlefield.

Piketty, Thomas, and Emmanuel Saez. 2003. "Income Inequality in the United States, 1913–1998." *Quarterly Journal of Economics* 118(1): 1–39.

Priceonomics. 2016. "Ranking the Most (and Least) Diverse Colleges in America." Accessed September 7. https://priceonomics.com/ranking-the-most-and-least-diverse-colleges-in/.

Pryor, John H., Sylvia Hurtado, Victor B. Saenz, Jose Luis Santos, and William S. Korn. 2007. *The American Freshman: Forty-Year Trends, 1966–2006.* Los Angeles: Higher Education Research Institute, UCLA.

Quillian, Lincoln. 2006. "New Approaches to Understanding Racial Prejudice and Discrimination." *Annual Review of Sociology* 32: 299–328.

Remnick, Noah. 2016. "Yale Defies Calls to Rename Calhoun College." *New York Times,* April 27 (http://www.nytimes.com/2016/04/28/nyregion/yale-defies-calls-to-rename-calhoun-college.html).

Richeson, Jennifer A., and Richard J. Nussbaum. 2004. "The Impact of Multiculturalism versus Colorblindness on Racial Bias." *Journal of Experimental Social Psychology* 40(3): 417–423.

Rivera, Lauren. 2015. *Pedigree: How Elite Students Get Elite Jobs.* Princeton, NJ: Princeton University Press.

Rockquemore, Kerry Ann, and David L. Brunsma. 2002. "Socially Embedded Identities: Theories, Typologies, and Processes among Black/White Biracials." *Sociological Quarterly* 43(3): 335–356.

Rockquemore, Kerry Ann, David L. Brunsma, and Daniel J. Delgado. 2009. "Racing to Theory or Retheorizing Race? Understanding the Struggle to Build a Multiracial Identity Theory." *Journal of Social Issues* 65(1): 13–34.

Ross, Louie E. 1997. "Mate Selection Preferences among African American College Students." *Journal of Black Studies* 27(4): 554–569.

Royster, Deirdre A. 2003. *Race and the Invisible Hand: How White Networks Exclude Black Men from Blue-Collar Jobs*. Berkeley: University of California Press.

Ryan, Carey S., Jennifer S. Hunt, Joshua A. Weible, Charles R. Peterson, and Juan F. Casas. 2007. "Multicultural and Colorblind Ideology, Stereotypes, and Ethnocentrism among Black and White Americans." *Group Processes & Intergroup Relations* 10(4): 617–637.

Saenz, Victor B. 2010. "Breaking the Segregation Cycle: Examining Students' Precollege Racial Environments and College Diversity Experiences." *Review of Higher Education* 34(1): 1–37.

Saenz, Victor B., Hoi Ning Ngai, and Sylvia Hurtado. 2007. "Factors Influencing Positive Interactions Across Race for African American, Asian American, Latino, and White Students in College." *Research in Higher Education* 48(1): 1–38.

Schuman, Howard, Charlotte Steeh, Lawrence Bobo, and Maria Krysan. 1997. *Racial Attitudes in America: Trends and Interpretations*. Cambridge, MA: Harvard University Press.

Sears, David O. 1988. "Symbolic Racism." Pp. 53–84 in *Eliminating Racism: Profiles in Controversy*. Edited by P. A. Katz and D. A. Taylor. New York: Plenum Press.

Sears, David O., and P. J. Henry. 2003. "The Origins of Symbolic Racism." *Journal of Personality and Social Psychology* 85(2): 259–275.

Shapiro, Thomas M. 2004. *The Hidden Cost of Being African American: How Wealth Perpetuates Inequality*. New York: Oxford University Press.

Shelton, J. Nicole, and Jennifer A. Richeson. 2006. "Ethnic Minorities' Racial Attitudes and Contact Experiences." *Cultural Diversity and Ethnic Minority Psychology* 12(1): 149–164.

Shelton, J. Nicole, Jennifer A. Richeson, and Jessica Salvatore. 2005. "Expecting to be the Target of Prejudice: Implications for Interethnic Interactions." *Personality and Social Psychology Bulletin* 31(9): 1189–1202.

Sherif, Muzafer. 1966. *In Common Predicament: Social Psychology of Intergroup Conflict and Cooperation*. Boston: Houghton Mifflin.

Sidanius, Jim, Shana Levin, Colette van Laar, and David O. Sears. 2008. *The Diversity Challenge: Social Identity and Intergroup Relations on the College Campus*. New York: Russell Sage Foundation.

Smedley, Audrey, and Brian D. Smedley. 2011. *Race in North America: Origin and Evolution of a Concept*. Fourth edition. Boulder, CO: Westview.

Smith, Darryl G. 2016. "The Diversity Imperative: Moving to the Next Generation." Pp. 375–400 in *American Higher Education in the 21st Century: Social, Political, and Economic Challenges*. Fourth edition. Edited by Michael N. Bastedo, Phillip G. Altbach, and Patricia J. Gumport. Baltimore: Johns Hopkins University Press.

Soares, Joseph. 2007. *The Power of Privilege: Yale and America's Elite Colleges*. Stanford, CA: Stanford University Press.

Solorzano, Daniel, Miguel Ceja, and Tara Yosso. 2000. "Critical Race Theory, Racial Microaggressions, and Campus Racial Climate: The Experiences of African American College Students." *Journal of Negro Education* 69(1/2): 60–73.

Stark, Tobias H. 2015. "Understanding Selection Bias: Social Network Processes and the Effect of Prejudice on the Avoidance of Outgroup Friends." *Social Psychology Quarterly* 78(2): 127–150.

Stearns, Elizabeth, Claudia Buchmann, and Kara Bonneau. 2009. "Interracial Friendships in the Transition to College: Do Birds of a Feather Flock Together Once They Leave the Nest?" *Sociology of Education* 82(2): 173–195.

Steele, Claude M. 1997. "A Threat in the Air: How Stereotypes Shape Intellectual Identity and Performance." *American Psychologist* 52(6): 613–629.

———. 2010. *Whistling Vivaldi: How Stereotypes Affect Us and What We Can Do*. New York: W. W. Norton.

Steele, Claude M., and Joshua Aronson. 1995. "Stereotype Threat and Intellectual Performance of African Americans." *Journal of Personality and Social Psychology* 69(5): 797–811.

———. 2004. "Stereotype Threat Does Not Live By Steele and Aronson (1995)." *American Psychologist* 59(1): 47–48.

Steinberg, Stephen. 2007. *Race Relations: A Critique*. Stanford, CA: Stanford University Press.

Stets, Jan E., and Peter J. Burke. 2000. "Identity Theory and Social Identity Theory." *Social Psychology Quarterly* 63(3): 224–237.

Stevens, Mitchell L., Elizabeth A. Armstrong, and Richard Arum. 2008. "Sieve, Incubator, Temple, Hub: Empirical and Theoretical Advances in the Sociology of Higher Education." *Annual Review of Sociology* 34: 127–151.

Stoll, Laurie C. 2013. *Race and Gender in the Classroom: Teachers, Privilege, and Enduring Social Inequalities*. Lanham, MD: Lexington.

Sue, Derald W., Christina M. Capodliupo, and Aisha M. B. Holder. 2008. "Racial Microaggressions in the Life Experiences of Black Americans." *Professional Psychology: Research and Practice* 39(3): 329–336.

Swarns, Rachel L. 2016. "Georgetown University Plans Steps to Atone for Slave Past." *New York Times*, September 1 (http://www.nytimes.com/2016/09/02/us/slaves-georgetown-university.html).

Swidler, Ann. 1986. "Culture in Action: Symbols and Strategies." *American Sociological Review* 51(2): 273–286.

Tajfel, Henri. 1982. "Social Psychology of Intergroup Relations." *Annual Review of Psychology* 33: 1–39.

Tajfel, Henri, and John C. Turner. 1997. "The Social Identity Theory of Intergroup Behavior." Pp. 7–24 in *Psychology of Intergroup Relations*. Edited by S. Worchel and W. G. Austin. Chicago: Nelson-Hall Publishers.

Taylor, Marylee C., and Thomas F. Pettigrew. 2000. "Prejudice." Pp. 2242–2248 in *Encyclopedia of Sociology, Volume 2*. Edited by E. F. Borgatta and R. J. Montgomery. New York: Macmillan Reference.

Taylor, Marylee C., and Matthew B. Schroeder. 2010. "The Impact of Hispanic Population Growth on the Outlook of African Americans." *Social Science Research* 39(3): 491–505.

Teranishi, Robert T. 2010. *Asians in the Ivory Tower: Dilemmas of Racial Inequality in American Higher Education*. New York: Teachers College Press.

Thelin, John R. 2004. *A History of American Higher Education*. Baltimore: Johns Hopkins University Press.

Thoits, Peggy A., and Lauren K. Virshup. 1997. "Me's and We's: Forms and Functions of Social Identities." Pp. 106–133 in *Self and Identity: Fundamental Issues*. Edited by R. D. Ashmore and L. Jussim. New York: Oxford University Press.

Torres, Kimberly C., and Camille Z. Charles. 2004. "Metastereotypes and the Black-White Divide: A Qualitative View of Race on an Elite College Campus." *Du Bois Review* 1(1): 115–149.

Tropp, Linda R. 2007. "Perceived Discrimination and Interracial Contact: Predicting Interracial Closeness among Black and White Americans." *Social Psychology Quarterly* 70(1): 70–81.

Tropp, Linda R., and Thomas F. Pettigrew. 2005. "Relationships Between Intergroup Contact and Prejudice Among Minority and Majority Status Groups." *Psychological Science* 16(12): 951–957.

Tuch, Steven A., and Michael Hughes. 2011. "Whites' Racial Policy Attitudes in the 21st Century: The Continuing Significance of Racial Resentment." *Annals of the American Academy of Political and Social Sciences* 634: 134–152.

Turner, John C., Michael A. Hogg, Penelope J. Oakes, Stephen D. Reicher, and Margaret S. Wetherell. 1987. *Rediscovering the Social Group: A Self-Categorization Theory*. New York: Blackwell.

Tyson, Karolyn. 2011. *Integration Interrupted: Tracking, Black Students & Acting White after Brown*. New York: Oxford University Press.

Van Ausdale, Debra, and Joe R. Feagin 2001. *The First R: How Children Learn Race and Racism*. Lanham, MD: Rowman and Littlefield.

Wagner, Ulrich, Oliver Christ, Thomas F. Pettigrew, Jost Stellmacher, and Carina Wolf. 2006. "Prejudice and Minority Proportion: Contact Instead of Threat Effects." *Social Psychology Quarterly* 69(4): 380–390.

Warikoo, Natasha K. 2016. *The Diversity Bargain: And Other Dilemmas of Race, Admissions, and Meritocracy at Elite Universities*. Chicago: University of Chicago Press.

Warikoo, Natasha K., and Sherry L. Deckman. 2014. "Beyond the Numbers: Institutional Influences on Experiences with Diversity on Elite College Campuses." *Sociological Forum* 29(4): 959–981.

Warikoo, Natasha K., and Janine de Novais. 2015. "Colour-blindness and Diversity: Race Frames and Their Consequences for White Undergraduates at Elite US Universities." *Ethnic & Racial Studies* 38(6): 860–876.

Weber, Max. 1930. *The Protestant Ethic and the Spirit of Capitalism*. London: Allen and Unwin.

Whitt, Elizabeth J., Marcia I. Edison, Ernest T. Pascarella, Patrick T. Terenzini, and Amaury Nora. 2001. "Influences on Students' Openness to Diversity and Challenge in the Second and Third Years of College." *Journal of Higher Education* 72(2): 172–202.

Wilder, Craig Steven. 2013. *Ebony & Ivy: Race, Slavery, and the Troubled History of America's Universities*. New York: Bloomsbury Press.

Williams, Robin M. 1947. *The Reduction of Intergroup Tensions: A Survey of Research on Problems of Ethnic, Racial, and Religious Group Relations*. New York: Social Science Research Council.

Wilson, William J. 1978. *The Declining Significance of Race: Blacks and Changing American Institutions*. Chicago: University of Chicago Press.

Wise, Tim. 2008a. "Majoring in Minstrelsy: White Students, Blackface, and the Failure of Mainstream Multiculturalism." Pp. 63–71 in *Speaking Treason Fluently: Anti-Racist Reflections From an Angry White Male*. Edited by T. Wise. Berkeley, CA: Soft Skulls Press.

Wise, Tim. 2008b. "Racism, Free Speech, and the College Campus." Pp. 165–174 in *Speaking Treason Fluently: Anti-Racist Reflections From an Angry White Male*. Edited by T. Wise. Berkeley, CA: Soft Skulls Press.

Worthington, Roger L., Rachel L. Navarro, Michael Loewy, and Jeni Hart. 2008. "Color-blind Racial Attitudes, Social Dominance Orientation, Racial-ethnic Group Membership and College Students' Perceptions of the Campus Climate." *Journal of Diversity in Higher Education* 1(1): 8–19.

Wright, Stephen C., Arthur Aron, Tracy McLaughlin-Volpe, and Stacy A. Ropp. 1997. "The Extended Contact Effect: Knowledge of Cross-Group Friendships and Prejudice." *Journal of Personality and Social Psychology* 73(1): 73–90.

Yale University. 2015. "Yale Launches Five-year, $50 Million Initiative to Increase Faculty Diversity." *Yale News*. November 3 (http://news.yale.edu/2015/11/03/yale-launches-five-year-50-million-initiative-increase-faculty-diversity).

Zuberi, Tukufu. 2001. *Thicker Than Blood: How Racial Statistics Lie*. Minneapolis: University of Minnesota Press.

Zweigenhaft, Richard L. 1993. "Prep School and Public School Graduates of Harvard: A Longitudinal Study of the Accumulation of Social and Cultural Capital." *Journal of Higher Education* 64(2): 211–225.

Zweigenhaft, Richard L., and G. William Domhoff. 1991. *Blacks in the White Establishment? A Study of Race and Class in America*. New Haven, CT: Yale University Press.

INDEX

Note: page numbers followed by *t* and *f* refer to tables and figures respectively. Those followed by n refer to notes, with note number.

ABOUT THE AUTHOR

W. CARSON BYRD is an assistant professor of Pan-African Studies at the University of Louisville. He is also a faculty affiliate in the Anne Braden Institute for Social Justice Research. His research examines educational inequalities, particularly the experiences of black students in higher education, racial identity and ideology formation, inter- and intraracial interactions, and how racial ideology shapes scientific innovation and knowledge production. His research has appeared in journals including the *Annals of the American Academy of Political and Social Science, Biodemography & Social Biology, Du Bois Review, Equity & Excellence in Education, Ethnic and Racial Studies, Humanity & Society,* and *Journal of African American Studies,* among others.

9 780813 589367